TACTICS FOR TEACHING

Second Edition

Thomas C. Lovitt
University of Washington

Merrill,
an imprint of Prentice Hall

Englewood Cliffs, New Jersey   Columbus, Ohio

Library of Congress Cataloging-in-Publication Data

Lovitt, Thomas C.

      Tactics for teaching / Thomas C. Lovitt.—2nd ed.

          p.   cm.

      Includes bibliographical references.

      1. Elementary school teaching. 2. Education, Elementary—Curricula.

I. Title.

LB1555.L82   1995

372.11'02—dc20   93-45870

Cover art: Courtesy of Southeast School, Columbus, Ohio
Editor: Ann Castel Davis
Production Editor: Linda Hillis Bayma
Text Designer: Ed Horcharik
Cover Designer: Steve Shaw
Production Manager: Deidra M. Schwartz
Electronic Text Management: Marilyn Wilson Phelps, Matthew Williams, Jane Lopez,
   Karen L. Bretz

This book was set in Century Schoolbook BT by Prentice Hall and was printed and bound
by R.R. Donnelley & Sons Company. The cover was printed by Phoenix Color Corp.

 © 1995 by Prentice Hall, Inc.
A Simon & Schuster Company
Englewood Cliffs, New Jersey 07632

Earlier edition © 1984 by Merrill Publishing Company.

Printed in the United States of America

10 9 8 7 6 5 4 3 2 1

ISBN: 0-02-371813-7

Prentice-Hall International (UK) Limited, *London*
Prentice-Hall of Australia Pty. Limited, *Sydney*
Prentice-Hall of Canada, Inc., *Toronto*
Prentice-Hall Hispanoamericana, S. A., *Mexico*
Prentice-Hall of India Private Limited, *New Delhi*
Prentice-Hall of Japan, Inc., *Tokyo*
Simon & Schuster Asia Pte. Ltd., *Singapore*
Editora Prentice-Hall do Brasil, Ltda., *Rio de Janeiro*

PREFACE

There are 105 tactics in this second edition of *Tactics for Teaching*. They are categorized into six sections: reading, writing, spelling, mathematics, classroom management, and self-management. Four of these categories were included in the first edition; the writing and spelling sections are new.

There are 50 tactics in the reading section, 10 each in writing, spelling, and mathematics, 15 in classroom management, and 10 in self-management. I kept 22 tactics in reading from the first edition, 5 in mathematics, 10 in classroom management, and 9 in self-management. There are 59 new tactics in this edition. Any tactics used from the first edition have been revised. One of these revisions is the inclusion of a section on monitoring in each tactic. This monitoring section was not a component of the tactics in the first edition. Moreover, I have included an additional reference for each of the "old" tactics. The new citation either validates the original technique's continued popularity or it describes a new wrinkle on the original approach. I tried to select research dated later than 1986 for the updated references and for the new tactics as well.

The sources for the majority of these tactics are journal articles in education and psychology. In fact, one of the primary considerations in selecting a tactic was that it was supported to some extent by data. Whenever possible that is the case. Some tactics that are included in this edition were carried out by students or others but the results were not published. In those instances, some data were still available to suggest that the procedures were effective. There were a few times, however, in which I selected a tactic that was simply written up but that did not have supporting data. These instances are rare, and when they did occur, I made a professional judgment that these tactics would be effective if the procedures outlined were followed properly.

The format for each tactic is the same throughout, and is very much like the design of the first-edition tactics. Each begins with a brief statement about the rationale for or background of the tactic, in which I explain (when appropriate) its derivation. The next section describes the type of pupils with whom the tactic was used in the cited study, as well as the type of students with whom the tactic would be most appropriately arranged. The third section is an outline of procedures for implementing the technique. In this part I tried to include enough detail so that teachers could put the idea into practice. The next section is on monitoring. There, suggestions are given for acquiring data on the effectiveness of the procedure. The next section of each tactic is on possible modifications and considerations. In this segment I discuss how the tactic can be altered for use with a wider range of pupils or with children whose behaviors differ from those originally documented. I have also noted aspects of the tactic that teachers might want to consider as they arrange its implementation. Each tactic ends with a citation or two giving the research that stimulated it.

Acknowledgments

I have a number of folks to thank for helping me out as I worked on this second edition. I will note the last names of a few—Martin, Benge, Mahillion, Tuchman, Mencken, Gould, Will, Turner, Marsalis, and Bartoli—and some first names—Richard, Tina, Al, and Zelda.

I would also like to thank the reviewers of this edition—Jane Adams, Washburn University; Jeanne Bauwens, Boise State University; Ann Rapp Garvin, College of Utah, St. Joe; Zoe Locklear, Pembroke State University; and Kathleen Tomaino-Knops, North Central College—for their helpful suggestions.

CONTENTS

Part 2   Writing   172

Part 3   Spelling   208

TACTICS FOR TEACHING

READING

There are 50 tactics in this section on reading, which makes up the major portion of this book. The first eight tactics pertain to the assessment of various reading skills (e.g., prereading skills and aspects of comprehension) and represent different ways in which to monitor these skills, such as with proposition analysis and portfolios. The next three tactics are concerned with aspects of early reading (e.g., phonemic awareness). In the next group of eight tactics, the focus is on oral reading. Included in this group is a tactic on placement and several that apply to increasing fluency. Next are four tactics that focus on vocabulary development. Silent reading and scanning are covered in the next two tactics. The group of 15 tactics that follows focuses on ways to enhance reading comprehension. This is one of the most important sections of the entire book. As with all the other sections in this second edition, newly researched techniques are included along with some tried-and-true procedures from the original edition. The next section includes six tactics that deal with reading in the content areas. Following this section is a tactic concerned with learning about other languages. In the final group, there are three tactics especially written for parents.

1 ASSESSMENT: PRECISE SCREENING OF EARLY READING SKILLS

Background

The steps in this technique* are to first identify the important prereading behaviors that first graders should develop, then determine the extent to which these skills should be attained, and finally, to schedule extra help for youngsters deficient in these skills.

One assumption behind this project is that there <u>are</u> important prereading behaviors, and when children can execute them proficiently, they are more likely to become successful readers. Another assumption of this approach is that certain prereading behaviors require auditory skills, whereas others rely on visual acuity. In other words, before a child can read, he or she must be able to discriminate between certain sounds and between certain visual symbols. Another feature of this screening technique is its reliance on a practice-sheet format.

Who Can Benefit

This is an appropriate technique for first graders, or possibly kindergartners, if it is done late in the year. The teacher could administer this screening test to an entire class at the beginning of the year, and once again at the end. More frequent data should be kept on children who are less proficient in these skills and for whom special assistance should be arranged.

Procedures

1. Design four types of practice sheets (8 1/2" × 11"):

   a. *See letter, name letter.* Print the various letters of the alphabet randomly on a page. The child's task is to say the letter names as fast as he or she can for one minute.

*In 1970, Linda Esmay developed this project for a special education class at the University of Washington in Seattle.

    b.   *See letter, name sound.*   The same sheet is used to assess this skill as was used for the preceding activity. For one minute, the pupil says the most frequent sounds of the letters.

    c.   *See picture, name sound.*   In order to evaluate this skill, draw a number of small pictures on the practice sheets. The pictures should be of objects with names that begin with the most frequent sounds of different letters. The student's task is to look at each picture and say the sound of the first letter of the object's name.

    d.   *Hear word, write first sound.*   Develop a list of common words that begin with the most frequent sounds. Read the words to the student for one minute and have him or her write the letter that corresponds to the initial sound.

2.   Require pupils to respond to the preceding four tasks for one minute per task. The first three tasks are administered individually, and the fourth may be given to an entire group.

3.   Chart the correct and incorrect rates per minute for all the pupils.

4.   Study these data to determine the following:

    a.   The target scores for each skill. Based on the data from other first graders, correct rates on the four skills at the beginning of the school year should be about 40, 25, 15, and 5 responses per minute, respectively.

       By the end of the year, the rates for the first three tasks should be about 100 per minute, and for the fourth, 25 or so. The rate for the fourth skill is to some extent dependent on the speed with which the teacher pronounces the words.

    b.   The skill that is most poorly developed by many of the pupils.

    c.   The pupils whose rates are generally lower than the others.

5.   Based on 4b and 4c, design instruction for the entire class and for certain pupils.

Monitor

In line with the procedures explained here, the teacher should keep track of each pupil's correct and incorrect rates as he or she performs each of the four skills. These rates should be charted each time the pupils perform, and their rates should be compared to those of exemplary performers in order to determine how far off the mark they were. By consulting these data, the teacher would know when to arrange special treatments for a pupil or would know when the pupil had achieved the goal and could move on to more advanced aspects of reading.

Modifications/Considerations

Other skills related to reading can be selected and assessed using similar techniques. For example, a teacher might design a sheet of consonant-vowel-consonant (CVC) words or one of consonant clusters, or might focus on digraphs, diphthongs, short or long vowels, familiar but irregular words, or short phrases. Other teachers might consider this method of assessment with various pinpoints in math, spelling, handwriting, or other subjects. Drake (1990) suggested that an informal reading inventory be developed based on the following five skills: oral cloze, oral cloze with initial consonant, sound/symbol relationships, knowledge of letter names, and instant recognition of high-frequency words. Her choice of critical skills was not very different from the ones described here.

The frequency with which these assessments are administered can certainly vary. For this example, the teacher gave them to all pupils at the beginning and end of the year, and more often to youngsters who were off the mark. Other teachers could assess their youngsters on a monthly, weekly, or even daily basis throughout the year.

Research

Drake, S. V. (1990). Why not an informal reading readiness inventory? *Academic Therapy, 25*(3), 315–319.

2 ASSESSMENT: MAINTAINING PORTFOLIOS

Background

According to some authorities, portfolio assessment is the answer to all of our assessment needs. Portfolio assessment has certainly been <u>the</u> alternative to standardized assessments of reading. The idea behind portfolio assessment comes from the files or portfolios kept by artists, architects, and photographers who assemble them to display their work. When such individuals apply for positions or simply wish to show others their work, they can pull out these visual records; they do not have to rely on indirect or synthetic measures of their abilities.

Who Will Benefit

Portfolios have been developed successfully for children and youth of all ages. Although these records have been created most often for elementary-school-age children who are learning the subjects of reading and writing, portfolios could be quite useful for older students, and in other subjects.

Procedures

If portfolios are to be used to satisfactorily monitor aspects of reading and writing, the following steps must be considered:

- The portfolios belong to the students; they should have some choice (more and more as they mature into independent readers and writers) as to what goes into them. The teacher serves as a consultant; he or she, first of all, explains to the students the importance and function of the files.

- The portfolio is a growing repository of developing performances and ideas. Periodically, the contents are reviewed. As part of that process, some materials are discarded and others revised. The teacher and student should hold conferences about what is in the file and what will be put into it in coming days. During conferences, the student should be encouraged to identify areas that need improvement and should be made aware of other performance aspects that have been developing satisfactorily.

- The portfolio should contain a variety of materials that reflect students' performances in reading and writing. Reading logs that report ongoing reactions to books and articles make valuable contributions to the collection.

- The portfolio should be the basis of conferences with parents. During these sessions, the student and teacher should explain to parents what the portfolio is all about. Parents should be encouraged to question why certain items are in the file and to comment on the different materials and the ways in which they were developed. Moreover, parents should be asked to suggest other items that might be included in the portfolio.

Following are five aspects of reading in general that lend themselves to portfolio assessment:

1. *Strategic reading, comprehension, and metacognition.*   Students could be asked to perform five types of reading exercises: *identifying* the topic before reading, *predicting* the content based on information in previous passages, *inferring* from the text, *monitoring* the meaning of a new word, and *summarizing* important information. Data on the extent to which students responded to these strategies could be kept.

2. *Additional measures of comprehension.*   *Cloze tasks* are well-suited to comprehension assessment, especially since they can be developed from regular curricular materials. Although *retellings* take more time and are not as suitable with groups of children, they should be included in instruction and assessment. For a further discussion of the cloze procedure and of retelling techniques, see Tactics 28 and 33, respectively, in this section.

3. *Additional measures of metacognition.*   Children should be asked to inform others as to *how* they decided whether or not they liked a book they had read or listened to. As students read and respond to queries, the teacher should record their comments and determine whether and how they used such strategies as skimming or bringing in prior knowledge.

4. *Motivation.*   Students could be asked several questions that have to do with their reading abilities and habits:
   - Are you a good reader?
   - Do you enjoy reading?
   - How often do you read at home?
   - Do your parents read, and if so, what?

5. *Literate environments.* Create lists of books, magazines, and other materials and ask students to circle or otherwise indicate the ones they read. Ask them if they know where to find certain books, newspapers, magazines, or other reading materials.

Monitor

This tactic has to do with monitoring. The worthiness of this approach for assessing reading, writing, and other subjects is determined by whether or not students become better, more motivated, or more thoughtful about the subject. Teachers should keep in mind as they rely on this type of assessment that some students will read so well and so often that their portfolios (if they have one) should look quite different from the ones kept by average or struggling students.

Modifications/Considerations

Portfolios are applicable to students of all ages and in many subject areas, particularly if portfolios are perceived as metaphorical as well as literal. Seen literally, a portfolio is simply a folder into which papers are included. Those papers, in the context of reading, could pertain to a student's performance on worksheets, answers to comprehension questions, as well as impressions of what he or she has read. If, however, a portfolio is viewed as something beyond a manila folder, that is, metaphorically, then other, more natural and imaginative, records of performance can be gathered. Evaluators could obtain impressions via video or audio recordings, pictures taken by observers, or recorded interviews from individuals who live or work with the student.

Research

Farr, R. (1992). Putting it all together: Solving the reading assessment puzzle. *The Reading Teacher, 46*(1), 26–37.

Paris, S. G. (1991). Portfolio assessment for young readers. *The Reading Teacher, 44*(9), 680–682.

3 ASSESSMENT: PROPOSITION ANALYSIS

Background

This approach is based on the work of Kintsch (1974), who defined propositions as "n-tuples" of word concepts, one of which serves as a predictor and the others as arguments. Predictors are usually verbs (e.g., John sleeps = [sleep, John]) but may also include adjectives (e.g., The man is sick = [sick, man]) and other parts of speech. The first proposition in a set is always superordinate and thus allows other propositions to be linked into a hierarchy of major and supporting ideas.

This tactic, like many others, has two functions. First, it can be used to assess the abilities of students; in this case, an aspect of their comprehension is evaluated. Second, this tactic can be used to teach readers to better comprehend (at least according to the rules of proposition analysis) the material they read or hear. It gives them another strategy to draw upon.

Who Can Benefit

The study selected to illustrate proposition analysis was conducted by Hansen (1978). There were two sets of pupils in her research. One group was classified as learning disabled and attended special classes; the other group comprised regular students. All the youngsters were fifth or sixth graders.

This tactic is also appropriate for pupils in elementary or secondary grades, particularly those who have problems comprehending what they read.

Procedures

1. Select a passage and list the propositions in it. Following is an example from a third-grade-level story:

    Six boys put up a tent by the side of the river. They took things to eat with them. When the sun went down, they went into the tent to sleep. In the night, a cow came, and began to eat grass around the tent. The boys were afraid. They thought it was a bear.

2. Require the pupils to read the story orally and be prepared to retell it.

3. Ask students to retell the story. If they hesitate after a few statements, ask them to tell you more.

4. Record what they say.

5. Following their reading, transcribe what they told you. The following is an example of a pupil's retelling of the preceding story:

These six boys went camping and they put up a tent and the sun went down. They went into the tent and they ate something and then a cow came and she was eating grass and that scared them. They thought it was a bear.

6. Explain the meaning of propositions and tell the pupil that he should identify as many of them as possible in subsequent performances.

Monitor

Alongside the propositions actually contained in the passage, write the propositions the student identified. See Table 3.1 for an example. Count the number of propositions the student said and the total number in the story, then compare the two. Inform the pupil about his or her performance, that is, how many of the possible ones he or she mentioned and which ones were overlooked.

Modifications/Considerations

Proposition analysis is rather time-consuming when all the usual steps are followed. There are, however, a number of ways to modify this technique to make it more easily manageable in an ordinary classroom.

First of all, instead of listing the propositions, one could enumerate events, circumstances, or other elements found in the stories. This is similar to listing items in the Comprehension Inventory shown in Tactic 4 of this section, except that the incidents are specific to each story. In Tactic 4, the listed items are applicable to several stories of a similar level.

Another modification would be to check the pupil's statements against the listed events at the same time as the pupil retells the story, rather than recording his or her description, transcribing it, and then comparing it with the original. With this modification, a paraprofessional or student tutor might be able to check the retellings of students.

TABLE 3.1
Comparison of Propositions
Derived from a Story and
Those Contained in a
Student's Retelling

SOURCE: From "Story Retelling
Used with Average and Learning
Disabled Readers" by C. Hansen,
1978, *Learning Disability Quarterly, 1,* p. 65. Copyright 1978
by Learning Disability Quarterly.
Reprinted by permission.

Propositions	
Text	**Student**
(put, boys, tent) = A*	(put, boys, tent)
(six, boys)	(six, boys)
(location: A, by [side of] river)	
(took, boys, things)	
(things, eat)	
(go, boys, tent)	(go, boys, tent)
(time: sundown)	(go, sun, down)
(sleep, boys)	
(come, cow)	(come, cow)
(eat, cow, grass) = B	(eat, cow, grass)
(location: B around tent)	
(time: night)	
(afraid, boys) = C	(scared, boys) = C
(C, cow)[+]	(C, cow)
(thought, boys, bear)	(thought, boys, bear)
(not bear)	
(animal, cow)	(animal, cow)
	(go, boys, camping)[++]
	(eat, boys, something)[++]

[*]The letters indicate base propositions that are later embedded in other
propositions.
[+]Inference in text
[++]Inference in student's retelling

    Kintsch (1988) has greatly expanded on his work with proposition analy-
sis. Initially, he envisioned propositions as a simple and literal translation of
words and phrases from text; there could be only a finite number of propositions in a body of text. He has elaborated that belief to indicate that base
propositions trigger all sorts of underlying and related propositions, many of
which are dependent on the reader's background or schemata.

Research

Hansen, C. (1978). Story retelling used with average and learning disabled readers as a
measure of reading comprehension. *Learning Disability Quarterly, 1,* 62–69.

Kintsch, W. (1974). *The representation of meaning in memory.* Hillsdale, NJ: Lawrence
Erlbaum.

Kintsch, W. (1988). The role of knowledge in discourse comprehension: A construction-
integration model. *Psychological Review, 95*(2), 163–182.

4 ASSESSMENT: A COMPREHENSION INVENTORY

Background

One reason for considering this tactic is that it can save considerable time when it comes to assessing children's story comprehension. Once the narrative features to which pupils should respond are listed on a form, and that form is reproduced, the teacher is prepared; he or she does not have to write comprehension questions for the dozens of stories his or her children will read. Another motive for this technique is that it requires pupils to respond to a set of questions common to several stories. A third idea behind this approach is that it makes keeping data on children's performances easier. The teacher can better keep track of students' progress and intervene, if necessary, when specific types of problems arise.

Who Can Benefit

This tactic can be arranged for children of any age or ability level. As mentioned in the Modifications/Considerations section, items that children must explain can be chosen to fit the comprehension abilities of any level. This tactic is particularly appropriate for the teacher who wants his or her pupils to comment on a number of story features.

Because a partial script is available with this technique, this is an especially good tactic to use in pair- or peer-tutoring or when paraprofessionals, parents, or senior citizens are enlisted to instruct youngsters. These amateur teachers can easily check off the features of the story as the pupil comments on them, and they do not have to come up with test items on their own.

Procedures

1. List several features of the stories on which you would like the pupils to comment. The number and type of features will depend on the difficulty of the material and on how extensively you wish the child to describe it.

Comprehension Inventory Form:
Literal Items

Name _____

Book _____

	Page																				
	Date																				
Names the title or author																					
Names characters																					
Gives details of appearance of characters																					
Gives details of personalities																					
Gives details of the setting																					
Gives details of when the story takes place																					
Tells whether fact or fantasy																					
Tells plot in sequence																					
Gives main idea of the story																					
Gives details of feelings of characters																					
Number correct																					
Number possible																					
% of possible items correct																					

Comments:

FIGURE 4.1 Comprehension Inventory Form: Literal Items

SOURCE: The inventories shown in Figures 4.1 and 4.2 were developed by Kathryn Fantasia when she worked on project CHARTS (**CH**anging **A**chievement **R**ates of **T**eachers and **S**tudents), which was headquartered at the Experimental Education Unit at the University of Washington from 1976 to 1980.

**Comprehension Inventory Form:
Interpretive Items**

Name _____

Book _____

Page

Date

| Main idea of story |
| Tells whether fact or fantasy |
| Predicts outcome of future events |
| Gives an opinion of author's purpose |
| Relates story to personal experiences |
| Draws conclusions |
| Infers character traits and emotions |
| Interprets ideas, implied not stated |
| Makes classifications |
| Identifies cause and effect relationships (not directly stated) |
| Number correct |
| Number possible |
| % of possible items correct |
| Comments: |

FIGURE 4.2 Comprehension Inventory Form: Interpretive Items

2.   Write these items on a form and include spaces for a number of dates. Form 1 (Figure 4.1) has a listing of literal terms, and Form 2 (Figure 4.2) has an array of interpretive items.

3.   Go over each of these features with the child until the child understands them. You may need to give several examples of some terms before he or she is certain about their meanings.

4.   Tell the pupil to read a story or passage, and remind the student that after the story is read, he or she will be asked to comment on the story's various features.

5.   Ask the student, after he or she has read the story, to respond to as many items as possible. When the student identifies a feature correctly, make an *X* next to it on the form. Be certain the child sees you do this. After the student has commented on as many of the points as he or she can, discuss each of the other features, one at a time. For example, if the child did not relate the story to a personal experience, ask him or her to do so. Mark with a / any cued items to which the student responded correctly.

Monitor

Following the session, the pupil and teacher could mark the answers together, or the teacher could do this alone and later inform the pupil about his or her performance. Then, either the teacher or the pupil could chart the number of items that were addressed properly, and could compare that day's performance to scores at other sessions. As we carried out this project, we checked the unaided and aided responses differently. Others might decide to score each type of answer the same, or not to give credit for those items that were cued.

Data could also be kept on the specific features to which the pupil responded correctly and incorrectly. The forms are, in fact, laid out to facilitate this type of record keeping. Depending on which features are routinely omitted or incorrectly addressed, the teacher could provide a mnemonic aid or some other such technique to help the student respond more accurately.

Paradis, Chatton, Boswell, Smith, and Yovich (1991) developed a similar type of matrix to assess the comprehension abilities of youngsters. Following are the features on which they acquired data:

● makes predictions about story
● participates in the discussion
● answers questions on all levels
● determines word meanings through context
● reads smoothly and fluently

- retells selection using own words
- comprehends after silent reading
- reads "between the lines"
- possesses broad background knowledge

They rate each youngster's ability on those features in one of four ways: often (+), sometimes (S), seldom (–), and not observed (N).

Modifications/Considerations

As pointed out earlier, this tactic is quite versatile; a variety of features can be printed on the form. For beginning readers, or those having difficulty remembering what they read, the teacher might include only two or three items, such as "Who were the main characters in the story? What was the story about? Was the story fact or fantasy?"

Later, the teacher might include the usual "who," "what," "where," and "when" items on the form. For more advanced students, you might ask about imagery, the author's use of language, identification with characters or incidents, and emotional responses to the content (to borrow from the taxonomy of Barrett, 1968).

Several possible modifications to this tactic involve cuing, scoring the features, and providing feedback. In the example here, if pupils did not respond we gave them cues by asking them to comment on the omitted features. The teacher might instead provide cues for all the features <u>before</u> the pupils respond, or elect never to cue them on any of the features.

Research

Barrett, T. C. (1968). Taxonomy of cognitive and affective dimensions of reading comprehension. In T. Clymer (Ed.), *What is "reading"?: Some current concepts. Innovation and change in reading instruction, Sixty-seventh yearbook of the National Society for the Study of Education, Part II.* Chicago: University of Chicago Press.

Paradis, E. E., Chatton, B., Boswell, A., Smith, M., & Yovich, S. (1991). Accountability: Assessing comprehension during literature discussion. *The Reading Teacher, 45*(1), 8–17.

5 ASSESSMENT: USING "THINK ALOUDS" TO ASSESS COMPREHENSION

Background

The type of reading assessment explained here is an alternative to standardized assessment, the result of which is a product. The rationale for the think aloud technique is that reading is an active construction of meaning. The interactive process between the text and the reader's background knowledge explains how good "comprehenders" process text so rapidly.

Who Can Benefit

The assessment approach described here is designed to identify comprehenders of five types: good comprehenders, non-risk takers, non-integrators, schema imposers, and storytellers.

The *good comprehender* makes reasonable inferences about the topic of the passage, recognizes when more information is needed to confirm a hypothesis, and abandons original ideas in favor of ones that better account for information in the text.

The *non-risk taker* is a bottom-up processor who assumes a passive role by not going beyond the text to develop hypotheses. When readers of this type do formulate hypotheses, they often pose their theories in the form of a question.

The *non-integrator* develops new hypotheses for every segment of the text, and does not relate the hypotheses with one another. These readers are a mixture of bottom-up and top-down processors.

The *schema imposer* is a top-down processor who holds on to an initial hypothesis in spite of incoming information that conflicts with it.

The *storyteller* is an extreme example of a top-down processor. A reader of this type tends to draw far more on prior knowledge than on information found in the text.

Procedures

Preparing the Text

1. Choose a short passage (from 80 to 200 words) in either expository or narrative form.

2. Select text that is new to the reader but that pertains to a topic with which he or she is familiar.

3. Select text that is at the reader's instructional level.

4. Modify the text so that the topic sentence appears last, and occlude the title, if there is one. (Altering the text in this way encourages the reader to use strategies for making sense of the passage and inferring the topic.)

Administering the Think Aloud Procedure

1. Tell the reader that he or she will be reading a story in short segments of only a few sentences each.

2. Inform the reader that after reading the section, he or she will be asked to tell what the story is about.

3. Ask the student to read a segment aloud. After reading it, ask him or her to summarize what is happening. If necessary, ask nondirective probing questions that encourage the reader to generate hypotheses (i.e., "What is it about?") and to describe or identify the basis for the hypotheses (i.e., "What clues do you find?").

4. Continue this procedure until the entire passage is read. Ask the reader to retell the entire passage. The reader may reread the story first.

5. Ask the reader to find the most important sentences in the passage.

6. Tape-record the session and transcribe it.

Instructional Strategies

For *bottom-up processors,* encourage pupils to draw on prior knowledge to enhance understanding. Place emphasis on developing relevant background knowledge before reading. Assist pupils in visualizing and developing semantic maps that show relationships among ideas.

For *top-down processors,* emphasize cognitive flexibility and comprehension monitoring. One approach would be to ask students to write down reasonable hypotheses and then test them against the text.

Monitor

Ask the following questions about each reader:

1. Does the reader generate hypotheses?
2. Does the reader support hypotheses with information from the passage?
3. What information from the text does the reader use?
4. Does the reader relate material in the text to his or her previous experience?
5. What does the reader do if there is information that conflicts with the schemata he or she has generated?
6. How does the reader deal with unfamiliar words?
7. What other observations can be made about the reader's behavior?

Modifications/Considerations

As youngsters become more proficient in summarizing short passages, the length of the text could be extended. Likewise, as students become adept at discerning the main idea of passages when the essential theme is explicitly stated, they could be asked to identify the main thought of a passage when that thought is rather vague, or when there are actually multiple main ideas. For this project it is recommended that the sessions be tape-recorded and later transcribed. Although this procedure provides accurate and detailed information, it is a very expensive process. An alternative approach might be to keep accurate notes of the pupils' responses.

Research

Wade, S. E. (1990). Using think alouds to assess comprehension. *The Reading Teacher*, pp. 442–451.

6 ASSESSMENT: PRINCIPLES FOR MONITORING COMPREHENSION

Background

The notions offered here are founded on the idea that reading is a process of constructing meaning through the dynamic interaction among a reader's present knowledge, the information in the passage being read, and the context in which the reading takes place. This interpretation of reading is a dramatic shift from earlier definitions that view reading as being simply text-driven, suggesting that reading is primarily the faithful decoding of words.

Who Can Benefit

When the principles of comprehension assessment that are described here are acknowledged, the primary beneficiaries will be children and youth who, as a result of these principles, will be instructed not only to understand and comprehend materials they read, but also to incorporate these materials into their previous experience and awareness. Although children of intermediate age will probably benefit the most, children in other age groups—such as those in the primary grades and older students in middle school, junior high, or high school—would also profit.

Procedures

Noted here are five principles that should guide reading comprehension assessment. The principles are derived from advances in reading theory, research, and instruction since about 1975. These advances have formed the basis of the interactive definition of reading that was cited earlier.

Principle 1: Reading assessment must acknowledge the complexity of the reading process. As for *topical knowledge,* the more knowledge one has about the content and organization of the passage, the more easily meaning is constructed. The *situational context* must be taken into account when assessing comprehension; that is, the place in which reading takes place and the purposes for reading that have been assumed or suggested must be considered during assessment.

Principle 2: Reading assessment should focus on the orchestration of many kinds of knowledge and skills rather than on the knowledge and skills themselves.   Enabling skills are pedagogically useful only to the degree that they assist students in constructing meaning from text. With respect to *ecological validity,* reading assessments must not only come from texts and other materials that students read at school, but also from magazines, newspapers, advertisements, and other common materials.

Principle 3: Reading assessment must allow us to assess the dynamic quality of the comprehension process.   Teachers must keep in mind that variability among students and variability within students from one passage or type of reading to another is to be expected, and it is the process, not the product, of reading that deserves our careful attention. Therefore, it is necessary to develop assessment strategies that are dynamic rather than static.

Principle 4: In optimal classroom assessment situations, the teacher becomes a partner—an advocate for students in their progress toward expert reading.   It is important to assess students' typical performance rather than potential competence. The point of assessment is to maximize rather than typify student performance. Student learning is enhanced when students participate in taking responsibility for their own instruction.

Principle 5: Because reading is a complex, dynamic process and because students are continually growing and changing, we must employ a variety of measures for making instructional decisions.   Restricting reading assessment to a single measure presents a narrow picture of the complex and diverse nature of reading.

Following are five types of assessment recommended by the authors that are based on the principles just discussed:

- *Find a number of acceptable answers.*   Students are asked to find several answers to a query.
- *Rate acceptability of choices.*   Using a multiple-choice format, youngsters are required to rate the acceptability of <u>all</u> the options.
- *Generate questions.*   Students are asked to come up with questions that would help them understand or better organize the material.
- *Summarize information.*   Students verbalize what they consider to be the most important ideas. Or, in a recognition format, they rate or evaluate a set of questions about a passage.
- *Construct meaning.*   Students predict what will occur next in a passage; note the likelihood that certain events could happen; change their predictions as more material is read; and explain why predictions were altered, if they were.

Monitor

The principles identified and explained in this write-up deal entirely with the monitoring of students' ability to comprehend.

Modifications/Considerations

The research authors offered certain classroom indices that signal when effective assessment efforts are in progress:

- Teachers are critical consumers of available reading curricula and assessment tools.
- Teachers work closely with students and interact with them.
- Evaluations are based on the type of support students require to learn new material.
- Students are engaged in a variety of "real-world" reading materials and activities during instruction and assessment.
- Assessments focus on the "big" goals of reading (e.g., understanding).
- Continual reevaluation of students' progress occurs.
- A cumulative file containing anecdotal records of several reading activities is kept and is consulted periodically by the teacher and the student.

Research

Valencia, S. W., & Pearson, P. D. (1988). Principles for classroom comprehension assessment. *Remedial and Special Education, 9*(1), 26-35.

7 ASSESSMENT: PUTTING IT ALL TOGETHER

Background

The public disappointment with student achievement has led to increased assessment. There is a growing concern that students in U.S. schools are not doing as well as are students in other industrialized countries. This is especially true in reading, and with literacy in general.

In a related issue, there has been widespread and growing dissatisfaction with normative or standardized tests. These latter criticisms have led educators to devise alternate assessments, which have led to even more assessments. Numbers of educators have been critical of most forms of assessment because they have not "done the job." They have not satisfied the needs of various individuals who have a stake in developing reading skills. In the manuscript paraphrased here, a plan is outlined to assemble the pieces of the assessment puzzle so that all parties are informed about reading in ways that are most appropriate for them.

Who Can Benefit

When assessment approaches, and methods of reporting data from those assessments, are designed in accord with the audiences who should consider those data, then all concerned will profit—the general public, school administrators, parents, teachers, and students. Too often, educators attempt to come up with <u>one</u> test or a <u>single</u> battery of tests to pull together data to respond to all those individuals' needs. As is true of most "one-size-fits-all" schemes, the matter of assessment is not that simple.

Procedures

Different audiences need different information with regard to reading. (See Table 7.1.)

Public.   Members of the general public, who make decisions through elected officials and school boards, have a decided interest in the future of children and in their education.

Administrators.   School administrators need measures that compare student performance against a clearly defined curriculum. They also need norm-referenced comparisons of their students' performances against performances from other locales.

TABLE 7.1   Assessment Audiences

Audiences	The Information Is Needed To:	The Information Is Related To:	Type of Information	When Information Is Needed
General public (and the press)	Judge if schools are accountable and effective	Groups of students	Related to broad goals; norm- and criterion-referenced	Annually
School administrators/staff	Judge effectiveness of curriculum, materials, teachers	Groups of students and individuals	Related to broad goals; criterion- and norm-referenced	Annually or by term/semester
Parents	Monitor progress of child, effectiveness of school	Individual student	Usually related to broader goals; both criterion- and norm-referenced	Periodically; 5 or 6 times a year
Teachers	Plan instruction, strategies, activities	Individual student; small groups	Related to specific goals; primarily criterion-referenced	Daily, or as often as possible
Students	Identify strengths, areas to emphasize	Individual (self)	Related to specific goals; criterion-referenced	Daily, or as often as possible

SOURCE: From "Putting It All Together: Solving the Reading Assessment Puzzle," by Roger Farr, *The Reading Teacher,* September 1992, p. 29. Reprinted with permission of Roger Farr and the International Reading Association.

Parents. Parents are mainly interested in their own children. Parents want criterion-referenced reports; they are also interested in how their children perform on normed tests in comparison to other children throughout the United States.

Teachers. The primary concern of teachers is to help students in their classes. They are mostly interested in the type of information that will support the daily instructional decisions that need to be made. This information is generated by criterion-referenced tests and other types of assessment that are closely related to the demands of actual classrooms and life generally.

Students. If students are to improve their literacy skills they need to become good self-assessors. Students need to select, review, and think about the reading and writing in which they are involved. When students understand their needs, they will improve.

Monitor

This entire program has to do with monitoring.

Modifications/Considerations

Following are points from good reading theory that should be incorporated into an overall assessment program:

- *Authentic assessment.* The reading required on tests should be reminiscent of actual reading.
- *Performance assessment.* Reading assessment should monitor reading in process and should judge comprehension of text in a realistic way.
- *Observations.* Teachers should periodically observe children as they read and must learn to organize data from those observations in a way that enables them to make instructional decisions.
- *Portfolios.* The idea of portfolios is to demonstrate a student's progress in reading, thinking, and writing. Portfolios should be reviewed regularly by the student and teacher.
- *Integrated assessment.* Assessments should be designed to emphasize the use of information from particular reading selections in a realistic and interesting writing task.

Although the suggestions offered here pertain specifically to reading, the general notion that there must be different types of assessment for different audiences is pertinent to all other academic offerings and many other skills and behaviors as well.

Research

Farr, R. (1992). Putting it all together: Solving the reading assessment puzzle. *The Reading Teacher, 46*(1), 26–37.

8 ASSESSMENT: MONITORING MINIMUM COMPETENCY

Background

This technique is based on the idea of Minimum Competency Testing (MCT), an approach that has received considerable attention in a number of states. The rationale behind MCT is self-explanatory. Advocates of these tests seek to ensure that graduates from schools are at least minimally competent in the basic skills that enable them to be productive citizens. Although most of the public and some educators agree with the idea of MCT, one of its problems is in defining the areas that comprise "basic skills." Another uncertainty is the extent to which students need to attain these skills.

Who Can Benefit

This tactic, which is based on the work of Wells Hively (1980), is suitable for youngsters in every grade and is particularly appropriate for students approaching graduation. It would be an especially suitable way in which to monitor aspects of reading of students with disabilities, who may need extra help with reading.

Procedures

Certainly there are a number of important attributes of reading that should be assessed, but the focus of this tactic is on oral reading. With respect to reading, one could argue that if individuals are to become informed citizens, they should be able to read passages from newspapers. Therefore, one way in which to determine whether youngsters are learning to read—to the extent that they can read newspapers—is to directly assess their ability to do so. Not only does the form of assessment described here fulfill the requirements of "good assessment" as suggested by educators, it satisfies the requirements of those who advocate direct, functional, alternative, and authentic assessment.

The following are a set of procedures for gathering data as youngsters read from newspapers:

1. Select a newspaper passage that is not about a current happening; it should be one that describes some situation about which individuals know nothing. Many human interest stories would fill the bill.

2. Require a number of average youngsters at every grade level—1 through 12—to read the passage orally for one minute. Gather similar data from a dozen or so average citizens. Count the number of correctly and incorrectly read words these youngsters and adults read.

3. Chart the average correct and incorrect rates for the readers in each of the grades and for the adults. The average correct rate for the first graders will probably be about 20 correct words per minute; for grades four, six, eight, and twelve, those rates should increase to averages of about 130, 175, 200, and 300, respectively. The correct rates for the average adults will be about the same (perhaps a little lower) as those of the high-school students.

4. Establish the rates of the adults as the MCT criterion rates, ones that all graduates should attain (and preferably surpass) in order to be minimally competent. Meanwhile, the rates of the students from first grade on could serve as benchmarks along the way toward minimum competency. By comparing the rates of youngsters at any grade level with the standard rates obtained from that level, you can determine whether students are progressing satisfactorily.

5. Use these comparison or discrepancy scores (the differences between a specific pupil's score and the criterion rate) to (1) design special programs for readers who are off the mark, (2) compare the effects of one type of instruction with that of another, and (3) track the improvement of pupils over time. These periodic benchmarks might also be used with children with disabilities. Over time, a teacher can learn the extent to which a special youngster is falling behind or whether he or she is catching up to the standard.

Monitor

The essence of this tactic is assessment and monitoring. In order to get the most out of this procedure, data of two types should be gathered on each reader: correct and incorrect oral reading rates. Teachers could, of course, ask readers to retell as much as they can about the passage, and to count as many facts, words, or other features that they can during a set period of time. In order to make this procedure a fair comparison across grade levels, the teacher would have to read aloud to students the parts of the passage that they were unable to cover during the set time period.

Modifications/Considerations

In this example, only one skill—reading orally from a newspaper—was discussed; however, the same approach could be considered for other basic skills. Some of these might include reading street signs, recipes, bus schedules, or billboards; making change; filling out application forms; writing notes or letters; remembering facts or figures; using the telephone book, yellow pages, dictionary, or catalogs; telling time; and estimating costs and time periods. Indeed, a few years ago, a doctoral student and I (Lovitt & Davidson, 1989) gathered several types of oral reading data from youth with and without disabilities. We had those individuals read from six "functional" areas: a television guide, a recipe, directions on a bleach bottle, a manual on fire prevention, a bus schedule, and a want ad. Those data showed that for every type of reading, the average rates for the youth without disabilities were higher than those for the youth with disabilities. There was a great deal of overlap between the ranges of the two groups, however, for all of the types of reading; that is, some of the youth with disabilities read better orally than did some of the youth without disabilities.

Research

Hively, W. (1980). *Fluency in reading aloud from the newspaper: A promising measure of growth in reading competency.* Unpublished manuscript.

Lovitt, T. C., & Davidson, M. (1989). *Functional reading rates of youth with and without disabilities.* Unpublished data, University of Washington, Seattle.

9 DEVELOPING PHONEMIC AWARENESS

Background

Phonemic awareness is the ability to examine language independently of meaning and to manipulate its component sounds. Phonemic awareness requires the ability to concentrate on a sound in the context of other sounds in a word.

Who Can Benefit

Phonemic awareness is essential for early readers, that is, youngsters in kindergarten and first grade. Although phonemic awareness is not synonymous with phonics, it is unlikely that children who lack this awareness will benefit fully from phonics instruction since they do not realize what letters and spellings represent. Phonemic awareness has a positive effect on the development of children's word-recognition and spelling abilities, and is generally a powerful predictor of later reading achievement.

Procedures

Offered here are suggestions for assessing phonemic awareness and for developing that type of awareness.

Assessing Phonemic Awareness

1. Determine the pupil's ability to rhyme words. Pronounce several pairs of words and ask if they rhyme.

2. Assess the student's ability to blend speech sounds into words. Say the words in a "secret language" (e.g., *sh-i-p*) and ask the child to say the word.

3. Determine the child's ability to isolate speech sounds. Say words and ask the child to say the sounds of particular parts of the words (e.g., beginning or end).

4. Assess the pupil's ability to completely segment phonemes. Say several simple words to the child; ask him or her to say the words in a "secret language," that is, phonemically.

Developing Phonemic Awareness

1. In your teaching, involve literature that plays with the sounds in language. For example, in alliteration and assonance the same sound occurs in two or more words of text (e.g., *lethargic lions lounging in lots of local libraries*).

2. Schedule opportunities to write. Children should be allowed to write using "invented" spellings. They should be encouraged to grasp the transition of going from thoughts to saying words to writing words. The more children write, the better they become at segmenting sounds in words.

3. Help students develop the ability to hear sounds in words. Training begins with the segmentation of spoken language into words and syllables. Children could match words and syllables to physical movements such as clapping, marching, and walking in place.

Monitor

The teacher could measure a child's ability to perform any of the activities outlined in the Procedures section by arranging a number of exercises and simply crediting the child with the ones performed correctly. Those data could be kept over time. Of equal importance, however, the teacher should keep track of the stories the child reads and writes and should note his or her specific decoding, spelling, and comprehending problems.

Modifications/Considerations

Boxes could be used with some children to teach phonemic segmentation, which is perhaps the highest level of phonemic awareness and the most difficult to master. To use boxes, the teacher slowly articulates a word while pushing counters into the boxes, sound by sound. Initially, it may be easier for children to hear continuant consonants at the beginning of words. Gradually, the child takes over that activity.

An important caution: Phonemic awareness activities will not be helpful to children unless they are placed in a context of real reading and writing. A significant amount of the time allocated for language instruction should be devoted to reading, writing, and listening.

Research

Griffith, P. L., & Olson, M. W. (1992). Phonemic awareness helps beginning readers break the code. *The Reading Teacher, 45*(7), 516–523.

10 NINE GUIDELINES FOR PHONICS INSTRUCTION

Background

The idea behind the paraphrased research in this tactic is that quality phonics instruction should be a part of a reading program, but should be integrated and relevant to the reading and writing of actual text. It should be based on and built upon children's experiences with texts.

Who Can Benefit

According to the research author, phonics instruction should begin in kindergarten and end at the second grade. Obviously, some youngsters will require more phonics instruction than others. For those who have been read to and have considerable familiarity with print, the need for phonics instruction will be less than for those children who have had fewer experiences with books and print in general.

Procedures

Following are nine components of exemplary phonics instruction:

1. *The instruction builds on a child's rich concepts about how print functions.*   Phonics instruction must build on a child's concept of the process of reading. The child must know that instruction in phonics is not an end, but that it leads to something much bigger, much more exciting.

2. *The instruction builds on a foundation of phonemic awareness.*   Phonics is the relation between letters and sounds in written words, and is an important precursor to success in reading.

3. *The instruction is clear and direct.*   Instruction should go right to the basic concept that a letter in a word represents a particular phoneme. Since circling pictures, coloring, and cutting and pasting do not usually convey this concept, they should be avoided.

4. *The instruction is integrated into a total reading program.* At least half of the time set aside for reading instruction should be devoted to actual reading. No more than 25 percent of the time should be given to phonics instruction.

5. *The instruction focuses on reading words, not learning rules.* Children recognize new words by comparing them, or the spelling patterns within them, to words they already know. Good readers see words not in terms of phonics rules, but in terms of patterns of letters that are used to aid in identification.

6. *The instruction may include onsets and rimes.* *Onsets* are the parts of the syllable before the vowel, and *rimes* are the parts from the vowel onward.

7. *The instruction may include invented spelling practice.* Practice in writing during which students may use invented spellings might be a good substitute for direct phonics instruction.

8. *The instruction develops independent word-recognition strategies, focusing attention on the internal structure of words.* The point of phonics instruction is to get children to notice orthographic patterns in words and to use those patterns to read words.

9. *The instruction develops automatic word-recognition skills so that students can devote their attention to comprehension, not words.* The goal is for children to recognize words quickly and automatically, so that they can turn their attention to comprehension of the text.

Monitor

Although the teacher might keep some data on the extent to which children master certain phonics elements (e.g., onsets or rimes), more attention should go toward assessing how well students read and how well they understand what they read or listened to. Data should be kept on their rates of reading orally and silently and their ability to retell or explain text they have read or listened to.

Modifications/Considerations

Stahl (1992) makes a strong case for changing the beliefs of many teachers about phonics instruction. For one, he argues that phonics instruction should be guided by the context of reading; it should not be thought of as a set of discrete skills to be mastered one at a time. For another, he maintains that the arguments about whether or not we should teach phonics should end. According to Stahl, there is no getting around phonics instruction, regardless of what method or philosophy of reading instruction is espoused, whether it be instruction from basal texts, instruction with a whole-language emphasis, direct instruction, or any other method.

Research

Stahl, S. A. (1992). Saying the "p" word: Nine guidelines for exemplary phonics instruction. *The Reading Teacher, 45*(8), 618–625.

11 TEACHING ELEMENTARY STUDENTS TO USE WORD-PART CLUES

Background

Much of the vocabulary explosion that begins around the fourth grade is due to exposure to words with prefixes, suffixes, or both (most prefixed words also have a suffix). Whereas some educators recommend that long lists of suffixes and prefixes be taught, the authors of the cited research in this tactic make a case that only the most important ones should be taught.

Who Can Benefit

The research authors maintain that systematic instruction on affixes should begin in the fourth grade and continue through the fifth grade. According to them, instruction on affixes could begin a year or so earlier for more advanced pupils.

Procedures

Affix teaching can be limited to nine frequently occurring prefixes and ten frequently occurring suffixes. These affixes cover about 75 percent of the prefixed words and 85 percent of the suffixed words in printed textbooks for grades 3 through 9.

Prefixes

Four prefixes—*un-, re-, in-* (meaning "not"), and *dis-*—account for 58 percent of prefixed words.

Three pitfalls to teaching prefixes

1. *Inconsistent meanings.* Each of the "big four" prefixes has at least two distinct meanings.

2. *False analysis.* False analysis occurs when the removal of a prefix leaves no recognizable base word (e.g., *intrigue*).

3. *Misleading meanings.* For example, *unassuming* does not mean "not supposing."

Lessons on prefixes

1. Explicitly define and teach the concept of a prefix by presenting examples and nonexamples.

2. Teach the negative meanings of *un-* and *dis-*.

3. Teach the negative meanings of *in-* and *non-*.

4. Focus on the two meanings of *re-*: "again" and "back."

5. Return to *un-, dis-,* and *in-,* teaching their less common meanings.

6. Present three more prefixes and their meanings: *en-, over-,* and *mis-.*

Suffixes

Plural and/or third person singular *-s/-es* account for 31 percent of the suffixes used in the sample texts. Three inflectional suffixes, *-s/-es, -ed,* and *-ing,* account for 65 percent.

The primary focus of suffix teaching during the middle elementary grades is suffix removal and root identification.

Lessons on suffixes

1. Teach the concept of a suffix in the same manner as the prefix concept.

2. Present suffixed words that show no spelling change from the base word (e.g., *blows, boxes, talking*).

3. Illustrate each of the three kinds of spelling changes that occur in suffixation: consonant doubling (e.g., *thinner*), *y* to *i* (e.g., *worried*), and deleted silent *e* (e.g., *baking*).

Monitor

The most obvious way in which to assess pupils' ability to identify and give meanings to affixes is to print lists of affixes and ask students to write meanings or give examples of each. Another way to monitor progress would be to ask students to search for certain affixes in assigned reading passages. In addition to these obvious and direct ways to monitor students' ability to understand affixes, have students read passages in which these affix forms appear. Then determine how well students understand and can define not only the word that contained the affixes, but also the meaning of the larger narrative units.

Modifications/Considerations

If in their reading children come across a prefix or suffix that has not been included on the list of those they were taught, it should be taught, especially if the children are inquisitive about its meaning. Moreover, children could be asked to search for other instances in which that affix is used.

As pointed out here, some prefixes have multiple meanings. Teachers could take advantage of this fact and ask students, ones who are rather advanced in their awareness of prefixes, to look for examples of these inconsistencies in books or other materials they are reading.

Research

White, T. G., Sowell, J., & Yanagihara, A. (1989). *The Reading Teacher, 42*(4), 302–308.

12 ORAL READING: IDENTIFYING PROPER READING LEVEL PLACEMENT FOR STUDENTS

Background

The main idea behind this research is that *student placement,* that is, identifying the proper level at which to begin reading instruction, is extremely important. The goal is to place pupils at levels that are *just right*: not too high, not too low, not too difficult, and not too easy. The teacher wants to challenge the students, not frustrate or bore them.

There are a number of approaches for placing children in various reading levels. One is to begin all students in the appropriate reader for their grade (e.g., fourth graders are given fourth-grade books). Another approach is to use achievement tests. A third method is to rely on the placement tests that accompany the chosen basal series; and a fourth, to use an informal reading inventory.

The latter two approaches are the most direct because they require pupils, during placement, to read from material that is identical to or much like the passages they will eventually read during their instruction. The problem with both these methods is that the stories in the basal texts are not appropriately sequenced; the progression of difficulty from one story to the next is not steady. Yet youngsters are generally required, during placement, to read only a few stories, and each of these only once. Therefore, a pupil easily could be placed improperly because he or she read a story that was especially hard or one that was uncommonly easy. In order to preclude that possibility, the technique described here requires that several reading samples be taken.

Who Can Benefit

In the research that serves as our example, the pupils were elementary-age students who had learning disabilities. The technique is appropriate, however, for all students who need to improve their oral reading skills.

Procedures

1. Select a basal series. In the example research, the Lippincott Reading Series was used.

2. Choose three 200-word passages from various parts of each book. Choose sections that are complete so that there is a sensible flow of narration.

3. Prepare copies of these passages and put them between acetate sheets.

4. Write six comprehension questions for each passage—two each on recall, sequence, and interpretation. (Do not forget to make a teacher's copy that has the answers.) Put these between acetate sheets.

5. Make an initial judgment as to the child's reading level.

6. Require him or her to read orally and answer comprehension questions from three levels: the one you suspect is appropriate (e.g., 2-1), one below (1-2), and one above (2-2). Do this over a three-day period. On the first day, begin with the lowest level; on the second, the intermediate level; and on the third, the highest.

7. As the pupil reads each passage orally, pronounce any of the words the student mispronounces or does not try to pronounce. At the end of one minute, circle the last word on your copy that the student read. Allow him or her to continue reading until the passage is finished.

8. Ask the student the six comprehension questions and write down his or her answers.

9. Count the number of words the student correctly read as well as the number of errors. Mark down the number of comprehension questions answered correctly.

10. Chart the correct and incorrect oral reading rates per minute and the number of comprehension questions answered correctly.

11. Evaluate all the charted data from the three days (the oral reading rates and the comprehension scores).

12. Place the pupil in the highest level book in which the following are noted:
    - Correct rates are generally between 45 and 65 words per minute (wpm).
    - Incorrect rates are from 4 to 8 wpm.
    - Comprehension scores are between 3 and 4.

Monitor

Once a pupil is placed at a certain level, continue to keep data on the three features just noted. If these data indicate that the pupil is generally improving from one session to the next, the placement is a proper one. If he or she does not improve satisfactorily, however, the student should be placed at a lower level.

Modifications/Considerations

There are a number of variations on this theme. One modification is to use a different number of books from which the pupils are to read. In this tactic, three books were used; in the cited research, eight. Another possible change might involve the number of times the pupil reads from each book. In this tactic's procedure, students read three times; in the published research, they read five times. For another variation, the reading samples could be chosen based on different criteria. In the previous example they were selected randomly from a book. In the research study, the first stories in the texts were chosen. Another possible modification lies in developing different types and/or numbers of comprehension questions.

If it is the intent of informal reading inventories to assess a pupil's ability to detect main ideas from paragraphs or to determine his or her knowledge of vocabulary, it is important to design questions that fulfill the requirements for doing so. Duffelmeyer and Duffelmeyer (1989) and Duffelmeyer, Robinson, and Squier (1989) have presented discouraging data in this respect from their analyses of informal reading inventories.

Research

Duffelmeyer, F. A., & Duffelmeyer, B. B. (1989). Are IRI passages suitable for assessing main idea comprehension? *The Reading Teacher, 42*(6), 358–363.

Duffelmeyer, F. A., Robinson, S. S., & Squier, S. E. (1989). Vocabulary questions on informal reading inventories. *The Reading Teacher, 43*(2), 142–148.

Lovitt, T. C., & Hansen, C. L. (1976). Round one—placing the child in the right reader. *Journal of Learning Disabilities, 9*, 347–353.

13 ORAL READING: CORRECTIVE FEEDBACK

Background

The main idea of the corrective feedback approach is that although most children of intermediate age have been exposed to a number of word-attack techniques, many of them do not know how best to use them. Therefore, the teacher is responsible for instructing students on how to draw upon these ideas to decode unknown words.

The corrective feedback technique is a linguistic approach in that it encourages students to use syntax and semantics while they read. Children are encouraged to anticipate forthcoming words and to confirm their choices by integrating them with ongoing narration.

When this technique is used, the teacher or manager provides a sequence of cues to help children detect and correct the reading errors they make. Beyond its merit as an instructional aid, this technique is a valuable method for teaching problem solving. Children can, with proper training, rely on this same sequence of steps as they read silently.

Who Can Benefit

The pupils in Hansen's (1976) study, the basis of this tactic, were 9- to 13-year-old boys with learning disabilities. They had been classified as learning disabled because, although they were of normal intelligence, they achieved significantly below expectation (particularly in reading). This tactic would be particularly good for many youngsters of primary or intermediate age who are struggling with oral reading and who have been given a few tactics to use in deciphering unknown words.

Procedures

Table 13.1 lists the six steps of corrective feedback. While the child reads orally, use the first cue when he or she makes a mistake or cannot pronounce a word. If, after the prompt, the child is unable to come up with the correct word, use the second cue, then the third, and so forth.

Included in the table alongside each step are explanations for the cues and their theoretical bases.

TABLE 13.1   Corrective Feedback Hierarchy and Linguistic Rationale for Correction Cues

Cue	Explanation	Rationale
1. "Try another way."	Tell the student that he read a word incorrectly.	The student should be allowed to first choose own method of his correction.
2. Say, "Finish the sentence and guess the word."	Tell the student to use context to help decode the unknown word.	Syntax and semantics are the basic methods of word recognition.
3. Say, "Break the word into parts and pronounce each one."	Help the student to analyze the segments of the word.	Morphological elements are the largest units of words that have meaning.
4. Cover over parts of the word and ask the child to decode each.	Give the student an aided visual cue to decrease the amount of stimuli.	Aided visual cues provide a transition between morphological and phonological cues.
5. Say, "What sound does it make?"	Provide the student with a phonic cue to indicate the location of his error within the word.	Phonological elements are the smallest sound-bearing units in words.
6. Say, "The word is _____."	Provide the student with the correct word.	After the child has analyzed the word unsuccessfully, it should be given to him.

SOURCE: From "The Generalization of Skills and Drills vs. Corrective Feedback Instruction to the Independent Reading Performance of Intermediate Aged Learning Disabled Boys" by C. Hansen, 1976. Unpublished dissertation, University of Washington, Seattle.

Monitor

Before arranging the treatment and during the period this strategy is in effect, data regarding oral reading and comprehension should be kept. Specifically, those data should pertain to correct and incorrect oral reading rates and the frequency or percentage of comprehension questions answered correctly.

Modifications/Considerations

This tactic can be administered by a paraprofessional, such as a parent or unskilled aide, or by an intelligent intermediate- or secondary-age youngster. Because a script is provided, these individuals know what to do; they do not have to be creative. They know that the instructional cues should be used in the order they are printed. Pupils quickly become accustomed to this routine.

One modification of this approach is to have the administrator start by using a cue other than the first one with some youngsters. It may be more expedient for certain pupils to begin with the second or third cue rather than beginning at the bottom of the hierarchy and working up.

Pany and McCoy (1988) indicated that research on corrective feedback used with young children who had learning disabilities showed that corrective feedback enhanced recognition of isolated words on both immediate and delayed tests, improved word recognition in context, reduced the number of meaning change errors in context, and improved comprehension.

Research

Hansen, C. (1976). *The generalization of skills and drills vs. a corrective feedback instruction to the independent reading performance of intermediate aged learning disabled boys.* Unpublished doctoral dissertation, University of Washington, Seattle.

Pany, D., & McCoy, K. M. (1988). Effects of corrective feedback on word accuracy and reading comprehension of readers with learning disabilities. *Journal of Learning Disabilities, 21*(9), 546–550.

14 ORAL READING: REINFORCEMENT PROCEDURES

Background

Everyone is motivated by something. In fact, most individuals are reinforced by millions of events, items, and relationships. In this tactic, it is assumed that teachers and parents are in a position to identify reinforcers of children and are able to either grant or deny them.

When proper reinforcers are arranged for individuals, they are better able to focus on certain activities. Said another way, reinforcement often sharpens an individual's attention or concentration for certain tasks. (It is quite likely that if teachers and others spent more time identifying the motivational events of youngsters with attention deficit disorder (ADD), and more time in consistently arranging these reinforcing events, they would not have to rely so heavily on pharmaceuticals or other synthetic means to control these students' behavior.)

Who Can Benefit

Reinforcement procedures can be effective with pupils who seem unmotivated. In reading, this lack of motivation can be displayed in several ways: (1) children simply refuse to read, (2) pupils will read, but stall and fidget in the process, (3) youngsters read but have absolutely no enthusiasm for the activity, and (4) children try to read but have great difficulty in concentrating on the task; they lack endurance.

The following procedures can also be used with pupils who are erratic (a common phenomenon with exceptional children). Erratic youngsters may read a passage quite adequately one day, but the next day their performance is poor.

Procedures

There are two general methods of arranging reinforcement. One is to give something, the other is to take something away. The "something" could be a star, token, sticker, mark, point, or any other item or event. Furthermore, these things can be given or taken away for either correct performance or for incorrect efforts. The following are some examples of reinforcing activities:

- *Giving for correct performance.* Grant the child something if he or she pronounces a certain number of words correctly during a session or reads orally at or beyond a prescribed rate.

- *Taking away for correct performance.* Take away a workbook drill or a phonics activity if the pupil's performance matches or surpasses a predetermined level. The pupil, in other words, escapes some assignment.

- *Giving for incorrect performance.* Give more practice if the youngster's performance is not satisfactory. If, for instance, the child mispronounces more words while reading than is normal for the child, require him or her to read those words in another context for a number of minutes.

- *Taking away for incorrect performance.* This technique is particularly effective with the erratic performer. To use it, simply take away some item (e.g., a minute of recess time) for each error that is made (e.g., a misread word).

Monitor

As with many other reading tactics in this book, particularly those that focus on oral reading, three types of data should be obtained:

1. correct and incorrect words read per minute,
2. a measure of comprehension, and
3. the frequency of facts said per minute if the youngster is asked to retell what he or she read as a measure of comprehension.

These three types of data should be acquired throughout two or three phases. The first phase should be used to establish a baseline; during this phase, no intervention should be in effect (e.g., no reinforcement contingency is arranged). During the second phase, the intervention is put in place, and during a third phase, the intervention is either lessened or withdrawn totally.

Modifications/Considerations

One modification for this tactic is to combine the give and take-away techniques. For example, something could be given for correct responses and something else (or the same thing) could be taken away for incorrect responses. There are many choices, of course, as to what and how much of a reinforcer is given or taken away. Furthermore, you can change who decides what will be given or removed and who performs the operation.

Wiesendanger and Bader (1989) asked intermediate-age children to rate some popular classroom techniques that teachers arranged to encourage reading. The most popular rewards allowed students more flexibility and independence. The children also felt that instead of offering just one reward, teachers should present alternatives and let students select the ones they prefer. Higher ability students reported that they were not reinforced when stars were given or when their names were posted on the bulletin board for superior performance. Poorer readers said that they did not like their charts to be displayed publicly or to be compared with others.

Research

Lovitt, T. C., Eaton, M., Kirkwood, M. E., & Pelander, J. (1971). Effects of various reinforcement contingencies on oral reading rate. In E. A. Ramp & B. L. Hopkins (Eds.), *A new direction for education: Behavior analysis*. Lawrence, KS: Department of Human Development.

Wiesendanger, K. D., & Bader, L. (1989). Children's view of motivation. *The Reading Teacher, 42*(4), 345–347.

15 ORAL READING: PREVIEWING

Background

The idea behind this technique is that some pupils read haltingly simply because a few words block their flow. Some of these words may be consistently troublesome, whereas others may be words that the pupil has never seen.

Who Can Benefit

This technique has been used with pupils who generally read fluently, but who are blocked by certain words from time to time. When they stop at the word, the flow of the narration is disrupted as well as their train of thought. It is often difficult for them to pick up the reading again. This tactic is also good for youngsters who need a brief warm-up before reading. Practicing isolated words serves that purpose. Moreover, previewing is a good choice for pupils who need to concentrate more on certain word elements (e.g., prefixes). When the students are shown one word at a time, their focus is sharpened.

Procedures

1. Ask the pupil to read a passage aloud. When he or she mispronounces a word or omits it, correct the error. Require the pupil to say the word correctly, then encourage him or her to proceed.

2. Write down each word the pupil mispronounces or fails to pronounce. After the session, write each word on a 3" × 5" card.

3. Ask the pupil to practice these error words for 5 minutes following the reading session.

4. Put the index cards in a stack with other cards containing missed words from previous sessions.

5. Before the next session, scramble the error word cards, and require the pupil to identify them a few times. When he or she says a word correctly, put that card in a pile of "known words."

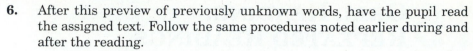

6. After this preview of previously unknown words, have the pupil read the assigned text. Follow the same procedures noted earlier during and after the reading.

7. On some occasions during the previewing session, select a few cards from the "known words" pile and present them with the cards from the "unknown words" pile. If the pupil has difficulty with an old word, put it in the "unknown words" pile for a time.

Monitor

The teacher might keep correct and incorrect rate data on the pupils' oral reading performances. These data could be acquired during a few sessions before a previewing technique is put into effect, then continued while the tactic is in use. By comparing the data from the two conditions, the teacher could determine the extent of the effects, if any, and when they might have occurred. The teacher should keep in mind as data are gathered on oral reading fluency that the prime reason for reading is not necessarily fluency, but the ability to comprehend text and to integrate that which has been read to prior experiences. Therefore, the teacher should periodically assess pupils' ability to understand and integrate information that has been read.

Modifications/Considerations

There are a number of ways in which to modify this technique. One method is for a teacher or some other good reader to read the passage to the pupil. Following, the student orally reads the same passage. Another modification is to have the passage recorded on tape. The pupil can listen to that taped passage, then orally read the passage (Rose & Beattie, 1986).

Yet another alteration is to preview words that are new to the pupil rather than error words. In many basal series, the new words for each story are printed in the back of the book or are included in the teacher's manual. The pupil could be required to rehearse these words before reading the story.

Another variation is to include either the error words or the new words in sentences or phrases and require the pupil to say them a few times before he or she reads the story. These phrases or sentences (or for that matter, the isolated words) could be recorded on language master cards. Using this device, the student is able to practice the items alone at any time.

Research

Jenkins, J. R., & Larson, K. (1979). Evaluating error-correction procedures for oral reading. *Journal of Special Education, 13,* 146–156.

Rose, T. L., & Beattie, J. R. (1986). Relative effects of teacher-directed and taped previewing on oral reading. *Learning Disability Quarterly, 9,* 193–199.

16 ORAL READING: REPEATED READINGS

Background

The rereading method is based, to some extent, on the automaticity theory proposed by LaBerge and Samuels (1974). According to this theory, a fluent reader decodes automatically, thus leaving him or her free to comprehend what is being read. Another idea to support this tactic is that a reading warm-up is helpful. Just as athletes, dancers, and musicians go through the same drills and exercises day after day, regardless of their level of proficiency, so should readers, particularly poor readers. Furthermore, this tactic is derived from the idea that children love the familiar; they enjoy doing what they can already do. Any music teacher will tell you that the songs their youngsters generally request are the ones they know, and parents who read stories to their children will inform you that they are asked to read the same stories over and over.

Moreover, more recent research (e.g., Dowhower, 1989) has given support to the fact that repeated reading is equal to or more effective than more complicated strategies such as note taking, outlining, or summarization. Repeated reading increases factual retention, leads to rapid reprocessing of text, enables pupils to remember more meaningful structures and idea units, and helps young children's story comprehension ability as well as encourages deeper questioning and insights.

Who Can Benefit

This tactic can be arranged to supplement the reading program of youngsters who have mastered some basic skills but who need to develop fluency. To gain the most from this approach, the student should know the names of the letters as well as their most characteristic sounds, and should be able to pronounce phonetically regular consonant-vowel-consonant (CVC) words and a few sight words. Furthermore, the pupil should be able to read a few words in succession and understand the notion of connected discourse.

This technique has been effective with a variety of pupils, many of whom failed badly in reading in the past and consequently dreaded reading. It has also been arranged successfully with youngsters who could not phrase properly; that is, they hesitated too much between some words and phrases. Generally, this tactic is an appropriate one for children whose reading rates are slow (less than 100 words per minute), because it gives them the idea that words can pop out at a more rapid rate.

Procedures

1. Determine what the pupil's average correct wpm rate is. This should be done over a period of two or three days. For illustration purposes, let us use 60 wpm.

2. Set a target rate that is above the average rate—one that challenges the youngster, but that is not so high that the child will not have a chance to reach it. As a rule, choose a standard that is 10 to 15 percent higher than the student's best rate on the material he or she is currently reading. In this example, the target rate would be set from 66 to 69 wpm.

3. Tell the pupil that he or she will learn to read faster, that you have identified a goal, and that when the goal is reached, he or she will advance to a new passage. Also explain what his or her reading rates have been and what they *should* be in order to move on.

4. Ask the student to read a passage. This could be an entire story, a page, a portion of a page, or a paragraph.

5. Time the pupil only for the first minute, but allow him or her to read the entire assignment. When the student finishes the passage, tell him or her what the timed rate was. If the pupil exceeded the target, move on to the next passage during that session.

6. Schedule some instruction or practice time if the pupil's rate was less than the target. Some teachers have required children to practice for a few minutes any errors committed in the session. Others have read portions of the passage to the child. Some have given instruction or advice such as "Look ahead as you read," "Try not to stall on certain words," or "Skip unknown words."

7. Tell the pupil what his or her rate was for the first reading and give praise if the rate was higher than the initial average rate. Remind the student again what the target rate is.

8. Ask him or her to read again and time this reading.

9. Continue this process for five readings. If the student reaches the target on one of these trials, move on to new material; if not, continue with the same passage, arranging instruction or practice following each reading.

10. Advance to a new passage after 10 attempts to reach the target, regardless of the pupil's performance.

Monitor

The method of assessment was explained as the procedures were outlined. The pupil's initial correct and incorrect oral reading rates should be entered on a chart. The goal rates also should be marked on the chart. Between the original rates and the goal rates, a record of each successive reading should be charted. After each data entry, the child should be encouraged to evaluate his or her own performance; that is, the child should explain how much he or she improved from the prior attempt, and estimate how much improvement is needed to reach the criteria.

Modifications/Considerations

One of the many possible modifications was already mentioned—altering the length of the passage. Another change could be the length of time the pupil reads. Ordinarily, children are timed for only one minute, but that period of time could be increased or decreased. Time between readings could also be changed. Some teachers merely tell the pupils what their rates were, whereas others arrange various exercises. The number of times per day that a pupil reads can also be changed. In this example, the pupil read five times; some teachers have scheduled from two to six readings.

Whichever of these options is selected, the entire session should last no longer than 20 minutes. During that time the pupil can read three or four times and practice on certain features for 10 minutes or so.

Lauritzen (1982) describes how this technique can be used with a small group. She suggests that teachers select passages for repeated readings that are highly motivating; for young readers these might include poetry, song lyrics, or folktales. She then recommends that pupils occasionally read the passage in unison as well as by themselves. She claims that in time, the children will ask to read their piece aloud.

Research

Dowhower, S. L. (1989). Repeated reading: Research into practice. *The Reading Teacher, 42*(7), 502–507.

LaBerge, D., & Samuels, S. J. (1974). Toward a theory of automatic information processing in reading. *Cognitive Psychology, 6,* 293–323.

Lauritzen, C. (1982). A modification of repeated readings for group instruction. *The Reading Teacher, 35*(4), 456–458.

Samuels, S. J. (1979). The method of repeated readings. *The Reading Teacher, 32*(4), 403–408.

17 ORAL READING: A LINGUISTIC METHOD OF SCORING ERRORS

Background

The research underlying this tactic was founded on the idea that a strong relationship exists between speaking and comprehending what is read. This tactic, which is an adaptation of Goodman and Burke's (1972) diagnostic schema, attempts to assess that relationship. Said another way, the purpose of this tactic is to determine whether the pupil (a) has an adequate knowledge of the grammatical relationship of words, and (b) knows the meanings of certain words.

Another purpose of this tactic is to simplify the Goodman and Burke method of assessment so that it can be regularly administered by teachers and still provide adequate linguistic information from which to design unique teaching approaches.

Who Can Benefit

This tactic is suitable for just about any reader. It would, however, be a particularly good approach for pupils with whom it is important to test not only their word-naming abilities, but also their understanding of language principles.

Since youngsters with learning disabilities often are delayed in acquiring language skills, they would certainly be good candidates for the use of this tactic. Moreover, many students in Chapter I, remedial, or English as a Second Language (ESL) situations would profit from this assessment. Another group of youngsters that might gain from this method are those with hearing problems, or more generally, children who simply have problems listening.

Procedures

1. Gather up the following materials: a pencil, two copies of a story, and one sheet of paper.

2. Ask the pupil to read orally from a copy of a familiar story.

3. Write the student's mistakes on your copy. For example, if the child reads "the dog" instead of "old dog," write the word *the* above *old*. Allow the student to read until he or she makes 10 mistakes.

4. When the pupil is finished reading, fold the sheet of paper into four columns. Label the first column "Unexpected readings"; the second, "Intended readings"; the third, "Language"; and the fourth, "Meaning." Then put the numbers 1 through 10 down the left side of the first column ("Unexpected readings").

5. List the student's 10 mistakes in the first column. In the second column, list the intended readings (what the words should have been).

6. Decide, for each mistake or unexpected reading, whether the word was grammatically correct. If it was, write "YES" in the third column; if not, write "NO." If the unexpected reading sounds like the child's speech, it is considered grammatically correct.

7. Examine the meaning of each unexpected reading. If the unexpected word means the same as the intended word, write "YES" in the fourth column; if not, write "NO."

8. Total the "YES" and "NO" responses in the two columns and decide whether to initiate training in grammar or meaning.

9. Begin instruction in either area if there are more than three "NO"s in a column. For grammatical instruction, you might (depending on the nature of the error) begin working on the construction of very simple sentences. For training in word meanings, you could develop a list of words and teach their meanings.

By administering this type of assessment a number of times, you might learn that there are particular grammatical or meaning errors that merit concentrated instruction.

Monitor

One way to monitor this tactic was explained in the procedures; that is, monitor progress by counting the number of grammar and meaning changes the pupil makes. If a treatment is scheduled, the teacher or the pupil might also keep a record over time of these data to indicate whether or not the instruction is succeeding.

Modifications/Considerations

At one time I combined this linguistic diagnosis procedure with the cloze approach. I blocked out every verb and then required a few children to read the story. As they read, I followed along in another book and made entries in two columns. One column was headed "Should be," and the other, "They said." In the first column I wrote down the actual word found in the text; in the second column I wrote the word they inserted. Later, I marked all the words in

Classroom Reading Miscue Assessment
Developed by Coordinators/Consultants Applying Whole Language

Reader's name _____ Date _____

Grade level assignment _____ Teacher _____

Selection read: _____

I. What percent of the sentences read make sense?

Sentence by sentence tally	Total

____ Number of semantically acceptable sentences

____ Number of semantically unacceptable sentences

____ % Comprehending score: $\dfrac{\text{Number of semantically acceptable sentences}}{\text{Total number of sentences read}} \cdot 100$ TOTAL ____

	Seldom	Sometimes	Often	Usually	Always
II. In what ways is reader constructing meaning?					
A. Recognizes when miscues have disrupted meaning	1	2	3	4	5
B. Logically substitutes	1	2	3	4	5
C. Self-corrects errors that disrupt meaning	1	2	3	4	5
D. Uses picture and/or other visual clues	1	2	3	4	5
In what ways is reader disrupting meaning?					
A. Substitutes words that don't make sense	1	2	3	4	5
B. Makes omissions that disrupt meaning	1	2	3	4	5
C. Relies too heavily on graphic clues	1	2	3	4	5

	No		Partial		Yes
III. If narrative text is used:					
A. Character recall	1	2	3	4	5
B. Character development	1	2	3	4	5
C. Setting	1	2	3	4	5
D. Relationship of events	1	2	3	4	5
E. Plot	1	2	3	4	5
F. Theme	1	2	3	4	5
G. Overall retelling	1	2	3	4	5
If expository text is used:	No		Partial		Yes
A. Major concepts	1	2	3	4	5
B. Generalizations	1	2	3	4	5
C. Specific information	1	2	3	4	5
D. Logical structuring	1	2	3	4	5
E. Overall retelling	1	2	3	4	5

FIGURE 17.1 Classroom Reading Miscue Assessment Form

SOURCE: From "Miscue Analysis in the Classroom" by Sheila W. Valencia, Lynn K. Rhodes, and Nancy L. Shanklin, *The Reading Teacher,* November 1990, p. 253. Reprinted with permission of Sheila Valencia and the International Reading Association.

the second column that were not verbs. This technique discriminated between some of the readers. Whereas some pupils consistently substituted verbs for verbs (if not the exact verb), others inserted nouns and other parts of speech for verbs. Certainly the first group of youngsters were more advanced linguistically than the latter and needed instruction according to their abilities.

Valencia (1990) has described a classroom reading miscue assessment. Figure 17.1 shows the form to use when administering this assessment.

Research

Goodman, Y., & Burke, C. (1972). *Reading miscue inventory kit, procedure for diagnosis and evaluation.* New York: Macmillan.

Tortelli, J. P. (1976). Simplified psycholinguistic diagnoses. *The Reading Teacher, 29*(7), 637–639.

Valencia, S. W., Rhodes, L. K., & Shanklin, N. L. (1990). Miscue analysis in the classroom. *The Reading Teacher, 44*(3), 252–254.

18 Oral Reading: Combining the Language Experience Approach and Cloze Procedures

Background

As its title indicates, this tactic combines the ideas from two familiar instructional procedures: the language experience approach (LEA) and the cloze technique. There are two bases for using the language experience approach. First, when a student practices reading words and phrases that he or she has chosen, there is a reasonable guarantee that the match between the student's spoken and written language will be nearly perfect. Another reason for arranging the LEA is increased motivation. Ordinarily, youngsters are excited about reading their own stories.

The motive for using *cloze procedures*—deleting certain words and requiring pupils to supply them—is that the readers are forced to deal with syntactic and semantic cues in order to come up with either the exact missing word or a reasonable substitute. Cloze procedures can be arranged in two ways. One method is simply to delete every *n*th word (e.g., every sixth word). Another approach is to take out words of certain types (e.g., verbs or "structural" words). In the former plan, the purpose is to improve comprehension in general; in the latter procedure, the aim is to concentrate on certain grammatical features.

Another consideration when embarking on the following procedures is that emergent literacy research suggests that learning to write complements learning to read. When the LEA approach is used, children are involved in real, relevant print; children realize that printed words are representations of events or thoughts that they already understand or have experienced.

Who Can Benefit

The study from which this tactic was developed dealt with young readers who have learning disabilities. This tactic also is suitable, however, for pupils who are not motivated about reading, who generally have problems understanding and remembering what they read, and who have vague notions about grammar and the appropriate uses of words.

Procedures

There are a number of modifications that are possible with this tactic, as we will cover later. The steps listed here are intended to help pupils recognize and understand structural words.

1. Ask the child to either dictate or write a story. At the beginning of this instruction, have the child try to keep the length between 100 and 150 words.

2. Type the story as it is presented. If you make changes, discuss them first with the child.

3. Prepare a cloze version of the story by deleting the structural words (e.g., *for, in, before, with, by*).

4. Tell the child what type of words have been left out, give an example or two, and explain that these are words that he or she commonly uses. Then ask the student to read the passage and to supply the missing words.

5. After the child reads the passage, compare the child's version to the passage that was originally typed. Discuss the following points:

    - How structural words function in our language.
    - What visual aspects or other cues in words might help in recognizing these words.
    - "Wrong" insertions and how they affect the meaning of the passage.
    - How structural words are used in other samples of the child's writing or in published materials.

Monitor

Data could be kept on the number of words read per minute, the number of perfect cloze responses, and the number of cloze responses that are at least plausible or linguistically correct in the context of the sentence. Data could also be kept on the number of correct alternatives a pupil could give for each cloze opportunity.

Modifications/Considerations

Whereas this example focuses on structural words, you might concentrate on other types of words such as adverbs/adjectives, action verbs, or nouns. To do so, delete words of the chosen category from the dictated passages.

Alternatively, you might instruct the pupil on general comprehension. For that purpose, delete every nth word, regardless of its type or function, and ask the youngster to fill in the blanks.

Not all story samples should be used for cloze procedures. For instance, if a child is deficient in a particular grammatical skill and the passage he or she dictates does not contain this skill, obviously this passage would not provide practice on the target item. Similarly, if a child needed to learn the meanings of certain words and they were not in his or her dictated stories, this approach would not be appropriate.

Research

Karnowski, L. (1989). Using LEA with process writing. *The Reading Teacher, 42*(7), 462–465.

Lopardo, G. S. (1975). LEA—cloze reading material for the disabled reader. *The Reading Teacher, 29*(1), 42–44.

19 ORAL READING: SKIP AND DRILL

Background

This tactic is based on some observations of basal readers. First, the stories in most basal readers have not been sequenced by degree of difficulty. In other words, the readability of the stories does not become progressively more complex from one story to the next. In some books, according to readability indexes, a few of the easier stories are located in the middle or toward the end of the text. This "scattering" is also true of some of the more difficult stories. Also, the words or phrases within the stories are not usually sequenced so that those in one passage must be mastered before advancing to the next.

A second observation is that most youngsters who are assigned texts that are at a lower level than the texts of their classmates are anxious to advance to a higher level. If, for example, a pupil is reading from a 2-1–level book while most of his or her friends are placed in 3-2 texts, the child probably would like to be promoted to that higher level.

Who Can Benefit

Several teachers have used this tactic effectively with exceptional or remedial students. It is best for students who can read at the first-grade level. These students know the letter names and sounds, can say most blends and CVC words, and can identify a few irregular sight words. This tactic has been particularly helpful for youngsters who read haltingly, make erratic errors, or have difficulty remembering what they read.

The Skip and Drill technique has been used successfully with several basal texts, including the Lippincott, Ginn 360, Holt, and Heath series.

Procedures

1. Place the child in the highest level book in which, generally, his or her correct rates are between 45 and 65 words per minute (wpm), incorrect rates are between 4 and 8 wpm, and comprehension rate is from 50 to 75 percent. (See the placement suggestions in Tactic 12.)

2. Divide the book into eight sections. If there are 150 pages in the book, for example, break the sections into about 18 or 19 pages each. Have each section begin with a different story or at least a logical starting point within a story.

3. Write 10 comprehension questions for each story or passage. They could be recall, sequential, inferential, judgmental, or other types of questions.

4. Gather baseline data for two or three days. Have the pupil read an entire passage or story, recording his or her correct and incorrect reading rates for only the first minute. After the pupil finishes the section, have him or her answer the comprehension questions. Keep data each day and perhaps chart the pupil's correct and incorrect oral reading rates and comprehension percentage scores.

5. Calculate the pupil's average scores and determine 25 percent improvement figures for each. If, for example, the child's three average scores during the baseline period were 50 wpm (correct rate), 8 wpm (incorrect rate), and 75 percent (comprehension), the improved scores would be 62.5 wpm (50 + 12.5), 6 wpm (8–2), and 93.75 percent (75 + 18.75).

6. Place marks on the pupil's chart to indicate these 25 percent improvement scores.

7. Begin the Skip and Drill phase. For a particular section, if the pupil's scores exceed the improvement scores, skip that entire section.

8. Schedule the following drills if none of the rates exceed the targets:
   - If the correct rate is not high enough, schedule five one-minute timings.
   - If the incorrect rate is too high, for five minutes have the pupil read several sentences that contain his or her errors.
   - If the comprehension percentage score is lower than the "improvement score," have the pupil reread the passage silently, locate the answers to the questions, and either write them or describe them to the teacher.

Monitor

Suggestions for monitoring this technique were included in the Procedures section; that is, after determining the student's baseline for correct and incorrect oral reading rates and percentage of correctly answered comprehension questions, set a 25 percent improvement goal for each area. During the phase when improvement goals are in effect, continue keeping data on the three aspects of reading performance and charting these rates. The teacher should also keep track of how many times the student skipped a section, how many times he or she did not, and how many times the student was asked to engage in one of the remedial exercises.

Modifications/Considerations

Skip and Drill can be modified in a number of ways. In one variation, the placement ranges could be changed by raising or lowering the correct or incorrect rate ranges. In another modification, the book could be divided into a different number of units. Some teachers have sectioned the book into four, five, or ten parts. Furthermore, the skip criteria can be changed. Instead of asking for 25 percent improvement, that mark could be higher or lower. Another variation is to use different criteria for the various scores. For example, the correct rate improvement might be set at 20 percent, the incorrect aim lowered by 30 percent, and the correctly answered comprehension questions percentage adjusted to 35 percent.

Rasinski (1989) detailed a number of techniques that have been successfully employed to increase the reading fluency of children. Following are the ones he noted: repeating the material several times, providing support for the student during reading, modeling fluent reading for the pupil, encouraging the pupil to read text units, and allowing the child to read easy materials. Other tactics in this collection discuss these approaches.

Research

Lovitt, T. C., & Hansen, C. L. (1976). The use of contingent skipping and drilling to improve oral reading and comprehension. *Journal of Learning Disabilities, 9*, 481–487.

Rasinski, T. V. (1989). Fluency for everyone: Incorporating fluency instruction in the classroom. *The Reading Teacher, 42*(9), 690–693.

20 VOCABULARY: DIRECT INSTRUCTION THROUGH MODELING

Background

This vocabulary development tactic is based on the following three features:

- maximizing engaged time on instruction,
- designing program steps (defining objectives, devising problem-solving strategies, developing teaching procedures, selecting examples, providing practice, and sequencing skills), and
- determining appropriate presentation techniques (small group vs. unison, oral responding, signaling, pacing, monitoring, diagnosing and correcting, and motivating).

Who Can Benefit

Teaching vocabulary through modeling is an appropriate approach for primary-age youngsters, particularly those who have a poorly developed vocabulary, or for children who have not been encouraged to learn new words at home. It is suitable for many youngsters with learning disabilities who have not amassed an adequate vocabulary. Moreover, this tactic would be quite useful for youngsters in ESL classes who can decode a number of words but do not always understand their meanings.

Modeling is the use of physical objects or demonstrations to convey the meaning of a word. This technique is often used when a verbal explanation of a new word would most likely include other words the student does not know or understand. Modeling is used primarily to teach the names for common objects, actions, colors, and shapes and attributes of size.

Procedures

The first step when using modeling to teach vocabulary is to formulate a set of statements about the word being taught. Develop three to six appropriate examples so that the student has enough information to generalize to other instances of the word's use. Use statements or questions that can be answered with a "yes" or "no."

TABLE 20.1   Format for Teaching Vocabulary Through Modeling

		Object	Adjective (Color)	Adverb	Adjective (Texture)
Step 1	Model positive and negative examples. Present 3 to 6 examples.	"This is a shoe" or "This is not a shoe." Examples: black sock, brown shoe, red shirt	"This is red" or "This is not red." Examples: 2" black disk 2" red disk 4" white disk	"This is running swiftly" or "This is not running swiftly." Examples: walk slowly, sing loudly, run swiftly.	"This is smooth." Examples: sandpaper, book cover, tree bark
Step 2	Test with yes/no questions. Give positive and negative examples until pupil gives 6 consecutive correct answers.	"Is this a shoe?"	"Is this red?"	"Is this running swiftly?"	"Is this smooth?"
Step 3	Test by asking for names. Offer examples until pupil gives 6 consecutive correct answers.	"What is this?" sock, shoe, shirt	"What color is this?" red, black, white	"Show me how you run swiftly."	"Find the smooth surface."

SOURCE: Reprinted with permission of Macmillan College Publishing Company from DIRECT INSTRUCTION READING, 2/e by Douglas Carnine, Jerry Silbert and Edward J. Kameenui. Copyright © 1990 by Macmillan College Publishing Company, Inc.

The second step is to test the pupil with yes/no questions about the word until he or she gives six consecutive correct responses.

The third step is to ask the student to provide the correct word for the modeled meaning. Do this until the pupil provides six consecutive correct answers.

Table 20.1 explains in more detail the steps a teacher should follow to teach an object, a color adjective, an adverb, and a texture adjective.

Monitor

One way to assess the effects of this technique on the development of vocabulary is simply to give a number of pretests and posttests. There could be 10 or so new words on each test. The pupil's scores on the two tests could be compared a few days following the treatment or when he or she had reached mastery during the intervention. The same test could be given a week or so following treatment to determine the extent to which the student had remembered the words. Another way to test a pupil would be to give the new words in a sentence rather than in isolation.

Modifications/Considerations

You may choose to give more or fewer examples to teach certain words. This would, of course, be determined by keeping data of some type on the pupil's progress.

These activities (or at least some of them) can be conducted with small groups. If the script for teaching various objects or words is laid out, it can be followed by paraprofessionals or pupil tutors. Parents can also use this approach with their youngsters during holidays and summer vacations to review existing vocabulary as well as to teach new words.

Blachowicz and Lee (1991) offer six guidelines for classroom vocabulary instruction:

1. Choose all vocabulary for instruction from contextual literary and content reading that is done in the classroom. In other words, focus on words that students will encounter in their regular curriculum.

2. Use maps or organizers of the reading material to help identify words for study. See Tactics 29 and 30 in this section for examples of such devices.

3. Plan prereading knowledge activation activities for the selection. See to it that children see and hear the important vocabulary words in a selection before the passage is read or studied.

4. Involve vocabulary in postreading discussion. One strategy is for the teacher to use the featured vocabulary words in questions asked the children. Another approach is to require children to use the appropriate focus words when answering questions.

5. Use contextual reinspection and semantic manipulation for words that are still unclear after reading and discussion. One way to do this is to identify the key words and ask children to search through passages that contain those words. Once students have found the words, ask them to underline or tell you about the words surrounding the key words that give clues to the meanings of the key words.

6. Use vocabulary in an integrated way. Encourage children to use the new words in retellings, responses, and in artistic, dramatic, or aesthetic ways.

Research

Blachowicz, C. L. Z., & Lee, J. J. (1991). Vocabulary development in the whole literacy classroom. *The Reading Teacher, 45*(3), 188–195.

Carnine, D., Silbert, J., & Kameenui, E. J. (1990). *Direct instruction reading* (2nd ed.). New York: Merrill/Macmillan.

21 VOCABULARY: PRECISION TEACHING (PT) SHEETS

Background

It is extremely important to learn the common vocabulary of a subject to fully understand it. For example, the following list of physical science words are ones that youngsters in intermediate classes are expected to know: *observation, experiment, probing, investigate, environment, chemistry, solution, amplify, voltage, molecule, compound, nuclear,* and *dissolve.* The approach described here for teaching vocabulary is based on features of Precision Teaching (PT): setting performance aims, charting performances, making instructional decisions from these data, and practicing with these materials until the performance aims are reached.

Who Can Benefit

Mastery of the specialized vocabulary of some content-area classes can be especially difficult for students whose reading abilities are below average. In one of the studies referenced here, pupils from several seventh-grade science classes were instructed with the PT sheets. Those students were taught in groups of six, each of which included two high-performing, two average-performing, and two low-performing students. The technique also would be suitable for younger students studying science and social studies.

Procedures

Constructing Vocabulary Sheets

1. Identify the key words in a chapter or passage in one of the following ways:

   - Select the words the publisher has highlighted (e.g., words that are italicized or that appear in bold).
   - Copy the words the publisher has included in a vocabulary section (often located at the end of the chapter).

- Pull out the essential words used in the introduction or summary section of the chapter.
- Select words that are identified in the book's glossary.
- Choose key words from the index.
- Require a few pupils to read the chapter and note words they cannot pronounce or for which they do not know the meaning.

2. Following these guidelines, write simple definitions for the words that were identified:

- Include words familiar to the students.
- Keep definitions short (4–10 words) with no unnecessary words.

3. Print the vocabulary words (no definitions) at the top of one side of the vocabulary sheet (see Figure 21.1). Below this list, write the definitions over and over again across the grid so that each definition appears three or four times.

4. On Side 2 of the vocabulary sheet, print the vocabulary words, along with their definitions, at the top. Below this section, print the vocabulary words over and over on the grid, with each word corresponding to the definitions written on the other side (see Figure 21.2).

Completing the Precision Teaching Package

1. Give each student a manila folder. Attach an acetate sheet to one of the inside flaps; on the inside of the other flap, tape a chart. (See the illustration of a Precision Teaching folder in Figure 21.3).

2. Personalize the folders. Ask students to write their names on the folders and decorate them according to a theme of their choice.

3. Establish a management system for storing and handing out folders. Choose methods that are smooth and fit in with your management style.

4. Purchase erasable marking pens for the students.

Teaching with the PT Package

1. Pass out folders and pens.

2. Give the following directions:

- Turn the folder lengthwise so that the hinge of the acetate sheet is in the middle and opens nearest to you.
- Place the practice sheets under the acetate with the "fill-in-the-blank" definitions facing you.
- Using the special pen, fill in the blanks on your sheets with the proper vocabulary words as fast as you can.
- Start with the item farthest to the left on the top row, move one at a time across that row, then move to the item on the left on the next row down. Do not skip around.
- Write as neatly and as rapidly as you can.

Unit 1, Sheet #1

Chapter 1: Measuring and Experimenting

Student _____
Date _____
Teacher _____
Period _____

buoyancy (buo)
displacement (dis)
SI (SI)
standard (stan)

hypothesis (hyp)
observing (ob)
inference (in)
scientific method (s.m.)

_____ is an international system of units (Metric System).

A _____ is a proposed answer to a question or tentative solution to a problem.

_____ is a way to determine the volume of an odd-shaped piece of matter.

A conclusion based on observation is called an _____.

A fixed quantity used in measuring is a _____.

_____ is taking notice and gathering data; using senses to find out things.

The upward push on an object placed in a liquid is called _____.

A fixed quantity used in measuring is a _____.

The _____ way to solve problems: observing, measuring, explaining, and testing.

_____ is an international system of units (Metric System).

A conclusion based on observation is called an _____.

A fixed quantity used in measuring is a _____.

A fixed quantity used in measuring is a _____.

A conclusion based on observation is called an _____.

The _____ way to solve problems: observing, measuring, explaining, and testing.

_____ is a way to determine the volume of an odd-shaped piece of matter.

A _____ proposed answer to a question or tentative solution to a problem.

_____ is taking notice and gathering data; using senses to find out things.

The upward push on an object placed in a liquid is called _____.

_____ is an international system of units (Metric System).

The _____ is a way to solve problems: observing, measuring, explaining, and testing.

_____ is a way to determine the volume of an odd-shaped piece of matter.

A _____ is a proposed answer to a question or tentative solution to a problem.

The upward push on an object placed in a liquid is called _____.

_____ is taking notice and gathering data; using senses to find out things.

FIGURE 21.1 Side 1 of a Precision Teaching Sheet Containing Textbook Terms at the Top Left and Their Definitions Below, Printed Randomly Three or Four Times Across Five Columns

buoyancy   = upward push on an object placed in a liquid
displacement   = way to determine the volume of an odd-shaped piece of matter
SI   = international system of units (Metric System)
standard   = fixed quantity used in measuring
hypothesis   = proposed answer to a question or tentative solution to a problem
observing   = taking notice and gathering data; using senses to find out things
inference   = conclusion based on observation
scientific method = orderly way to solve problems: observing, measuring, explaining, and testing

SI	observing (ob)	standard (stan)	displacement (dis)	SI
hypothesis (hyp)	buoyancy (buo)	inference (in)	hypothesis (hyp)	scientific method (s.m.)
displacement (dis)	standard (stan)	scientific method (s.m.)	inference (in)	displacement (dis)
inference (in)	scientific method (s.m.)	SI	observing (ob)	hypothesis (hyp)
standard (stan)	buoyancy (buo)	standard (stan)	observing (ob)	buoyancy (buo)

FIGURE 21.2 Side 2 of a Precision Teaching Sheet Containing Textbook Terms and Their Definitions at the Top, and the Terms That Match the Definitions Presented on Side 1 (Figure 21.1)

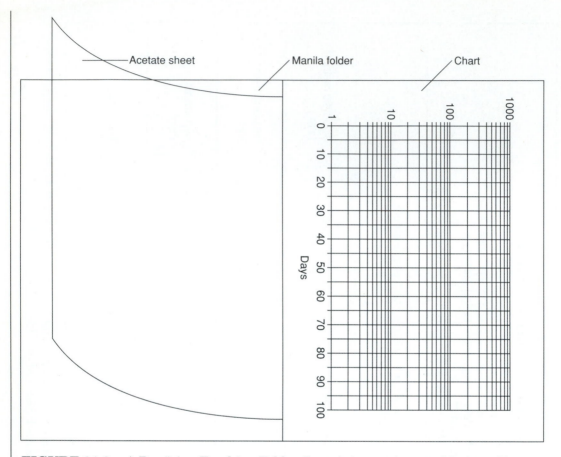

FIGURE 21.3   A Precision Teaching Folder Containing an Acetate Marking Sheet and a Standard Behavior Chart for Recording Student Performance

- Refer to the list of words at the top of the page if you need to check your spelling.[*]
- Flip the sheet over and look at the filled-in definitions if you cannot remember the meaning of a word.[*]

3.   Begin the timings. Allow students to work for one minute.

4.   When finished, instruct students to check and count their answers in the following manner:

- Flip the practice sheets over and compare your responses with the answers on the sheet.
- Circle incorrect answers and write in the correct word.
- Count the number of correct and incorrect answers.

5. Explain to students the components of a graph and how to chart their data:

- Vertical lines = Day *Lines* (Sunday is represented by heavy lines, with each succeeding line representing successive days of the week.)
- Horizontal lines = *Rate Lines* (Explain what the 1s, 10s, 100s, and the lines in between them indicate.)
- Place data from the first timing on the first day's line of the first week, and so on. (*Note:* Four timings, one after another, three times a week, are recommended.)

6. Ask students to evaluate their scores by comparing their best score with a classroom goal.

7. Collect folders and pens. This should be done quietly and quickly. File the folders so they can be accounted for and distributed easily the next session. Count pens to see that they have all been returned.

*Tell students to rely on this procedure only if absolutely necessary.

Monitor

Suggestions for monitoring appear in Procedure numbers 4 and 5, "Teaching with the PT Package." Pretests and posttests would provide an additional evaluation.

Modifications/Considerations

PT vocabulary sheets can be altered in several ways. For instance, the number of words could vary, or abbreviations might be used in place of whole words for definitions. The advantage to using the shortened form is that students can cover more ground during the one-minute timings. A word of caution, however: Test students periodically to make sure they still know what words the abbreviations stand for. The vocabulary sheets can be used for peer tutoring, pair teaching, homework, or review sheets. The classroom goal mentioned in Procedure number 6, "Teaching with the PT Package," may be based on the performance of one of the best students in the class. The suggested rate is about 20 correct answers per minute.

Research

Lovitt, T., Fister, S., Freston, J., Kemp, K., Moore, R., & Schroeder, B. (1992). *TRIP: Translating research into practice.* Longmont, CO: Sopris West.

Lovitt, T., Rudsit, J., Jenkins, J., Pious, C., & Benedetti, D. (1985). Two methods of adapting science materials for learning disabled and regular seventh graders. *Learning Disability Quarterly, 8,* 275–285.

22 VOCABULARY: CONSTRUCTING POSSIBLE SENTENCES AND PREDICTING WORD MEANINGS

Background

This technique for developing vocabulary draws on a number of characteristics of effective instruction. One such characteristic is eliciting students' prior knowledge. The Possible Sentences technique requires students to think about relationships between word concepts. Moreover, it involves interaction among the members of a class, and requires a great deal of active responding and processing.

Who Can Benefit

The research supporting this tactic was carried out with several fifth-grade classes, during which time the youngsters were expected to learn new words in science and social studies topics. This approach also would be an effective one with older youngsters in those or other content areas, and would be useful in assisting younger students to learn new words from narrative passages.

Procedures

1. From a science or social studies textbook, choose six to eight words that might cause difficulty for students. These *unfamiliar* words are usually key concepts (e.g., *front, barometer, humidity, air mass, air pressure, meteorology*).

2. Select an additional four to six words that are likely to be *familiar* to the students (e.g., *high, rain, clouds, predict*).

3. Write both sets of words on the chalkboard and offer a brief definition of each.

4. Direct students to think of sentences that contain at least two of these words.

5. Write their suggestions on the board. Include <u>all</u> the sentences, even those that do not make sense.

6. Ask the students to read the passage from which the words came.

7. Following the reading, return to the sentences on the board and discuss the sentences as a class. If a sentence is true, in that it agrees with information given in the passage, leave it. Otherwise, rewrite the sentence so that it does agree with the material just read.

Monitor

In the cited research, three types of measures were arranged:

1. Students were asked to *write* as many *facts* as they could about the passage they read. They were given credit for each fact that was in the story. This was a measure of literal comprehension.

2. Students were given a *sentence anomaly test* consisting of sentences containing the unfamiliar words. Some sentences were true and some were clearly false. Students were credited with each correctly identified sentence. This was a measure of the students' recall of specific information.

3. Students were given a *multiple-choice test* that featured the unfamiliar words.

Modifications/Considerations

Several modifications are possible with this tactic. For example, instead of merely crediting students for facts they write from the story, students could be credited with responses that come from other materials and experiences as well, so long as the responses are correct or at least plausible. Using this modified technique, the research authors carried out studies with groups of students and with individuals. Pupil performances were generally better in group situations than in individual ones.

The Possible Sentences technique should be included in the repertory of teachers dedicated to instructing vocabulary from content areas. It could be included with other worthwhile practices such as Semantic Mapping, Semantic Feature Analysis, and Quadrant Charts. (Most of these approaches are discussed in this book.)

According to the research authors, there are three general principles that are common to effective approaches for instructing vocabulary: (a) Effective approaches include both definitional and contextual information. (b) Effective approaches involve students in active word learning. (c) Effective approaches provide multiple exposures.

Research

Stahl, S. A., & Kapinus, B. A. (1991). Possible sentences: Predicting word meanings to teach content area vocabulary. *The Reading Teacher, 45*(1), 36–43.

23 VOCABULARY: LEARNING THROUGH READING

Background

According to the authors of the cited study as well as many others, there is a significant relationship between vocabulary knowledge and reading comprehension. This is not to mention the notable correspondence between vocabulary knowledge and performance on standardized and other tests. In spite of its importance, little classroom time is devoted to specifically instructing students in vocabulary. The notion supporting this tactic is that children can be taught the definitions and uses of words through context.

Who Can Benefit

The pupils in the cited research were fifth graders from four classrooms. The procedures explained here, however, are applicable for a wide range of youngsters and a broad range of words.

Procedures

1. Select the words that are to be taught. Following are the 18 words that were identified for instruction in the referenced study: *abhor, acquiesce, adroit, altercation, avocation, entice, disparate, eradicate, expedite, incarcerate, loquacious, meticulous, passive, potent, provocative, reform, transient,* and *virtuoso.*

2. Write at least 10 paragraphs for each word, with each paragraph comprising four to six sentences. The paragraph context should strongly imply the meaning of the target word and should contain a synonym for it. Following is an example sentence that features *avocation*.

    My aunt Alta's avocation is gardening. She works as a physician at a local hospital during the week. On weekends she spends time in her garden. Her hobby means a lot to her. Aunt Alta is extremely proud of the flowers she grows. She should be; they have been awarded a number of prizes at fairs.

3. As a class, go over the list of words and their meanings. Discuss the meanings and ask students to use the words in sentences.

4. Give the children the paragraphs for the words. The teacher may opt to concentrate on only one word at a time, or may decide to pass out paragraphs for three or four words at a time. If the latter plan is adopted, the teacher should target words that are as different as possible along several dimensions (e.g., spelling and meaning).

5. Ask the children to read each paragraph, and, as they do, have them identify the key word. This activity could be arranged individually, in small groups, or with the entire class.

6. Ask the children to write other paragraphs that use the key words once they have read and discussed the paragraphs prepared by the teacher.

7. Have some of the students read their paragraphs to the class. As a class, the pupils could comment on whether or not the key words had been used appropriately.

Monitor

In the cited study, four measures were scheduled to determine the effects of the vocabulary instruction:

1. *Supply definition.* All the target words were embedded in sentences and underlined, with one sentence being used for each word. The students were asked to read the sentences and then write the definitions for the key words.

2. *Select definition.* This was a multiple-choice test. Four choices were given for each key word and the students' task was to identify the proper one.

3. *Sentence completion.* This too was a multiple-choice test. The target words were provided in phrases (e.g., *An altercation is most likely to happen . . .*). Then, four phrases were provided for each target word, one of which would correctly complete the sentence (e.g., *between two people who don't like each other*).

4. *Reading comprehension.* Passages of about 200 words were written that contained six of the key words. Passages were constructed so that there were few if any context clues for the key words. Several questions then were developed from these narrations.

Modifications/Considerations

Several modifications are possible with this tactic. Certainly, the number of words identified for instruction in a period could be altered. In this example, there were 18. Moreover, the number and length of paragraphs used to display the target words could differ from the procedures used in this study. Another modification could be to give the students a few sentences in which the key words are used inappropriately. It would probably be a good idea to do this when the students were fairly secure in the meanings of the target words. It was pointed out in the cited study that an absolute minimum of 10 instances of offering the words in context should be used. For that reason it is wise to have the children prepare passages in which the key words are used correctly, as suggested earlier.

Research

Jenkins, J. R., Stein, M. L., & Wysocki, K. (1984). Learning vocabulary through reading. *American Educational Research Journal, 21*(4), 767–787.

24 SUSTAINED SILENT READING

Background

The idea to support this technique is that the best way to learn to read is to read. Once a pupil has the basic reading skills, he or she needs to practice them. Another thought behind this tactic is that teachers should also read, thereby serving as models for the youngsters. If teachers show interest in reading and children see their enthusiasm, the concern for reading may be contagious. It is hoped that children will become eager to read and will do more of it, improve in skill, read even more, become even more enthusiastic, and so forth.

Who Can Benefit

Sustained Silent Reading (SSR) is an appropriate technique for youngsters of all ages. Certainly the time allotted for SSR should be adjusted for children of different ages and abilities. Only 5 minutes or so is enough for first graders, increasing to 30 or 40 minutes for high-school youngsters. Even children who are unable to read can profit from SSR. They can be given picture books and then encouraged to look at them and imagine their own stories.

Procedures

There are a number of steps that the teacher or building principal can take to ensure that a class or school gets off to a good start with SSR. There is more to SSR than simply telling pupils to read silently for a few minutes and allowing nature to take its course.

Laying the Groundwork

1. *Advertise SSR.* Put up posters announcing that SSR is coming, tell pupils what it is, read portions of books to them, arrange book tables and bulletin boards that contain different book titles, set up display corners, group books by topics, and so forth.

2. *Collect reading materials.* Assemble books on a wide variety of topics at various levels; bring in picture books, magazines, catalogs, newspapers, and pupil-written books; ask parents to send books and magazines to school.

3. *Schedule an SSR time.* A period should be consistently set aside every day; students and teachers must be able to count on it. Some schools have chosen the period following lunch. This settles children down after talking and playing and prepares them for a few more hours of schoolwork. Some SSR programs might begin with a short time period that is gradually extended.

4. *Develop SSR guidelines.* Before starting the program, tell everyone concerned what SSR is all about and set a few rules and requirements. Emphasize that the reading period is for pleasure reading; inform the children that they can select any material they wish to read and that they will not be tested on it. Tell pupils that even the teachers will be reading.

Maintaining Interest

1. *Everyone reads.* The teacher can read a favorite book or a professional journal; the children can read whatever they choose; all other school personnel read as well (i.e., psychologists, janitors, cooks, principals).

2. *Materials selection.* Have children select what they want to read before the SSR time. Continually "sell" books and reading, and encourage children to sample books before they select them—they should find something they can read and that interests them.

3. *Variety is important.* Have students create a reading corner. Set up a bulletin board on which children can advertise their favorite books, and invite special people to come into the classroom and read silently with the youngsters (e.g., principal, a parent, the school psychologist). Teachers could talk with children about the books *they* have been reading (enthusiastically, of course).

Monitor

Perhaps the easiest way in which to monitor the effects of a SSR program is to have children make a list of the books, articles, or other types of material they read during this time. Yet another way, one that pertains more to function, would be to arrange a pretest prior to using SSR, one that tapped the children's ability to read orally or silently and to comprehend. Then later, after several weeks of being involved in SSR, readminister the tests. Yet another approach to evaluating the individual effects of SSR would be to ask the children questions about their reading. Hobbs (1989) suggests several questions:

- Did you have a good reading period today?
- Did you read better today than you did yesterday?
- Did the ideas in the book hold your attention?
- Did you want to read faster to find out what happened?
- Was it hard for you to concentrate on your reading today?
- Were there words in the passage today that you didn't know?
- Were you bothered by anything in the room today as you read?

Modifications/Considerations

Any number of choices can be made when a class or school arranges for SSR: the time of day the reading is scheduled, the length of time people read, the place(s) they can read, the publicity that goes into starting up and maintaining the program, and the extent to which the adults are involved in reading. Whatever the choices and whatever the difficulties, the important thing is to do it. Not only will children's reading abilities improve because of SSR, but when SSR is in effect, the result is one of remarkable peace and tranquillity.

Research

Gambrell, L. B. (1978). Getting started with sustained silent reading and keeping it going. *The Reading Teacher, 32*(3), 328–331.

Hobbs, M. (1989). Enhancing SSR. *The Reading Teacher, 42*(7), 548–549.

25 SCANNING

Background

Many pupils (and many adults) are unable to scan quickly through printed material to find certain facts. Often a person simply wants to locate a single piece of information and does not need to comprehend *all* the information in a chapter, article, or even a paragraph.

Rarely are time and effort devoted to instructing youngsters on how to scan. Although most teachers concentrate on the fundamentals of oral and silent reading and devote time to developing vocabulary and various comprehension skills, few instructors are seriously concerned about teaching children to scan through books or other materials to locate specific details.

Who Can Benefit

This tactic is appropriate for advanced readers in the primary grades who can read silently at comfortable rates and who comprehend most of what they read. Most assuredly this would be a suitable technique for pupils of intermediate and secondary age.

Procedures

First of all, set the stage for scanning. Inform the pupils that often it is not necessary to comprehend everything in a passage; one only needs to locate specific pieces of information. Then give examples of items that might be found by scanning: a date, a location, a person's name, an amount.

Next, begin in an organized way to help your pupils develop this skill.

Step 1. Develop several practice sheets on which 20 nouns appear at random. Select words such as *pen, pencil, cup,* and *eraser.* Type about 10 words per row and print 15 rows. Put these sheets in acetate covers and give each pupil a Vis-a-Vis™ marker or other type of erasable marking pen. Set a time limit of one minute and ask the pupils to circle a certain word each time they see it on the page (e.g., the word *pen*). At the end of the timing, ask them to count the number of *pen*s they circled. Schedule this exer-

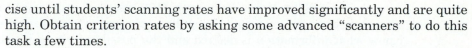

cise until students' scanning rates have improved significantly and are quite high. Obtain criterion rates by asking some advanced "scanners" to do this task a few times.

Step 2. Develop practice sheets on which 20 different short phrases are printed. These phrases should be on three different topics (e.g., math, baseball, and food). All the phrases should be different from one another, but should pertain to one of the three major themes. Put these sheets in acetate covers, and give the youngsters marking pens. See Tactic 21 for an illustration of this process. (By enclosing the printed phrases in Step 2 and the words in Step 1 in acetate covers, the teacher can reuse them.) Tell the pupils to circle all the sentences that pertain to one of the topics (e.g., food) for one minute. Schedule these sessions until the youngsters become proficient.

Step 3. Ask the students to get their social studies, science, or other content book. Tell them to take out a pencil and paper and write numbers 1 through 25 down the left side of a paper. Next, direct the pupils to turn to a certain page in the text. Ask them a series of questions that can be answered from materials between the pages you specify. Direct them to write the answers to the queries alongside the numbers on their papers. For example, begin by saying, "Number one: Find the date of _____ event." Wait for a short time and then give the next command: "Number two: Find the name of the person who did _____ ." Continue until all 25 questions have been asked.

Monitor

In line with the procedures noted for detecting words and phrases, teachers (or pupils) could, following a one-minute timing, count the number of correct and incorrect identifications. Moreover, by comparing the circled or underlined responses to those highlighted on a master copy, the teacher (or pupil) could indicate the number of times the pupil failed to mark a desired item. Thus three types of data could be kept: hits, misses, and skips per minute. These data could then be entered on a chart.

Modifications/Considerations

Dozens of modifications are possible with this tactic. One alteration is the number of items that must be found by scanning. Another could be the amount of time pupils are given to locate the answers. A third variable is the complexity of the search. Perhaps the easiest information to locate is that in bold print, in headings, or highlighted in some other manner. Moreover, it is usually easy to find dates, names, and places; however, it is more difficult to spot information regarding opinions or judgments, comparative or evaluative statements, or descriptive remarks. Children could be phased gradually into those latter discriminations.

Carnine, Silbert, and Kameenui (1990) suggest activities to teach scanning and skimming and note the skills necessary to maximize the process: (a) Know what information is desired and the possible form in which it might be found; (b) rapidly look over the page while limiting attention to the desired information; and (c) read the surrounding material to verify the applicability of the information to the question.

Research

Carnine, D., Silbert, J., & Kameenui, E. J. (1990). *Direct instruction reading*. New York: Merrill/Macmillan.

Ekwall, E. E., & Shanker, J. L. (1993). *Locating and correcting reading difficulties* (6th ed.). New York: Merrill/Macmillan.

26 COMPREHENSION: THE WHAT, WHY, HOW, AND WHEN OF INSTRUCTION

Background

This tactic is based on the ideas and principles of direct instruction; that is, when teachers are actively, intensively, and systematically involved with instruction in reading comprehension, students will learn to comprehend better than if instruction is incidental, undirected, or nonexistent. Furthermore, this tactic supports the notion that instruction in reading comprehension, in order to be comprehensive, should focus on three types of knowledge: declarative, procedural, and conditional.

Who Can Benefit

In the cited study, the sample lesson was carried out with fourth graders. The students had received prior instruction in identifying explicit ideas in the form of topic sentences. The four-step instructional strategy explained here also would be a suitable one for instructing youngsters in the fifth and sixth grades as they learned to comprehend expository materials.

Procedures

Following is a general description of the four steps of this instructional strategy.

Step 1: WHAT is the reading skill?

Step 1 communicates *declarative knowledge*. The teacher tells students what the reading skill is (e.g., identifying main ideas), and states directly what the instruction will involve.

Step 2: WHY is the reading skill important to learn?

Step 2 communicates *conditional knowledge*. The teacher tells students why the reading skill is important, and how its mastery will make them better readers.

Step 3: HOW does one use the reading skill?

This step involves *procedural knowledge*. The teacher tells, shows, models, or demonstrates how the reading skill operates. Generative or constructive components, such as composing rather than recognizing answers, are important elements of this step. During this step, the responsibility for skill acquisition should gradually be shifted from teacher to pupils.

Step 4: WHEN should the reading skill be used?

This step communicates more *conditional knowledge*. The teacher identifies the condition (e.g., purposes for reading) in which the skill should be used.

A Sample Lesson

Step 1: What

"Today we will learn more about paragraph main ideas. We will learn to find main ideas in paragraphs that do not have topic sentences."

Step 2: Why

"Learning to figure out unstated paragraph main ideas is an important skill. Finding the main idea will help you remember and learn the most important information in what you read. This will be particularly helpful when you read assignments in science and social studies books."

Step 3: How

"Following are three steps that will help you figure out unstated paragraph main ideas:

1. Decide what the topic of the paragraph is.
2. Decide what is said about the topic. Read through the paragraph to see what the rest of the sentences tell you about the topic.
3. Check yourself. Go through each sentence in the paragraph. Ask whether the sentence relates to the main idea you have selected. If it does, you have selected the correct main idea. If not, choose another main idea and carry out the same steps."

Step 4: When

"I have two more things to say about main ideas. One, finding main ideas works only when you have informational writing. Two, use this reading skill when you come to difficult or confusing paragraphs."

Monitor

Initially, data should be kept on the extent to which children master the four-step process to reading comprehension. Data should be gathered on how well they identify main ideas and support those ideas from sentences in paragraphs. In the beginning, such data might be kept while students read rather short and simple paragraphs. As students develop proficiency, the paragraphs used could be more complex and longer. Eventually, when students have demonstrated a rather thorough and consistent grasp of the technique, data should be kept on their abilities to comprehend, evaluate, and make judgments from text they have read.

Modifications/Considerations

Most reading comprehension instruction comes from commercial sources such as basal readers. The following list provides instances of using the four-step strategy so that commercial materials might be adapted for developing the three types of knowledge.

1.   If declarative knowledge is missing, give students a simple statement of what the reading comprehension skill is.
2.   If there is no "why" information in the material, tell students why mastery of this skill will make them better readers.
3.   If there is not sufficient direct instruction, elaborate on the existing instruction. Keep in mind the necessary transition from full-teacher to full-student responsibility and provide for the gradual exchange of responsibility for learning.

Research

Baumann, J. F., & Schmitt, M. C. (1986). The what, why, how, and when of comprehension instruction. *The Reading Teacher, 39*(7), 640–646.

27 COMPREHENSION: THE GUIDED READING PROCEDURE

Background

The Guided Reading Procedure (GRP) is, according to Manzo (1975), a relatively simple instructional procedure that is well- suited to group teaching. This technique is meant to help students improve their comprehension, recall, and organizational skills. One important characteristic of GRP is that it increases the proportion of student response compared to the commentaries and discussions of the teacher. The procedure also encourages students to use higher level comprehension skills.

Who Can Benefit

This procedure is recommended for pupils of all ages—elementary school through college. GRP is particularly useful in the content areas, such as science or social studies, in which narration is packed with facts.

Procedures

Following are the steps for practicing Manzo's GRP:

1. Explain the purpose for reading and tell pupils to remember all they can. When they finish reading the passage (ordinarily about 500 words), have them shut their books.

2. Ask the class members to tell everything they can about the selection. Write this information on the chalkboard in whatever order or fashion it is given.

3. Ask the students to read the information on the board and determine how consistent it is. Encourage them to look again at the passage they read. Then ask students to add to the information on the board and correct any inconsistencies noted in their first recall.

4. Tell the students to organize the information on the board. They can do this with an outline, a diagram, or with a semantic web. (See Tactic 30 for a discussion of semantic webbing.)

5. Ask several synthesizing questions. These questions should help students blend old and new information.

6. Administer a test (matching, multiple choice, essay, true/false, unaided recall) to assess the students' short-term memory.

7. Give another form of the test a few days later to assess students' long-term memory.

Monitor

To assess the effects of this approach, teachers could ask students to tell as much about the story as they can. Teachers could, of course, make more sophisticated requests of the children; for example, students could be asked to relate the story just read to other stories they have covered in class on a similar topic. Or, continuing up the line of difficulty and sophistication, children could be asked to evaluate or make judgments about the story, perhaps comparing it along certain stylistic features to other literature they have read.

Modifications/Considerations

You may need help in writing the pupils' recollections of the story, as some of them, after reading certain passages, can reel off a great deal of information. Organizing their comments can be accomplished as a group activity rather than having each member do it on his or her own. It may be particularly beneficial to organize comments as a group when the GRP is first used.

Synthesizing questions could be asked by the students, or they might share this responsibility with the teacher. Similarly, the short- and long-term recall tests could be developed by the youngsters, or they could at least share in this assignment.

Au and Scheu (1989) reported on how students were guided to interpret novels. In their project, teachers created opportunities for fourth-grade students to explore interpretations of novels. They assisted pupils in developing a sense of shared meaning and in exploring the personal significance of novels in their lives. This approach relied on the view that by understanding specific parts of text, the readers' vision of the text as a whole is broadened. According to these researchers, teachers should help pupils develop common understandings of specific ideas in texts, and then lead them to see the relationships of those ideas to the overall theme of the novel.

Research

Ankey, P., & McClurg, P. (1981). Testing Manzo's guided reading procedure. *The Reading Teacher, 34*(6), 681–685.

Au, K. H., & Scheu, J. A. (1989). Guiding students to interpret a novel. *The Reading Teacher, 43*(2), 104–110.

Manzo, A. V. (1975). Guided reading procedure. *Journal of Reading, 18,* 287–291.

28 COMPREHENSION: USING CLOZE PROCEDURES FOR INFERENCE TRAINING

Background

The basis for this technique is that reading is an interactive process and readers must be strategic learners who construct meaning from text and monitor their thinking to ensure comprehension. *Reading* means thinking about ideas while reading and using a variety of information to understand text.

Who Can Benefit

The strategy explained here has been used successfully with fifth- and sixth-grade classes including remedial learners. It has been used in nearly all curricular areas.

Procedures

The intentions of this technique are to focus attention on text clues and to relate text information to prior knowledge.

General Techniques

1. Explain carefully to students the purpose of the procedures—that it will help them answer inferential questions as they read. Inform them that this technique will help them in all subject areas, not just the ones they are taking now.

2. Model the procedure for the youngsters. The teacher should model and talk through each step of the process, explaining the importance of each step and how it relates to the other steps.

3. Schedule times for the students to practice the procedure on materials that progress in difficulty from simple sentences to more sophisticated paragraphs. Teachers should provide feedback about the students' logic and accuracy.

4. Encourage the students to proceed from situations of active teacher involvement to ones of supervision.

Specific Techniques

1. Begin with a simple cloze sentence: *The car skidded out of control, and crashed through the railing over the* _____ . In this example a variety of responses would be acceptable.

2. Include another sentence, one that provides more information to use when selecting a response: *The car skidded out of control, and crashed through the railing over the* _____ . *The boat below was half-way through the bridge and just missed being hit.* Students read beyond the first sentence to search for more specific clues.

3. Add more sentences.

4. Give the youngsters a self-monitoring checklist similar to the one following to use throughout this process. It could either be written on the chalkboard or attached to their desks.

   - Does the answer make sense in the passage?
   - Is the answer based on a combination of knowledge you had before you read the passage and clues in the passage?
   - Is there a forward clue in the same sentence, paragraph, or passage?
   - Is there a background clue in the same sentence, paragraph, or passage?
   - Did the clue make you change your answer or not?

Monitor

A simple way to monitor the performance of youngsters would be to count the number of correct and incorrect responses to the cloze procedure. A correct answer should be defined more liberally than usual; any response that is plausible should be accepted.

Modifications/Considerations

After students are adept with the cloze strategy and are familiar with the self-monitoring checklist, they should be encouraged to use similar strategies for drawing inferences from text. For this step, they might be required to complete a rather lengthy cloze passage. After completing the passage, the entire class could discuss the various responses for each blank. After the cloze answers and their clues have been discussed, the students and teacher can read the completed passage again.

Interspersed inferential questions prompt students to review previous text, search forthcoming text, and rely on background knowledge in their efforts to respond to the questions.

Research

Carr, E., Dewitz, P., & Patberg, J. (1989). Using cloze for inference training with expository text. *The Reading Teacher, 42*(6), 380–395.

29 COMPREHENSION: STORY GRAMMARS

Background

The primary idea behind this technique is that stories have structures; they have a form that is somewhat consistent and predictable. Most readers have notions, albeit unspecified, about these forms. Moreover, it seems that the clearer a person's ideas about these structures are, the better he or she understands what was just read.

Several reading experts have identified similar structures in reading. The structure selected here was advanced by Mandler and Johnson (1977). According to them, there are six major story elements.

Who Can Benefit

This technique would be quite appropriate for all youngsters who are learning to comprehend text, especially narrative-type stories. It is a useful approach for assisting pupils to understand stories they listen to or ones they read themselves. This method would also be appropriate for students who are beginning to write stories but whose narrations lack structure.

Procedures

The first step when instructing story grammars is to tell students that most stories are made up of six elements: setting, beginning, reaction, attempt, outcome, and ending. Explain the make-up or purpose of each section:

Setting: The main characters are introduced and statements often are made about the time or location of the story.

Beginning: Some precipitating event generally occurs.

Reaction: The main character's reaction to the beginning of the story and the formation of a goal are presented.

Attempt: A planned effort is made to reach the goal.

Outcome: The results of the attempts to reach that goal are given.

Ending: The long-range consequences of the action and the final response of certain characters in the story are presented.

Read several stories to the youngsters and identify these six elements. Later, ask students to identify the parts while the stories are read to them.

Following are five techniques to help children understand and identify story structures.

Prediction task.   Ask students to read incomplete stories, then say or write what they think comes next. They may read only the setting and beginning and then comment on what might follow.

Macro-cloze task.   In this activity, an entire section (e.g., reaction) is deleted. The pupils' task is to furnish a plausible section.

Scrambled stories.   Jumble the various parts of the story. Require pupils to put them in their proper order.

Sorting task.   Break the story into several sentences or phrases. Type these on strips of paper, and require pupils to sort the material for each of the elements into separate piles.

Retelling stories.   Tell children a story they know and then scramble up some of the parts (e.g., read the reaction section before the beginning). Ask the pupils to point out the misplaced sections.

Monitor

Following are the measures used in the Newby, Caldwell, and Recht (1989) study having to do with story grammars:

1.   the number of words read orally in one minute, starting at the beginning of the passage, not counting miscues;

2.   the percentage of words taught during the word-recognition component (they were taught five words for each new story) that were read correctly in list format; and

3.   the number of idea units recalled from the passage. (Idea units are based on propositional analysis. For a description of this type of measure, see Tactic 3.)

Modifications/Considerations

One modification of this technique is to have students mark (with stick-on tabs) the story elements in their texts as they read the stories. Another is to have them identify these elements as they write stories.

More advanced pupils could be instructed to look for additional elements or variations on the six elements presented here. In this vein, youngsters could read more sophisticated stories and identify such features as flashbacks, summaries, and recapitulations throughout the narration.

Newby and colleagues used a story grammar strategy to instruct young dyslexic children. The treatments for those youngsters corresponded to their type of dyslexia, either dysphonetic or auditory-linguistic. For the former children, the story elements were taught in a visual manner; representative pictograph boxes were used, along with the names of the story elements. The auditory-linguistic children were instructed by giving them a sheet on which the story elements were listed; arrows connected the elements to indicate the sequence in which they occurred in a story. Newby et al. showed that both treatments were effective; students increased their reading comprehension.

Research

Mandler, J., & Johnson, N. (1977). Remembrance of things parsed: Story structure and recall. *Cognitive Psychology, 9,* 111–151.

Newby, R. F., Caldwell, J., & Recht, D. R. (1989). Improving the reading comprehension of children with dysphonetic and dyseidetic dyslexia using story grammar. *Journal of Learning Disabilities, 22*(6), 373–380.

30 COMPREHENSION: SEMANTIC WEBS

Background

Semantic webbing is a process of organizing and constructing a visual display of information categories taken from textbooks, showing the contents of each category as well as how each relates to other categories. Semantic webbing is an effective way for teachers to present materials and concepts, as well as being an effective way to help students understand what they read.

The semantic web (or map) is made up of four elements:

1. The *core question* is the focus of the web and the purpose of the inquiry. The teacher chooses it.
2. The *web strands* are the students' answers to the core questions.
3. The *strand supports* are the facts, inferences, and generalizations that pupils select from the story to give clarity and validity to the strands and to differentiate them from one another.
4. The *strand ties* are the relationships among the various strands.

Who Can Benefit

This is an effective technique for most types of youngsters, including remedial or regular pupils of primary through secondary age. It is appropriate for use with basal texts or a variety of content-area books. According to some researchers, a number of students with learning disabilities are more apt to acquire and organize information if it is presented in a nonverbal format.

Procedures

To illustrate the use of semantic webbing with basal readers, an excerpt from a story such as *The Children's Story* could be read to the youngsters. This story describes how a new teacher comes into a class and begins to change their way of thinking. Following are the basic steps:

Step 1. Set a purpose for reading to encourage students to use a specific reading-thinking strategy. Decide also which part of the story students will read. Table 30.1 can help in choosing a strategy. In this table, the various reading-thinking strategies are printed vertically, and the optional reading units are laid out horizontally. In this example, the group read a paragraph in order to predict events (as indicated by the checkmark shown in the table). After the students read the first few paragraphs in the story, ask them to read a few more and then predict what happens next.

Step 2. Formulate a core question for the web based on the selected strategy and unit. "Now that you have read a few paragraphs, what do you predict the new teacher will do?" Symbolize this on the board, as shown in Figure 30.1.

Step 3. Elicit possible answers to the question from the students. Write all responses on the board, connecting them to the core question of the web. Then ask the students to accept, reject, or modify the answers (Figure 30.2.).

TABLE 30.1 Establishing the Reading-Thinking Strategy and the Reading Unit

	Reading Units				
Reading–Thinking Strategies	**Word**	**Sentence**	**Paragraph**	**Story Part**	**Story**
Getting main idea					
Drawing conclusions					
Making generalizations					
Using context clues for meaning					
Predicting events			✓		
Identifying author's purpose					
Identifying author's point of view					
Recognizing major characters					
Story setting					
Story theme					
Recognizing and evaluating author's use of:					
Alliteration					
Jargon					
Humor and puns					
Dialect					

SOURCE: From "Enriching Basal Reader Lessons with Semantic Webbing," G. Freedman and E. G. Reynolds, *The Reading Teacher, 33,* 1980, p. 679. Reprinted with permission of G. Freedman and the International Reading Association.

FIGURE 30.1 Core Question

Step 4. Build student support for the web strands. Write all suggestions on the board, as shown in Figure 30.3. Ask the pupils to examine the suggestions, and then accept, reject, or modify them. Before doing this, the pupils may reread the passage. As the students comment, probe for clarification.

Step 5. Guide the students in relating the various strands. Be careful not to produce a confusing mass of lines and labels. Generally, two or three relationships are enough. See Figure 30.4 for an example. You might ask, "Can you see any way in which some of your predictions can go together?"

FIGURE 30.2
Web Strands

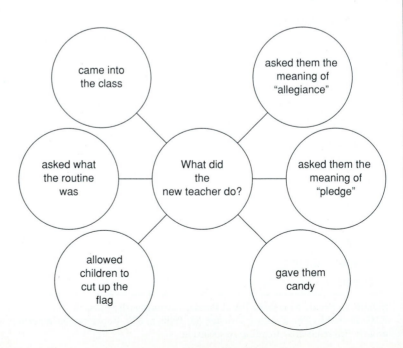

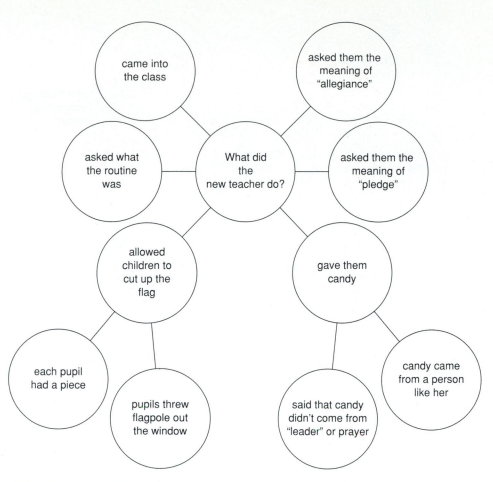

FIGURE 30.3   Strand Supports

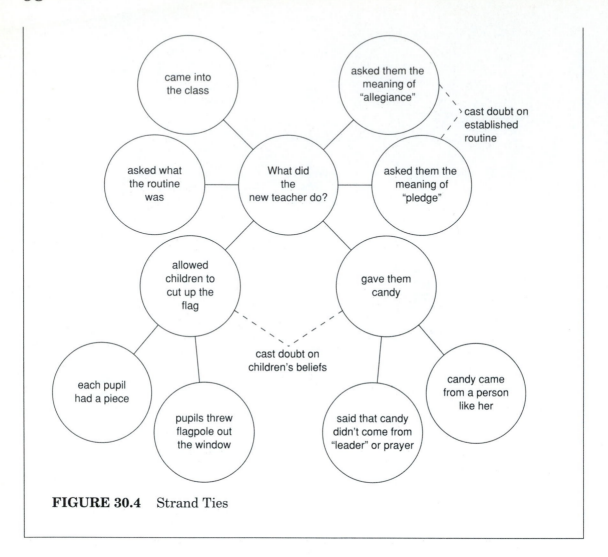

FIGURE 30.4   Strand Ties

Monitor

In order to evaluate the effects of arranging webs or maps, the teacher should use them for some stories and not for others. Perhaps the treatment could be scheduled for every other story or for occasional stories. Several types of data could then be gathered, one of which might be for students to retell as much as they could about the passage. With this measure, the teacher could count the number of words mentioned, or more importantly, the number of facts or inferences mentioned. The teacher, using these data, could compare the students' performance when the web or map treatment was scheduled, and their performance when it was not used.

Modifications/Considerations

Use semantic webs for any of the following activities: to set purposes for further reading in the same story; as a model for constructing webs for other stories; and to bring circumstances to life through art, drama, role playing, and other activities that relate the web concepts to students' other knowledge and experiences.

Semantic webs can also be constructed from children's story books. In this context, Cleland (1981) describes how to set up three types: the episodal, the inductive, and the emotions web. Moreover, webs or maps can be drawn to illustrate story grammars or structures.

Research

Clavell, J. (1981). *The children's story*. New York: Delacorte Press.

Cleland, C. J. (1981). Highlighting issues in children's literature through semantic webbing. *The Reading Teacher, 34*(6), 642–646.

Freedman, G., & Reynolds, E. G. (1980). Enriching basal reader lessons with semantic webbing. *The Reading Teacher, 33*(6), 677–684.

Sinatra, R., Berg, D., & Dunn, R. (1985). Semantic mapping improves reading comprehension of learning disabled students. *Teaching Exceptional Children, 17*(4), 310–314.

31 COMPREHENSION: RECIPROCAL TEACHING

Background

The concept of reciprocal teaching was developed by Palincsar and Brown (1984) to help students better comprehend what they have read. The technique follows a four-step procedure: generating questions, summarizing, predicting, and clarifying. The ultimate goal of reciprocal teaching is for students to apply the technique to content-area materials as a means to study and learn that material.

Who Can Benefit

This tactic would be beneficial for remedial as well as regular readers of intermediate and secondary age. It can be used with content-area texts as well as with basal readers.

Procedures

During the first few reciprocal teaching sessions, the teacher models all the steps to help students become familiar with them. Then the students take turns being the teacher, while the classroom teacher acts as a member of the group and assists the student teachers if they have difficulty with particular steps.

To begin the process, each member of the group silently reads a short passage or paragraph. When finished reading, each student silently generates answers to the four-step procedure in preparation for being the teacher. Once every member of the group has completed the reading, the classroom teacher selects one student to act as teacher. The student teacher works through the four steps orally and calls on other students when applicable.

Step 1: Question. The student teacher generates a question about the main idea of the paragraph. He or she might say, "The first step is a main idea question. A good main idea question about this paragraph is . . . " Once the question is posed, the student teacher may call on others for the answer.

Step 2: Summarize.   The student teacher summarizes the passage in a brief sentence or two. The summary should include the main idea as well as any important details. He or she might say, "The next step is to summarize the paragraph. This paragraph is about . . . "

Step 3: Clarify.   The student teacher asks if there are any words in the paragraph that are unfamiliar to anyone. He or she may generate the definition of a word to be clarified or may ask another student to give the definition. If no one is familiar with the word, the dictionary may be consulted.

Step 4: Predict.   The student teacher predicts what the next paragraph will be about. The prediction should be based on the information in the current passage and on previously read paragraphs in the text. He or she might say, "Because the third to last paragraph described ducks, and this paragraph noted what they ate, I predict that the last paragraph will be about where ducks live."

Students silently read the next paragraph or passage, and the classroom teacher selects the next student to act as teacher.

Monitor

This technique could be monitored by giving students a paragraph to read silently, removing the paragraph after they had read it, then giving them a worksheet of questions pertaining to the text. This could be done on a weekly or biweekly schedule. The students could also be asked to tell or write freely about what they had read. They could be asked to do this once in a while prior to reciprocal teaching and occasionally while the technique was in use. Teachers could count and chart the number of words said or written, the number of facts, or other features.

Yet another way to evaluate this technique, particularly as it influences comprehension, would be to take turns telling the story. The teacher might describe one part of a story (perhaps the first) and ask a student to tell about the next section. They could continue telling about alternate sections throughout the story. By so doing, the teacher and student would be reciprocally involved in a macro cloze technique.

Modifications/Considerations

Group size is an important consideration for this technique. The smallness of the group increases the turns each student will have and decreases the chance of any student becoming bored. The technique could be modified for a larger group by having different students act as teacher for each individual step.

The classroom teacher must be careful not to interfere unless absolutely necessary. He or she directs the lesson only when a student is unable to complete a step or completes the step incorrectly. Even then, the teacher should act only as a facilitator to help students generate correct answers or questions.

The steps can be modified and presented in any order. Some teachers might put the clarifying step first. The ultimate goal is for students to internalize the steps so that they can use them when studying content-area material.

Research

Herrmann, B. A. (1988). Two approaches for helping poor readers become more strategic. *The Reading Teacher, 42*(1), 24–28.

Palincsar, A. M., & Brown, A. (1984). Reciprocal teaching of comprehension-fostering and comprehension-monitoring activities. *Cognition and Instruction, 1*(2), 117–175.

32 COMPREHENSION: STRUCTURING DIALOGUE

Background

This tactic was designed to develop metacognitive skills during reading that would in turn increase students' comprehension. POSSE is an acronym for the five steps of the Structuring Dialogue tactic: predict, organize, search, summarize, and evaluate. The POSSE technique has the ability to quickly modify and adapt materials to various students' ability levels and for a variety of curricula in general education classes.

Who Can Benefit

This tactic could benefit a variety of students, from fourth grade on up. POSSE's systematic organization lends itself to focusing the curriculum for all students. It is particularly beneficial for those pupils who are having difficulty comprehending their textbooks. POSSE could be used by special education teachers in resource rooms to develop the independent reading comprehension skills of students, and is useful as the organizational base for establishing peer tutoring situations. Moreover, the POSSE technique could provide the needed structure for cooperative learning groups in general education classes.

Procedures

Introduction to POSSE
Initially, the teacher works from the POSSE worksheets (Figure 32.1). After providing information about the strategies that are being taught, the teacher provides rationales for their importance to students.

The POSSE Dialogue
Use the POSSE acronym to assist students in carrying out the following:

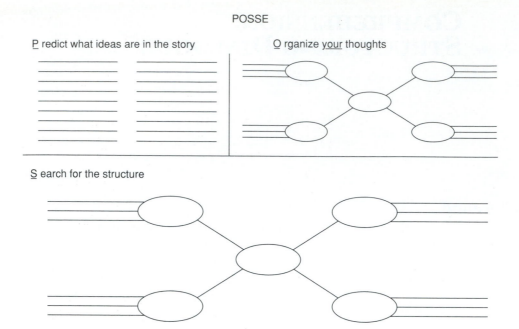

FIGURE 32.1 POSSE Strategy Sheet

SOURCE: From "Send for the POSSE: Structuring the Comprehension Dialogue" by C. S. Englert and T. Mariage, 1990, *Academic Therapy, 25*(4), p. 475. Copyright 1990 by PRO-ED, Inc. Reprinted by permission.

Prereading phase

1. **P**redict what ideas are in the story. Use cues from the title, headings, pictures, or initial paragraph to brainstorm the relevant information and to predict what the article will be about. Write the ideas on the POSSE worksheet.

2. **O**rganize your thoughts. Organize the brainstormed ideas list into categories. Use them to develop the semantic map on the worksheet.

During reading phase

3. **S**earch for the structure. Confirm the predictions developed in the semantic map by identifying the author's actual categories and details.

4. **S**ummarize the main idea in your own words. Identify short segments or paragraphs of the article that tell what the paragraph is about. Record the main idea in one of the category boxes and summarize supporting details on the adjacent lines of the worksheet.

Postreading phase

5. <u>E</u>valuate by asking a question about the main idea, then compare, clarify, and predict.

   a. *Question:* Change the main ideas recorded in the category boxes to questions in order to elicit the supporting details recorded on the adjacent lines.

   b. *Compare:* Compare the semantic maps generated during prereading and reading stages for new, confirmed, and unconfirmed information.

   c. *Clarify:* Ask questions about unfamiliar vocabulary, unclear referents, and information not provided by the author.

   d. *Predict:* Use the information in the semantic map to predict what the next section will be about.

Monitor

Ideas for monitoring or evaluating aspects of this technique were offered in number 5 of the Procedures section (Evaluate by asking . . .). Taking a cue from those suggestions, data could be acquired as to pupil's ability to change main ideas to questions, compare semantic maps from one stage to another, give the meanings of important vocabulary words, or predict upcoming events from available information.

Beyond these suggestions, one of the simplest ways to evaluate the technique is to set up a two-phase study. During the first part, prior to arranging POSSE, data should be kept on the students' ability to retell facts from stories. Then, during the second phase, while the strategy is in effect, the same type of data are taken. Data from the two phases for each participant are then compared to ascertain the effects on each individual.

If youngsters were placed in reciprocal teaching or cooperative learning groups (to improve either reading or writing), data regarding their individual contributions could be obtained. These data would be particularly important if an objective of setting up those situations was to increase the extent to which youngsters interacted with one another. Data regarding student contributions could pertain to either the frequency of their involvements or the quality of their comments.

Modifications/Considerations

With minor modifications this tactic could be effective for a variety of classroom activities, from cooperative learning groups in which students write fiction, carry out science projects and experiments, discuss civics questions, and debate political issues, to independent research projects in which students write papers and conduct laboratory experiments.

Whereas the purpose of the technique described here is to assist youngsters in comprehending material they read from texts, the identical procedures may be used to aid them with expressive writing.

Research

Englert, C. S., & Mariage, T. (1990). Send for the POSSE: Structuring the comprehension dialogue. *Academic Therapy, 25*(4), 473–487.

33 COMPREHENSION: FREE DESCRIPTION (RETELL)

Background

The Free Description tactic is based on three assumptions. The first assumption is that preparing written comprehension questions of many types and levels is a time-consuming and often inefficient task. To prepare such questions, someone must read through the materials, identify questions and answers, write or type them, then store them in some convenient place. Using the retelling technique is a time-efficient alternative.

A second thought to support this tactic is that often comprehension questions written by teachers (or for that matter, comprehension questions found in standardized tests) are not passage-dependent; some youngsters can answer a number of them correctly without bothering to read the narration.

The third idea behind the retelling method is that when children describe what they read, they must use language. Most special education and remedial teachers agree that many youngsters need help with language development. Therefore, when children describe (orally or in writing) what they have read, they are practicing two things: reading comprehension and language development.

Who Can Benefit

At the risk of belaboring the obvious, this tactic is a good choice for children who need to expand their descriptive language skills. This is a particularly good tactic for youngsters who rely heavily on cues from the stories' questions when formulating the answers. Furthermore, it is quite appropriate for children who have difficulty reading or understanding comprehension questions or who have problems writing out the answers.

This tactic has nearly universal utility. It can be used with young students with disabilities as they describe only the basic facts, as well as with older, more advanced children as they describe sophisticated aspects of a story.

Procedures

1. Define the characteristics of the passages you want children to describe. If, for example, you want them to list facts about the story, then explain what a fact is. Here is a detailed definition of a fact in this sense:

   - Any comment on the theme of the story counts as a fact (e.g., "It's a story about *lungs*.").
   - Each noun plus an action verb counts as two facts (e.g., "The *boy ran*.").
   - Each adjective or adverb that describes a noun or verb is a fact (e.g., "The *red* ball" or "She ran *fast*.").
   - Each preposition that describes a location is a fact (e.g., "The ball was *on* the table.").

   The following are not counted as facts:

   - Repetitions
   - Value judgments about the story (e.g., "I liked the story.")
   - Nonspecific statements (e.g., "She was doing something.")
   - Information about the pictures

   Count the following as incorrect:

   - Statements that go beyond the facts of the story
   - Incorrect information about events or circumstances
   - Incorrect numbers, names, times

2. Give the student examples of what a fact is and what it is not.

3. Model for the child how to say facts, one after the other. Read the same story the child reads. Then, you say facts: some correct, others incorrect. Occasionally repeat information.

4. Count the facts together. As you say the facts, count them with the student. After a few sessions allow the pupil to count on his or her own.

5. Discuss the merits of the information. As you and the student count the facts, ask the child from time to time to explain why he or she counted the fact as correct, incorrect, or did not count it at all. Continue these modeling sessions until you are certain the pupil knows what is being counted.

6. Ask the student to read a passage. Tell the child that after reading it, he or she will be asked to say facts for a period of time (with beginning readers, 30 seconds or 1 minute is enough).

Monitor

1. Count the number of correct and incorrect facts the child expresses. Tell the student, as you count, whether they are correct or incorrect.

2. Tell the child at the end of his or her description how many comments were correct and incorrect. Tell also how these numbers compare to past performances; for example, tell whether the correct rate has gone up, down, or has remained the same.

3. Plot these performance numbers on a chart. Either you or the pupil can do this. Regardless of who does the charting, it is important that the child sees the results and relates his or her performance to that of previous days.

4. Tell the student after each session about the quality of his or her recitation. Describe which types of facts the child included, which ones were omitted, and explain any mistakes that he or she made. Instruct the student on how to correct any errors, and suggest ways to improve his or her performance in general.

Modifications/Considerations

One modification of this extremely versatile tactic lies in the modes of input and output that are used. The pupil could read the passage before answering the questions, either orally or silently, or the passage could be read to the pupil. In respect to output, the student could either say the facts or other information, as in the example, or he or she could write the retelling.

In the example given here, the pupil identified facts for one minute. The student could also be asked to describe story features for longer periods or until he or she had no more to say.

A third alteration might be what type of information is requested from the pupil. You might require the student to give other, more complex information as well as facts. For example, you might ask the pupil to do any of the following: describe a sequence of events, locate and identify likenesses and differences in characters, describe the reasons for certain happenings, place people or events in categories, paraphrase statements or events, consolidate ideas or information, conjecture about the facts of the story, hypothesize about motivations of the characters, predict outcomes, interpret figurative language, discriminate between fact and opinion, express feelings about the passage, or react to the author's craftsmanship.

Still another modification is for the teacher to tell facts and untruths about the story. The pupil's task would be to identify the true and the false information. This is a particularly good exercise for a pupil who needs to develop both comprehension and listening skills.

In a study by Angeletti (1991), second- and fifth-grade children were asked to retell and write about what they had read. Then, Angeletti had the students respond to question cards that pertained to several layers of comprehension: comparison and contrast, opinion, inference, drawing conclusions, characters, author's style, author's purpose, and type of literature.

Research

Angeletti, S. R. (1991). Encouraging students to think about what they read. *The Reading Teacher, 45*(4), 288–296.

Hansen, C., & Lovitt, T. (1977). An applied behavior analysis approach to reading comprehension. In J. T. Guthrie (Ed.), *Cognition, curriculum, and comprehension* (pp. 160-186). Newark, DE: International Reading Association.

34 COMPREHENSION: PUPILS ASK QUESTIONS

Background

The main idea behind this tactic of having pupils ask questions is to encourage pupils to be more active in assessing and developing their comprehension skills. Some studies have shown that when students know they will be required to ask questions about what they have read, they will concentrate on their reading more than they would otherwise.

Another motive for this tactic is to increase the passage dependency of the task. If children are to ask specific questions about a story, they must first read it to be able to compose questions about it.

This tactic is also a time saver. The teacher does not have to prepare items ahead of time about stories the students will be reading. The teacher must, however, read the story beforehand before assigning it to the students (or at least must follow along carefully as students read it).

Who Can Benefit

This tactic is particularly useful for youngsters who rely too much on cues from traditionally prepared comprehension questions. In such cases, the teacher often is uncertain whether students have read the story or not. This would also be an appropriate technique for pupils who need to improve their general language skills or, specifically, their ability to ask questions.

Procedures

1. Ask the pupil to read a passage either silently or orally. Tell the student that when he or she finishes, he or she will be expected to compose questions about the story.

2. Give examples of various types of questions and discuss the differences between them.

3. Tell the student that the questions he or she asks must be specific. The questions that the student creates should not be, for example,

> "Was the story good or bad?", "What are the characters' names?", or "What is the main idea?" Also instruct the student not to ask questions that can be answered with a "yes" or "no." (Teachers can get away with this, but not students!)
>
> 4. Students should be told to offer questions about the whole story, not just the beginning or end. Moreover, tell the student to ask questions in a sequential order; that is, first ask some questions about the beginning, then others about the middle, and so forth. Explain that the questions can be connected with "and"s.

Monitor

Explain to the pupil that he or she should ask questions for one minute. As the child does so, record the number of questions that are correct and incorrect. After the one-minute period, tell the student how many questions were asked, and of those, how many were "correct." Coach the student on specific aspects of his or her performance. If he or she failed to ask questions about the whole story, or repeated some questions, point this out. Ask the pupil to evaluate his or her performance relative to earlier sessions.

Modifications/Considerations

The time allotted for asking questions could be adjusted, ranging from 20 seconds to several minutes. This would depend on the difficulty and length of the assigned passage, the student's ability, what objectives were set for the student, and other such factors. The pupil could be asked to either verbalize or write the questions. Furthermore, the student could be requested to ask questions of specific types (e.g., judgmental or inferential).

Davey and McBride (1986) trained young students to generate inferential-type questions from expository texts. The findings from their study pointed to overall positive effects of the training "on the accuracy of comprehension question responses, and on the accuracy between actual and predicted comprehension question performance" (p. 260). They claimed further that their findings suggested "that effective question generation can provide readers with a metacognitive strategy (heightening awareness of their own comprehension adequacy) as well as a cognitive strategy (generating and answering higher level think-type questions)" (p. 260).

Research

Cupp, D. E. (1974). *Asking questions as a teaching strategy for reading comprehension.* Unpublished manuscript, University of Washington, Experimental Education Unit, Seattle.

Davey, B., & McBride, S. (1986). Effects of question-generation training on reading comprehension. *Journal of Educational Psychology, 78*(4), 256–262.

35 COMPREHENSION: PROVIDED AND GENERATED QUESTIONS

Background

Two theories form the basis of this comprehension tactic. One theory states that self-questioning enhances the ability to comprehend text because the reader is more actively involved with the text. The other view suggests that self-questioning is most effective when learners are aware of the structure (e.g., compare and contrast) of the text they are reading. Combining these views, it might be suggested that the effectiveness of active processing produced by self-questioning depends on the kinds of questions generated (e.g., factual or conceptual), and that the questions depend on the metacognitive awareness of the learner.

Who Can Benefit

Students in the cited research study were in grades 5, 8, and 11. All the students were of average or above-average ability. This technique would be especially helpful for readers having difficulty organizing the thoughts and ideas of successive paragraphs.

Procedures

- Provide each student with a text booklet appropriate for his or her grade level. Each reading segment should be about 10 paragraphs in length. Students should be able to read the passage in at least 20 minutes.

- On the cover of the passage, write the instructions for carrying out the activity.

- Write one conceptual question for each paragraph of the story. (*Conceptual questions* require the reader to organize the paragraph details according to a main concept, which is contained both in the questions themselves and in the topic sentence of the paragraph to which the questions refer.) These questions are printed below their associated paragraphs.

- As students read the paragraphs, ask them to respond to each of the questions. After reading the entire passage, ask students to respond to the conceptual questions a second time.

- Ask students to respond to the corresponding cued recall measure. Students are allowed to refer back to the associated text paragraphs when answering the questions. (The *cued recall test* is developed by using sentences identical in phrasing to the passage sentences, but with an important word or phrase omitted from each one. Ten of the items test recall of the main ideas found in the topic sentences of each paragraph. Thirty items measure recall of the factual details from all the paragraphs.) Students are required to fill in the blanks as best they can and to try to guess the answer if they are uncertain.

Monitor

To receive credit for answering a question, the student must fill in the omitted word or phrase, or its semantic equivalent. Variations in phrasing and synonyms should be considered correct if the students do not alter the meaning of a given sentence.

Modifications/Considerations

Rather than the teacher writing a conceptual question for each paragraph, students could be asked to write questions for each paragraph, placing each question underneath the paragraph from which it was derived. Students should be told to write questions that will help them remember the important information in the paragraphs.

The research authors reported that in their study, the questions written by students were mainly factual-level questions. In keeping with one of the theories about this type of research, it could be that if youngsters are trained to identify text structures (see Tactic 40), they may be better able to interact with text at more sophisticated levels; that is, knowledge of text structure might allow them to write questions beyond the factual level. The authors also mentioned that this treatment was more effective in assisting youngsters to comprehend text than was a read-only treatment.

Denner and Rickards (1987) reported that when questions were provided by the teacher, the students' comprehension measures were generally better than when students came up with the questions themselves. The provided conceptual questions enhanced comprehension and retention of both main ideas and subordinate facts. Furthermore, the provided questions produced more efficient recall of passage ideas than did the other two treatments mentioned in the previous paragraph. This finding seemed to be particularly true for younger students.

Since most students seemed to gain more from questions written by teachers, it might be a good plan to continue with this approach until students are quite adept at answering comprehension questions of various types. Then, and after they have received training in identifying text structures, the teacher occasionally might ask the students to write their own questions. The plan, obviously, is to gradually turn the task of asking questions over to students, thus assisting them to not only be better "comprehenders," but also to be more independent ones.

Research

Denner, P. R., & Rickards, J. P. (1987). A developmental comparison of the effects of provided and generated questions on text recall. *Contemporary Educational Psychology, 12,* 135–146.

36 COMPREHENSION: DETECTION AND IDENTIFICATION OF TEXT INCONSISTENCIES

Background

According to the authors of the cited research, comprehension monitoring consists of at least two components: evaluation and regulation. Specifically, students need to keep track of their understanding of text and identify any failures to comprehend (the evaluative component), and then take appropriate action to remediate those failures (the regulation component). In this study, youngsters were given instruction in using a cross-referencing technique to evaluate text inconsistencies.

Who Can Benefit

Some of the students in the Chan, Cole, and Barfett (1987) study were 11-year-old boys and girls with learning disabilities who attended remedial classes. Other students were about 8 years old and were in the third grade. The technique explained here is probably most appropriate for youngsters in third grade and up.

Procedures

- Prepare a number of stories that are about 15 sentences and 150 words in length. The authors of the cited research selected adventure stories.

- Write an inconsistent version of each story. There should be two versions of each story: the original one which is presumably consistent, and the one written with inconsistencies.

- In the episodic and internal response sections of each inconsistent story, write two anomalous sentences. (*Anomalies,* or irregularities, of several types may be found in sentences: inconsistent information, structural incohesiveness, incomplete information, propositional incohesiveness, syntactical errors, violations of prior knowledge, and lexical inconsistencies.)

- Inform students that they will be given stories to read, some of which will contain sentences that do not fit properly into the stories, and that they will be asked to look for these ill-fitting sentences.
- Ask students to read the first passage silently as the instructor reads it aloud.
- Explain to the students, following the reading, why the given sentences are inconsistent.
- Ask students to read the passage a second time. As they read, the instructor should point to the first anomalous sentence, note that it does not fit properly into the story, and then explain why (e.g., the sentence deals with one topic while the story as a whole deals with another topic).
- Have students underline the anomalous sentence.
- Repeat these procedures with the next ill-fitting sentence and with a second demonstration passage.
- Give students a set of test passages and ask them to help look for the ill-fitting sentences. Tell them that there are two sentences in each passage that do not fit.
- Ask the students to read a passage, and following, ask them if they detected any sentences that did not fit. If they did, ask them to mark the sentences by underlining them.
- Ask students if they thought there was something generally wrong with the story.
- Have the students respond to seven multiple-choice comprehension questions for each passage.

Monitor

In the Chan et al. study, three types of measures were obtained: identification, detection, and comprehension. The extent to which students underlined the anomalous sentences was the identification measure. Students' responses to the question, "Did you think there was something wrong with the story?", provided the detection measure. Responses to the multiple-choice questions formed a measure of comprehension competence.

Modifications/Considerations

The steps outlined in the Procedures section make up what the research authors call the *specific instruction condition*. An alternate treatment that was used in this study is referred to as the *general instruction condition*. For this condition, an explanation is not given as to why the sentences are inconsistent, but they are underlined. Data from this study revealed that whereas students with learning disabilities performed better on all three measures in the specific instruction condition, the general education students performed equally well during both treatments.

Research

Chan, L. K. S., Cole, P. G., & Barfett, S. (1987). Comprehension monitoring: Detection and identification of text inconsistencies by LD and normal students. *Learning Disability Quarterly, 10,* 114–124.

37 COMPREHENSION: PARAGRAPH RESTATEMENTS

Background

In this study the authors provided students with a strategy (restating the main ideas of paragraphs) that would enable them to achieve the goal of comprehending more from material they had read. A more important goal was to demonstrate that if students were encouraged to rely on this strategy during certain times, they would voluntarily use the strategy in situations when they were not prompted to use it.

Who Can Benefit

The students in this study were in grades three through six; all of them had significant deficits in decoding and comprehension. The authors' data revealed that generally, the students' comprehension improved not only under conditions which closely matched the training task, but also under those which demanded some generalization of the strategy.

Procedures

First phase
- Select narrative-type stories and retype them, inserting a lined space between paragraphs. In the cited research the stories were about 400 words in length.
- Instruct students—through modeling, practice, and corrective feedback—to name the most important person and the major event that occurred in each paragraph.
- Inform students to rely on two questions as they formulate restatements: (a) "Who?" and (b) "What's happening?" (The research authors note that if the purpose is to improve students' comprehension of expository-type material, the questions should be altered to take that into account.)

- Require students to read the paragraph a second time if they do not generate a restatement.
- To evaluate whether or not students realize the significance of certain events in the paragraph, when students formulate a restatement, ask them to evaluate the restatement's importance.
- Record the student's oral restatements on the chalkboard.

Second phase
- Point out that restatements should involve the fewest possible words needed to convey the gist of the event.
- Require students to work individually as they write brief restatements on the lined spaces following each paragraph.
- Check students' work and give corrective feedback as required.
- Remove the reading material when students have finished; read each restatement to them, and ask them to elaborate on the paragraph's content.

Third phase
- Give students regular narrative passages without spaces for writing notes.
- Tell them to write restatements on a separate sheet of paper.

Monitor

For the first phase of monitoring, the *test of training,* administer a set of 12 comprehension questions to the students. In addition, ask students to retell the story. Scoring of the retellings could be based on a pausal unit analysis, in which the stories and the units are rated for their structural importance, yielding four categories of rated importance ranging from 1 (least important) to 4 (most important).

For the second phase, *near transfer test,* students are asked to respond to 12 comprehension questions.

For the third phase, *remote transfer test,* students answer 12 comprehension questions and retell the story.

Modifications/Considerations

The research authors mentioned that their restatement training program would have been more comprehensive had they included a fourth phase during which students learned to construct mental rather than written restatements. The fact that effects were observed during the remote transfer test, when students had no writing materials, suggests that students <u>were</u> adopting a covert form of the restatement procedure. Certainly students should be assisted in covertly interacting with the text, since the writing requirement and the time the procedure consumes could easily detract from its appeal.

Of some interest is the fact that many students in the control group, according to the researchers, wrote notes on the blank papers they were given even though they were not prompted to do so. This would indicate that those students were rather eager to comply with the teacher's instructions, if they just knew what they were!

Research

Jenkins, J. R., Heliotis, J. D., Stein, M. L., & Haynes, M. C. (1987). Improving reading comprehension by using paragraph restatements. *Exceptional Children, 54,* 54–59.

38 COMPREHENSION: MENTAL IMAGERY

Background

Reading experts agree that mental imagery has a definite relationship to cognition and language; and the ability to use imagery in an effort to comprehend written discourse is central to differentiating good from poor readers. Moreover, experts are in accord that reading must involve active monitoring of one's own comprehension. Mental imagery is one way to become involved in what is read.

Who Can Benefit

In the cited study, the students were below-average readers in the fourth and fifth grades. However, this tactic would also be an appropriate one for teaching comprehension of text to younger, average readers, because children in this group seem to be unaware that it is necessary to expend additional effort to make sense of the words they have decoded. Ordinarily, when younger or poorer readers are asked what they could do to improve their comprehension or understanding—that is, to expend more of an effort—they say they could read the material again. Sadoski (1985) has successfully explored this technique with third- and fourth-grade average readers. Teaching students to rely on mental imagery is one among many ways to assist children in expending effort and in becoming more involved with their reading, and hence, in getting more out of it.

Procedures

The idea behind this technique is to teach children to use mental imagery to detect inconsistencies (i.e., contradictory information) in text. In fact, children were asked to locate inconsistencies that were *explicitly* and *implicitly* stated.

- Inform students in small groups that they will read sentences and paragraphs silently, and they should try to understand and remember what they read.

- Tell them that one way to understand and remember what they read is to make pictures of the story in their minds.

- Ask the students to read the sentences, one at a time, and remind them to make pictures in their minds. Following is an example of a high-imagery sentence: The little green car raced up the narrow, winding road.

- Ask children questions such as the following: "What kind of car was mentioned?" and "Can you describe the road?"

- Review the sentences and remind students when they omit important elements.

- Follow the same procedures when using a few high-imagery paragraphs. Following is an example of such a paragraph:

    Pete opened a door. The room was empty except for a large white furry cat who was sleeping on the hearth. Pete walked to the fire and warmed his hands. He then stroked the cat.

Monitor

- Inform the students that they will be asked to read a few passages that are rather poorly written. Tell them that it is up to them to identify the places that contain information that does not fit with other information in the story.

- Inform them also to make pictures in their minds as they read the passages. This will help them to determine if there is anything about a passage that is not clear and easy to understand.

- Require the students to read two passages: one containing an explicit inconsistency, the other containing an implicit inconsistency. (In the explicit passage, the contradictory information should be clearly stated in adjacent sentences. In the implicit passage, the contradictory information should not be located in adjacent sentences, but should be implied across two sentences.)

- Administer a 10-item questionnaire following each passage. Questions on this instrument should fit into one of three categories: (a) detects inconsistency without prompting, (b) detects inconsistency during indirect confrontation, (c) detects inconsistency during direct confrontation.

- Schedule several more stories for some of the youngsters, depending on how well they did on the test.

Modifications/Considerations

Children do not typically encounter text that contains glaring inconsistencies. They will, however, read text that is laced with redundancies, is vague and unclear, is poorly sequenced, and is generally "inconsiderate." It is a goal of this technique that if youngsters are explicitly informed that not all text is clear and easy to understand, but that it is still necessary or important for them to read it, they will be able to sort out the irregularities and make sense of the passage after they have been trained to do so.

Research

Gambrell, L. B., & Bales, R. J. (1986). Mental imagery and the comprehension-monitoring performance of fourth- and fifth-grade poor readers. *Reading Research Quarterly, 21*(4), 454–464.

Sadoski, M. (1985). The natural use of imagery in story comprehension and recall: Replication and extension. *Reading Research Quarterly, 20*(5), 658–667.

39 COMPREHENSION: SUMMARIZATION TRAINING

Background

This tactic is based on evidence that summarization training can transfer to general reading comprehension, particularly when instruction in this technique is thorough and explicit. Summarization training is just one type of instructional program designed to improve students' metacognitive control of the reading process. The type of instruction explained here teaches children to pay greater attention to the text.

Who Can Benefit

The participants in the cited study were sixth-grade students. The technique can be used with an entire class of children. Although all types of readers can participate, this type of instruction, and other forms of metacognitive training, is especially effective with poorer readers.

Procedures

Foundation of Summarization Training
In order to maximize the effectiveness of summarization training, two design principles were adopted: direct instruction and self-control. Four summarization operations were directly taught:

1. identifying/selecting main information
2. deleting trivial information
3. deleting redundant information
4. relating main and important supporting information

Schedule of Summarization Training
Day 1. Define *summary* as the important information from a reading, and explain that writing a summary is useful when reading and studying. The

teacher models the process, followed by student "talk throughs." The checklist of steps (i.e., the four operations noted earlier) is on display.

Day 2. The teacher reviews the steps involved in producing appropriate paragraph summaries. The teacher actively monitors the students' work.

Day 3. When students are proficient with the process for single paragraphs, they are asked to summarize a series of paragraphs. First they write summaries of individual paragraphs, then a summary of those individual summaries. The teacher models the process, followed by student "talk throughs."

Day 4. Students now write summaries about groups of paragraphs without writing summaries of individual paragraphs.

Day 5. Students write summaries of each section of the chapter as if they were taking notes. The checklist is not made available at this time.

Monitor

As with several tactics in this book, it is advisable to acquire data of two types. First, data regarding the extent to which youngsters engage the technique should be kept. In this case, such data would pertain to how well they identified main bits of information, deleted trivial information, deleted redundant information, and related main and supporting pieces of information. For the second measure, data should be kept on how well the youngsters comprehended text. Several types of measures may be used: having students retell what they read, requiring students to ask questions about the text, having students respond to certain features of text, or having students respond to teacher-prepared questions.

Modifications/Considerations

The research authors noted that it would have been a good idea to have taught the students to "invent" or name a main idea in paragraphs when the main idea was not explicit or clearly stated. Quite possibly, this type of training would apply to note-taking activities as well as reading from text, another important behavior at the intermediate and secondary level.

Research

Rinehart, S. D., Stahl, S. A., & Erickson, L. G. (1986). Some effects of summarization training on reading and studying. *Reading Research Quarterly, 21*(4), 422-438.

40 COMPREHENSION: TEXT STRUCTURE AND SUMMARIZATION INSTRUCTION

Background

Experts contend that children generally have more difficulty reading expository text than they do narrative passages. Several theories have been advanced to explain this: insufficient prior knowledge, lack of interest, and lack of motivation. Another factor that could contribute to this difficulty is that children may lack sensitivity to text structures. The following are text structures for expository text that are ordinarily identified: comparison/contrast, cause/effect, temporal sequence, problem/solution, description, and enumeration. The purpose behind the cited study was to instruct students to recognize the problem/solution structure and to use it to organize written summaries of what they had read.

Who Can Benefit

Students in the cited research were fifth graders. However, the procedures outlined here to enhance comprehension of expository text would be useful for students in the fourth and sixth grades as well, since these groups are being instructed more and more from content-area textbooks.

Procedures

Materials
Prepare booklets for the students. In each booklet include the following:

1. a definition and description of the problem/solution text structure and a schematic representation of that structure (Figure 40.1)
2. rules for writing a summary of problem/solution passages, including a pattern for writing and guidelines for checking the summary (Figure 40.2)

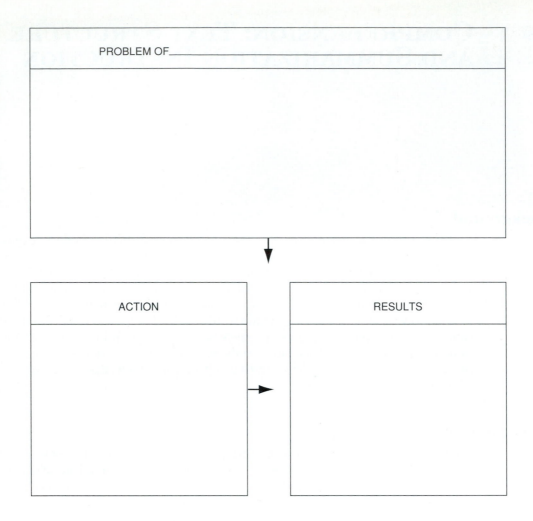

PROBLEM = something bad; a situation that people would like to change

ACTION = what people *do* to try to solve the problem

RESULTS = what happens as a result of the action; the effect or outcome of trying to solve the problem

FIGURE 40.1   Problem/Solution Frame

SOURCE: From Figure 1 of "Does Text Structure/Summarization Instruction Facilitate Learning from Expository Text?", Bonnie B. Armbruster, Thomas H. Anderson, and Joyce Ostertag, *Reading Research Quarterly, 22*(3), 1987, p. 335. Reprinted with permission of Bonnie B. Armbruster and the International Reading Association.

FIGURE 40.2

Guidelines for Summarizing Problem/Solution Passages

SOURCE: From Figure 2 of "Does Text Structure/ Summarization Instruction Facilitate Learning from Expository Text?", Bonnie B. Armbruster, Thomas H. Anderson, and Joyce Ostertag, *Reading Research Quarterly, 22*(3), 1987, p. 337. Reprinted with permission of Bonnie B. Armbruster and the International Reading Association.

How to Summarize Problem/Solution Passages

Sentence 1— Tells who had a problem and what the problem is.

Sentence 2—Tells what action was taken to try to solve the problem.

Sentence 3—Tells what happened as a result of the action taken.

Pattern for Writing a Summary of a Problem/Solution Passage

_____ had a problem because _____

Therefore, _____

As a result, _____

Guidelines for Checking Summaries of a Problem/Solution Passage

Check to see that:

1. Your summary has all of the information that should be in a summary of a problem/solution passage. (See "How to Write a Summary of a Problem/Solution Passage.") Compare your summary with the original Problem/Solution passage to make sure that the summary is accurate and complete.

2. You have used complete sentences.

3. The sentences are tied together with good connecting words.

4. The grammar and spelling are correct.

3. 13 problem/solution passages from fourth- and fifth-grade social studies textbooks, ranging in length from 100 to 500 words

4. multiple copies of problem/solution frames that contain blank lines for students to use in writing summaries of the passages

Instructional Procedures

Day 1

- Offer a rationale for the project. For example, "Social studies texts discuss many problems and solutions. Learning about those structures will help you to focus on main ideas and to remember important information."

- Use the first example story. Ask the following questions: "Who has a problem?" and "What actions were taken to solve the problem?"
- Introduce the problem/solution frame (Figure 40.1) and tell students that the diagram will help them organize their answers to the questions.

Day 2

- Conduct a review, then lead a discussion of the second passage in the workbook.
- Explain that one way to learn from reading texts is to summarize the information read.
- Explain the guidelines for summarizing problem/solution passages (see Figure 40.2).

Days 3 through 9

- Require students to work consecutively through the workbook, following three steps for each passage: (1) read the passage silently, looking for information that answers the problem/solution questions; (2) record notes on the passage in the provided problem/solution frames; (3) write a summary of the framed information.

Days 10 and 11

- Return students to their regular textbooks.
- Ask students to read a passage, then discuss it using the problem/solution frame.
- Record the discussion points in a frame on the chalkboard, then ask students to summarize the frame orally.

Monitor

The authors used two categories of measures:

Tests of learning from independent reading   There were three of these. The first was designed to assess students' comprehension of the higher order structure of a passage about homesteading. The test was an essay question: "What were the problems that settlers faced on the Great Plains? How did they solve those problems?" The second measure was a 10-item, short-answer test intended to tap more specific information from the passage. The third test was designed to assess students' ability to write summaries of problem/solution passages. For this, students summarized two 200-word passages, one on the problem of obtaining food in Haiti, the other on the problem of getting oil from Alaska.

Tests of learning from structured discussion   Students were asked to respond to an essay question about a passage from their regular textbooks. The topic was the settlers in Jamestown and the question was: "Describe two problems that the English colonists faced in the early years of the Jamestown settlement. How did they solve those problems?"

Modifications/Considerations

The research authors mentioned that although the low-ability students did as well as the high-ability students on the dimensions of integration, focus, and support/elaboration, they did not do as well on the dimension of organization. The authors recommended, therefore, that the instruction for those students should provide considerably more practice and feedback.

Research

Armbruster, B. B., Anderson, T. H., & Ostertag, J. (1987). Does text structure/summarization instruction facilitate learning from expository text? *Reading Research Quarterly, 22*(3), 331–346.

41 CONTENT READING: PRIMARY GRADES

Background

According to the authors of the cited study, a number of factors account for young children's difficulties with expository text, among them: limited background knowledge to link with new information, unfamiliar text organizational structures, and a limited vocabulary.

Who Can Benefit

The approaches reviewed here would be helpful for all students engaged in reading content or expository texts, but particularly for youngsters in the primary levels: grades one, two, and three.

Procedures

The research authors compiled a list of 17 general practices often used to assist students in acquiring and assimilating information from content texts. Primary-level teachers were asked to rate these practices according to which ones they believed were most suited to their youngsters. The following is the list of techniques in the order that they were placed by primary teachers:

preview vocabulary/concepts

manipulations (maps, pictures, etc.)

retelling

individual or class summary

visualization

brainstorming

narratives on same content topic

audio or computer materials

act/role play

graphic overview

SQ3R

glossary use

study guide

partial outline

read aloud; students follow along

cloze passages

who, what, when, where, how, why

The research authors then outlined six strategies for assisting children to acquire information from content materials. To do so they combined features of the techniques preferred by the primary teachers. Of the six strategies that they formulated—semantic mapping, using concrete manipulatives and experiences, participating in visual imagery, using expository paragraph frames, group summarizing, and using K-W-L: What I **k**now, what I **w**ant to learn, what I **l**earned—the last three are summarized here.

Expository Paragraph Frames
This strategy is based on evidence that when children retell what they have read, comprehension is improved. Expository frames aid children with retelling. See Figure 41.1 for examples of frames used to stress sequence and compare-contrast, two common text structures.

Group Summarizing
The following is an example of group summarizing: Prior to students reading about armadillos, it is decided to read for descriptions of armadillos, information about their food, about their homes, and other interesting facts. A sheet such as the one shown in Figure 41.2 is given to the students and they fill in the information as a part of a class activity, in small groups, or individually.

K-W-L: What I Know, What I Want to Learn, What I Learned
Prior to reading, label three columns, as is shown in Figure 41.3, on the chalkboard (or have each child draw the columns on their own papers). Next, ask the students as a group (or individually) to give as much information about the first two columns as they can. Students then read the passage, and finally, they fill in information in the third column, "What we learned and still need to learn."

Sequence frame (Based on a passage about how cloth is made.)

I learned many interesting things about how cloth is made.

First, I learned that _____

_____

Next, I learned that _____

_____

Third, I learned that _____

_____

Finally, I learned that _____

_____

As you can see, it is interesting to learn how cloth is made.

Contrast frame (Based on a passage comparing oceans and lakes.)

Oceans and lakes are different in several ways. They are different in size. Oceans are _____ than lakes. Their water is different too. Ocean water is _____ while lake water is _____. Different kinds of fish live in oceans and lakes. _____ and _____ fish live only in ocean water while _____ and _____ fish live only in lakes. It is interesting to learn how oceans and lakes are different.

FIGURE 41.1   Sample Expository Paragraph Frames

SOURCE: From Figure 2 of "Content Reading Instruction in the Primary Grades: Perceptions and Strategies," Mary W. Olson and Thomas C. Gee, *The Reading Teacher,* December 1991, p. 303. Reprinted with permission of Mary Olson and the International Reading Association.

Description	Food
Nine-banded armadillos are about 2 feet long and weigh about 15 pounds. They have strong claws for digging and a shell of hard bony plates for protection.	Armadillos eat insects, earthworms, spiders, and landsnails by licking them up.
Home	**Interesting facts**
Armadillos live in a tunnel hole filled with leaves to keep them warm.	Armadillos protect themselves by digging a hole or curling into a ball. They have four babies at a time that are all males or females.

FIGURE 41.2   Sample Organizational Format for Group Summarizing Activity

SOURCE: From Figure 3 of "Content Reading Instruction in the Primary Grades: Perceptions and Strategies," Mary W. Olson and Thomas C. Gee, *The Reading Teacher*, December 1991, p. 304. Reprinted with permission of Mary Olson and the International Reading Association.

K What we know	W What we want to find out	L What we learned and still need to learn
Toads ① small animal ① gray ① has a long tongue ③ jumps ③ spits poison ② eats bugs ② eats spiders Categories 1. description 2. food 3. what toads do	Are toads the same as frogs? If not, how are they different? Where do toads live in the winter? In the summer? What do toads eat? How do toads protect themselves? How far can they jump?	

FIGURE 41.3 K-W-L Worksheet for a Science Selection on Toads

SOURCE: From Figure 4 of "Content Reading Instruction in the Primary Grades: Perceptions and Strategies," Mary W. Olson and Thomas C. Gee, *The Reading Teacher,* December 1991, p. 305. Reprinted with permission of Mary Olson and the International Reading Association.

Monitor

These three approaches could be evaluated simply by counting the number of relevant comments on the sheet that accompanies each activity. Alternatively, the children could be asked to retell about the passages. As they do so, the teacher could tally the number of correct facts, proper sequences, comparisons, judgments, or evaluations they provided.

Modifications/Considerations

When evaluating this research, the possibility should be kept in mind that most of the teachers who responded to the survey might not have adequately experienced all 17 of the listed techniques. It is possible that none of the teachers had actually used even 10 of the listed approaches. However, inservice providers or teachers of classes who set out to inform others about reading comprehension, particularly the comprehension of expository passages, will be able to arrange exciting and informative sessions by using the practices noted here. (Incidentally, many of the 17 listed techniques are explained in this volume.)

When presenting any of the various listed techniques to others, the presenters should first of all give a brief outline of each technique and then provide supporting information or research about it. Additionally, the presenter could demonstrate how each technique could be arranged for classes or for individual children, provide information regarding the limitations of each technique, and identify the types of youngsters with whom each technique would be most effective.

Research

Olson, M. W., & Gee, T. C. (1991). Content reading instruction in the primary grades: Perceptions and strategies. *The Reading Teacher, 45*(4), 298–307.

42 CLASSROOM ORGANIZATION FOR INSTRUCTION IN CONTENT AREAS

Background

The instructional approach explained here is much broader than most of the other tactics in this book; in fact, it might be more aptly categorized as a strategy. (Actually, it has to do with logistics.) The idea behind this approach is to identify ways in which classrooms can be organized to best teach content subjects. The research authors point out that although "ability grouping" has continued to be the most popular way in which to organize classes for instruction, there are scant data to suggest that it is the best way to go about instructing children. Conversely, considerable data are available showing that when children are heterogeneously assembled in small cooperative groups, their achievement increases. The authors identify three organizational groups and explain the types of instruction best suited for each arrangement.

Who Can Benefit

The class that served as the basis for the cited research was at the intermediate level. The suggestions regarding the three organizational approaches would be pertinent not only to fourth-, fifth-, and sixth-grade classes, but also to many situations at the middle-school, junior-high, and high-school levels.

Procedures

Three organizational approaches are discussed here: teacher-led, whole-class discussions; cooperative small groups; and individual. A few remarks are offered on each.

Teacher-led, Whole-class Discussions

There are several purposes for teacher-led discussions:

1. To introduce new strategies and concepts. (See, for example, those summarized in Table 42.1.)

K-W-L	This framework helps students build background knowledge and share common experiences. *K* stands for what do I already know? *W* stands for "What do I want to learn?" and *L* stands for "What have I learned?" It prompts students' thinking about: (1) their relevant background knowledge, (2) questions that reflect their purposes for reading, and (3) the information they learned from reading the text. Using K-W-L encourages students to attack informational text with a purpose, and recognize the information they have gleaned from it.
Focus journals	This type of journal encourages students to review their background knowledge, reflect on their previous learning, and predict their future learning. The journal focus is written on the board by the teacher each day before the students arrive. Students read the focus, reflect on their response and write in their journals. Frequently, the focus of the journal is on content area studies, though some days students choose their own topics. The focus journal helps students focus on their own learning and serves as a basis for discussion.
Concept maps	These visual organizers help students literally "map" their knowledge base. The maps can be used to help students understand a vocabulary term by having students identify the concept to be defined (e.g., communication); a superordinate category or phrase that helps them understand what it is (e.g., sending and receiving messages); traits (e.g., ideas from one person are shared with someone else; can be done in writing or out loud); and examples (e.g., newspapers, letters, telephone calls). Maps can also be used to organize information from different sources.
The author's chair	The author's chair provides students with a real audience as they share their journals, text, trade books, reports, and so forth. It is a special chair in the front of the room in which the child sits to read aloud to the rest of the class. During the time the child reads, she is speaking for the author. During content area study children may: (1) sit in the author's chair to read from their textbook to the rest of the class, (2) share their journal reflections and predictions with their peers, and (3) share their rough drafts for help in revisions and final drafts for general comments.
QAR	QAR teaches children about sources of information, helping students discover and use the many sources of information from which questions can be answered. It provides direction to those students who are overreliant on their background knowledge at the expense of information from texts, or those who are overreliant on the text as a sole source of information and do not consider their own background knowledge and experience.
CSIW	CSIW is a framework for guiding students as they plan, organize, write, edit, and revise expository texts. A set of "thinksheets" serves as a basis for the teacher to model strategies. The thinksheets act as prompts for students to take notes and keep records about the information for their reports, to sustain their thinking about topics and as a basis for discussion. Thinksheets may be adapted to serve the specific needs students have as they gather and organize their information.

TABLE 42.1 Selected Comprehension Strategies

SOURCE: From Table 1 of "Classroom Organization for Instruction in Content Areas," Laura S. Pardo and Taffy E. Raphael, *The Reading Teacher*, April 1991, p. 558. Reprinted with permission of Laura S. Pardo and the International Reading Association.

2. To share related background knowledge. Students could contribute information on the topic of the day (e.g., communication) before reading it or after they had read all or parts of it.

3. To build common experiences. If field trips, for example, are associated with the activity, the teacher could ask the children to speculate about what they might see on the trip.

4. To learn from difficult text. The teacher could model lessons on note-taking or summarizing, for example.

5. To schedule enrichment activities. Students could work on special projects (e.g., prepare a video) that pertained to the topic.

Cooperative Small Groups

Such approaches provide opportunities for students to:

1. Practice newly learned strategies (e.g., K-W-L) and apply newly learned concepts to further their study in a selected area.

2. Work collaboratively to create reports, questions, or information assembled from interviews.

3. Engage in discussions about the content and processes they are studying.

Individual

Four reasons are noted for allowing students to work alone:

1. To reflect on their ideas, the passages they are reading, and their discussions with the teacher and with other students. To stimulate these activities, children might be asked to respond to a few questions.

2. To set individual goals. Children could be encouraged to write down their goals.

3. To apply and practice strategies they were shown.

4. To provide information regarding their own progress. Periodically, the students could evaluate how much progress has been made toward their goals.

Monitor

Several skills or attributes could be measured with respect to the arrangements discussed here. For one, a measure of the extent to which the children learned or knew about the various strategies that were taught (e.g., K-W-L) could be gathered. The children could be asked to explain or write about the strategy, define its elements, and identify when it is best used. For another, a measure of the students' ability to tell about material they have just read or talked about could be obtained. Moreover, the teacher could assess the students' writing ability. For that, several measures come to mind: number of words or phrases per a particular unit of time, number of instances they criticize or make judgments about material they just read or discussed, or the extent to which they integrated the new material with material from previous lessons or from their experiences apart from school.

Modifications/Considerations

Although the three organizational approaches discussed here are perhaps the most common, there are others. Various tutoring arrangements could be set up, for example. Paraprofessionals, older students, or parents could be brought in to assist the youngsters, particularly those who are having the most trouble. Another organizational approach might be to set up a computer network. With such an arrangement, the teacher, at a controlling and central machine, could work with the entire class, portions of the class, or with students one at a time. It would certainly be possible to have more than one of the approaches in effect at the same time. For example, the teacher could be assisting several of the youngsters with the computer network, other children might be paired up for instruction, and a few others could work individually.

Research

Pardo, L. S., & Raphael, T. E. (1991). Classroom organization for instruction in content areas. *The Reading Teacher, 44*(8), 556–565.

43 MULTIPASS: A STRATEGY FOR COMPREHENDING

Background

The Multipass approach is based on the SQ3R technique advanced some years ago by Robinson (1946) to aid reading comprehension. The SQ3R method involves

- a quick survey (S) of the material
- a second pass through the material during which the student turns subtitles into questions (Q)
- a read-through (R1) of the material to locate answers to the questions
- a recitation (R2) of the answers as well as taking notes
- a final review (R3) of the material

Who Can Benefit

The students in the sample research were at the secondary level; they were enrolled in programs for children with learning disabilities. This approach is also appropriate for youngsters in the intermediate grades as they begin reading in the content areas.

Procedures

General Procedures

Step 1: Test to determine the student's current learning style.

In this step, the teacher uses two sets of materials to test the student's Multipass skills. One set of materials tests reading ability level, or the level at which the student can read; the other set of materials tests grade level, or the level at which the student should be reading. After testing, the teacher discusses test results with the student, often confirming that the child did

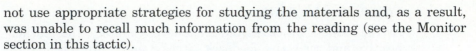

not use appropriate strategies for studying the materials and, as a result, was unable to recall much information from the reading (see the Monitor section in this tactic).

Step 2: Describe the learning strategy.

Next, the teacher describes to the student the steps involved in the Multipass strategy (see the *Multipass Procedures* section for an explanation of this strategy) and contrasts these steps with the student's current study habits. These steps include the specific behaviors to be followed. The explanation of each step should be accompanied by a rationale for its use and a description of how it will help the pupil learn the material more easily.

Step 3: Model the strategy.

The teacher models the Multipass approach for the student. He or she demonstrates the strategy by acting out each of the steps while "thinking aloud" so that the student can observe all the processes involved.

Step 4: Verbally rehearse the strategy.

The student verbally rehearses the steps involved in the Multipass strategy to a criterion of 100 percent correct without prompts. This step is designed to familiarize the student with all the phases so he or she can use self-instruction in the future when using this strategy.

Step 5: Practice with controlled materials.

In this step, the student practices applying the strategy while reading successive chapters in his or her ability-level book. Ability-level materials make fewer demands than do grade-level books, which allows the student to concentrate on learning the new approach. As the pupil becomes proficient, he or she is encouraged to progress from spoken to silent self-instruction while practicing the strategy.

Step 6: Provide feedback.

As the student applies the strategy to a new chapter in the book, the teacher gives both positive and corrective feedback. Steps 5 and 6 are repeated with additional chapters until the pupil learns to employ the strategy to a specified criterion.

Step 7: Test.

The tests administered during Step 1 are given to the student again, using different text chapters in both ability-level and grade-level texts. These tests give a measure of the student's progress in learning the Multipass technique. If the results indicate a need for more help, the student is assigned the next three instructional steps (8, 9, and 10). If, however, he or she meets criteria in both sets of materials, instruction ends.

Step 8: Practice in grade-level materials.

When this step is required, the student practices applying the Multipass strategy to successive chapters in grade-level materials.

Step 9: Provide feedback.

As the student practices the grade-level chapters, the teacher gives both positive and corrective feedback. Steps 8 and 9 are repeated until the student masters the strategy to a specific criterion.

Step 10: Test.

Once the student meets the criterion on grade-level practice, the tests administered in Steps 1 and 7 are scheduled again using different text chapters. These tests serve as final measures of the student's skills.

Multipass Procedures

The Multipass approach includes three substrategies: Survey, Size-up, and Sort-out. Each step, which is taught separately, requires the student to pass through the chapter for a particular purpose. Once the student masters the steps at his or her ability level, a posttest is given to assess what he or she has learned. The student then receives additional practice and, if ready, is advanced to grade-level material.

Survey pass

This pass is designed to familiarize the student with the main ideas and organization of the chapter. During this pass the student is required to:

1. read the chapter title
2. read the introductory paragraph
3. review the chapter's relationship to others by perusing the table of contents
4. read the major subtitles of the chapter and notice how the chapter is organized
5. look at the illustrations and read their captions
6. read the summary paragraph
7. paraphrase all the information gained in this process

Size-up pass

This pass is designed to help students gain specific information and facts from a chapter without reading it from beginning to end. This pass requires the pupil to first read the questions at the end of the chapter to determine which facts are the most important. If the student is able to answer some questions as a result of the survey pass, he or she puts a checkmark next to these questions.

The student now skims through the entire chapter with the following purposes in mind:

1. to look for textual cues (e.g., boldface print, subtitles, colored print, italics)

2. to turn these cues into questions (e.g., if the cue was the italicized vocabulary word *conqueror*, the student might ask, "What does conqueror mean?"; if the cue was the subtitle "The Election of 1848," the student might ask, "Who won the election of 1848?" or "Why was the election of 1848 important?")

3. to skim through the text surrounding the cue to find the answers to the questions developed by the student

4. to paraphrase the answers without looking back at the book

When the student—using these four steps for each textual cue—reaches the end of the chapter, he or she is asked to paraphrase as many facts and ideas from it as possible.

Sort-out pass

This pass requires the student to test him- or herself over the material in the chapter. In this final pass, the pupil reads and answers each question at the end of the chapter. If the child can answer a question immediately, he or she places a checkmark next to it. If not, he or she looks for the solution by

1. thinking about the section of the chapter in which the answer would most likely appear,

2. skimming through that section for the answer,

3. identifying another section if the answer was not located in the first, and

4. skimming this second section, and so on.

When the answer is located, the student places a checkmark next to the question and moves to the next item.

Monitor

Eight tests are given to students before and after training (see Steps 1, 7, and 10). The first six tests measure students' skills in the three substrategies of Multipass in both ability- level and grade-level materials. The final two tests, one in ability-level and one in grade-level material, require the student to apply the Multipass strategies to new materials.

For the two Survey tests (one in ability-level, the other in grade-level materials), the student is assigned a chapter in a text and is told to remember as much as possible about its main ideas and its organization, allowing one minute per page. The student's surveying procedures are observed by the teacher, who could use a checklist to record whether or not the student followed the behaviors listed under the *Survey pass* heading in the Procedures box. When the time is up, the student closes the book and tells everything he or she can about the main ideas and organization of the chapter. The teacher also asks the child to explain how he or she learned this information.

In the two Size-up tests, the student is instructed to gain as many specific facts from the chapter as possible without reading it. The child is allowed 12 minutes per page for this task. At the end of this time, the student closes the book, reports the cues he or she picked up in the chapter, and tells as many facts as possible about the material.

As for the pair of Sort-out tests, the pupil is instructed to show how he or she would self-test to see whether or not he or she knows about the information in the chapter. Using a behavioral checklist that contains the items listed under the *Sort-out pass* heading in the Procedures box, the teacher observes and records the student's self-testing process and records the number of questions the child correctly answers at the end of the chapter. (A new chapter is assigned each time the student receives the series of three substrategy tests.)

Finally, two other tests are given, one using ability-level materials and the other using grade-level materials. For these, the student is assigned a new chapter to read and study and a date is set for testing him or her on the chapter. The student is given a minimum of 24 hours to study for the test. (The length of study time allowed is the same for the pretest and the posttest.) The test is made up of 20 items written in an objective format. The student answers the questions without consulting the text or notes and is given 30 minutes to complete the test. The test is then graded and the percentage of questions answered correctly is recorded.

Modifications/Considerations

One obvious alteration of this tactic is to reduce or increase the number of passes a student is required to make through a passage. Another is to change the purpose of these scannings. Yet another modification is the number of steps used. There could be more or fewer than the 10 used in the research, and they might pertain to different topics.

Shoop (1986) describes a related reading and listening strategy referred to as the Investigative Questioning Procedure. Three steps comprise this strategy: read the story, role play a news conference, and evaluate the interview.

Research

Robinson, F. P. (1946). *Effective study*. New York: Harper and Brothers.

Schumaker, J. B., Deshler, D. D., Alley, G. R., Warner, M. W., & Denton, P. H. (1982). Multipass: A learning strategy for improving reading comprehension. *Learning Disability Quarterly, 5,* 295–304.

Shoop, M. (1986). InQuest: A listening and reading comprehension strategy. *The Reading Teacher, 39*(7), 670–674.

44 IMPROVING CONTENT-AREA READING BY USING INSTRUCTIONAL GRAPHICS

Background

The basis for the research that supports this tactic is that meaningful learning depends on three related processes—selecting, organizing, and integrating information (Mayer, 1984). This particular tactic focuses on the first of these two elements: selecting and organizing. Moreover, the research summarized here is based on the notion that it is important for students to participate actively in their instruction.

Who Can Benefit

The research of Armbruster, Anderson, and Meyer (1991) was carried out with several fourth and fifth graders in regular classrooms in a number of different schools. Since these youngsters were working from textbooks on social studies topics and from passages that would ordinarily be assigned to them, the procedures arranged by the researchers and the conclusions drawn from their results also should be applicable to other situations; for example, situations involving social studies at higher grades would be applicable.

Procedures

Constructing the Frames

1. Review the chapter or portions of the chapter to be framed. Identify the main concepts you intend to teach. Teachers could work in groups or individually.

2. Develop frames with the requisite information filled in, such as the completed frame shown in Figure 44.1. Frames should include page numbers to indicate where relevant information can be found in the text.

3. Type blank frames and give them to the students. The filled-in frames will serve as the answer key.

Name _____   Teacher _____

4. The Battle of Gettysburg
(Chapter 16, pp. 370–372)

GOAL:

The victory at _____Chancellorsville_____ gave the Confederacy confidence to try to invade the North. The Confederate goal was to end the war by _winning_ _____a clear victory on Northern soil_____ .

ACTIONS:

The Battle of Gettysburg

The high point was _____Pickett's Charge_____ , a moving wall of Confederate soldiers led by General George Pickett. The charge failed and the Confederate troops retreated.

RESULTS:

Casualties were high because of the advance in war _____technology_____ , including new kinds of cannons and guns called _____musket rifles_____ .

Lincoln gave a famous speech called _____The Gettysburg Address_____ .

The North was now fighting for 3 goals:

1. _preservation of the Union_
2. _freedom for slaves_
3. _defense of democracy_

FIGURE 44.1 Example of a Completed Fifth-Grade Frame

SOURCE: From Figure 4 of "Improving Content Area Reading Using Instructional Graphics," Bonnie B. Armbruster, Thomas H. Anderson, and Jennifer L. Meyer, *Reading Research Quarterly, 26*(4), 1991, p. 405. Reprinted with permission of Bonnie B. Armbruster and the International Reading Association.

Constructing Information Sheets

1. Leave chunks of information incomplete.

2. Arrange the information "out of order" on the students' sheets, as shown in Figure 44.2.

Information Sheet for "The Plains States—1"

Two landforms in the Plains states are the _____ and the _____ .	Two of the largest rivers are the _____ and the _____ .
Most of the land in the Plains states is not perfectly flat, but is _____ .	The four states in the Great Plains are _____ , _____ , _____ , and _____ .
Pumps, sometimes driven by _____ , bring groundwater to the surface. The water is used by _____ and _____ .	People of the Plains states also use groundwater, which is _____ .
The Plains states are in the Interior Plains, which are divided into the _____ and the _____ .	The two states in the Central Plains are _____ and _____ .

FIGURE 44.2 Information Sheet for a Fourth-Grade Frame

SOURCE: From Figure 3 of "Improving Content Area Reading Using Instructional Graphics," Bonnie B. Armbruster, Thomas H. Anderson, and Jennifer L. Meyer, *Reading Research Quarterly, 26*(4), 1991, p. 404. Reprinted with permission of Bonnie B. Armbruster and the International Reading Association.

Carrying out the procedures

1. Elicit prior knowledge from students; ask them to make predictions about the frames before reading the passage.

2. Ask students to read the passage.

3. Assign students to small groups; ask them to fill in the blanks on the answer sheet.

4. Ask students, in groups, to cut out each information chunk from the information sheet.

5. Decide where each chunk should be placed on the frame.

6. Lead a whole-class discussion about the frame.

7. Ask students to tape information chunks to their frames when a class consensus is reached.

8. Ask students to study the frames in preparation for a test. They can do this individually or in small groups. Tell them what type of test it will be (e.g., short answer).

Monitor

There are several ways in which to monitor the effects of this procedure. In the cited research, teachers gave the students short-answer tests. Another option might be to give them the original blank frames and ask them to fill them in. Yet another approach would be to simply require the youngsters to write as much as they could, in an organized fashion, about the topic and contents of the passage they had read and studied.

Modifications/Considerations

It may not be appropriate to ask middle-school or high-school students to cut out responses from information sheets and tape them to the frames. Instead, they could write or type their responses. For that matter, instructional sheets and frames could be entered on computers. Students' computers could be networked and as a group they could fill in the frames.

Research

Armbruster, B. B., Anderson, T. H., & Meyer, J. L. (1991). Improving content area reading using instructional graphics. *Reading Research Quarterly, 26*(4), 393–416.

Mayer, R. E. (1984). Aids to text comprehension. *Educational Psychologist, 19,* 30–42.

45 LOCATING INFORMATION IN TEXT

Background

Children are often asked to search text for answers to questions, to pursue evidence in support of a point, and to seek information on topics of interest. Related to these tasks, the ability to locate information is often assessed by standardized tests. According to the authors of the cited study, four elements are required to locate information: goal formation, text selection, information extraction and integration, and evaluation.

Who Can Benefit

Research on the various components required to successfully access information has been carried out with a wide range of students, from elementary to college age, and with "good" and "poor" reading habits. Being able to identify textbook information of various types is an extremely important skill, and one that is required of students as soon as they begin reading. From the fourth grade on, it is particularly critical to successfully demonstrate this skill.

Procedures

According to the authors of the cited research, there are three primary reasons why it is difficult for children to comprehend information from textbooks:

- Passages in textbooks are written in organizational patterns that many youths are not familiar with (i.e., description, comparison/contrast, temporal sequence, explanation, and problem-solution).

- Stories and passages in many textbooks are "inconsiderate"; they lack coherence, are poorly organized, and provide inadequate explanations.

- Many youngsters do not read very much, let alone attempt to search textbooks for essential information.

Armbruster and Armstrong (1993) claim that the search process is prompted by the reader's goals, that is, the information that he or she is searching for. To assist in focusing those goals, the authors developed a three-dimensional framework. One dimension of the frame is the *source* of the goal. The source may be external (e.g., questions asked by the teacher or the textbook) or internal (i.e., ones generated by the reader). The second dimension is the *time* in which the goal is made. The goal may be established before reading (to locate information in material that has not yet been read) or during or after reading (to locate information in text that has been read but perhaps forgotten). The third dimension of the process is how *specific* the goals are. This dimension represents goals that range from very specific (e.g., literal questions) to very general (e.g., broad research questions). In Figure 45.1, these framework dimensions are represented in a matrix that includes examples of tasks for elementary-age students.

Along with providing a framework to aid in forming the goals of reading, Armbruster and Armstrong offer suggestions for teachers that pertain to each of the four stages of locating information in text: goal formation, text selection, information extraction and integration, and evaluation.

		Time of Search		
		Before Reading	During/After Reading	
		Specific – – – – – – – ➤ General	Specific – – – – – – – ➤ General	
Source of Goal	External	text-explicit question	assigned research on general topic	text-explicit question	find evidence in support of conclusion
	Internal	locate fact	self-selected general research topic	spontaneous lookback to locate fact	spontaneous lookback to locate source of confusion

FIGURE 45.1 Types of Search Goals or Tasks

SOURCE: From "Locating Information in Text: A Focus on Children in the Elementary Grades," by B. B. Armbruster and J. O. Armstrong, 1993, *Contemporary Educational Psychology, 18,* p. 142. Copyright 1993 by Academic Press, Inc. Reprinted by permission.

Goal Formation

- Teach children about *question differentiation,* which is the process of discriminating types of tasks that require text search from ones that do not.
- Instruct youngsters to attend to the internal goal of "fixing up" a comprehension or memory failure. Convince them that text "lookbacks" are legal.

Text Selection

- Within the context of pursuing authentic search goals, inform students about the use of reference materials and book parts.
- Devote instructional time to explaining the procedures for *text sampling*, which is the process of scanning or skimming text for information relevant to questions.

Information Extraction and Integration

- Schedule time for distinguishing important from less important information by offering instruction on main ideas and summaries.
- Help students learn to summarize texts they have read. Initially, they could summarize paragraphs, then larger units of text.

Evaluation

- Assist pupils in becoming more proficient comprehension monitors. Encourage them to comment on the goals they want to attain and their progress toward reaching those goals.

Monitor

Start slowly with some children. Give them only short passages that are simply constructed and ask students to search for words. The words might even be highlighted. Gradually involve longer passages and ones that are more complex. The information sought could be more sophisticated. Throughout the process, keep track of students' correct and incorrect "identifications." Also keep track of the time it takes students to identify the pieces of information, tallying the correct and incorrect "identifications" per minute.

Modifications/Considerations

What with the technological advances of the past few years, individuals can access information from a broad range of sources, among them the commercial computer networks that are available. There are a number of networks and bulletin boards that are open to anyone with a computer, a modem, and some experience with accessing those sources. Indeed, individuals can access information from their own computers without going through an outside network by using existing software for encyclopedias, dictionaries, and almanacs.

Research

Armbruster, B. B., & Armstrong, J. O. (1993). Locating information in text: A focus on children in the elementary grades. *Contemporary Educational Psychology, 18,* 139–161.

46 CONTENT-AREA READING–WRITING LESSONS

Background

According to the research authors, the following are components of a good reading comprehension lesson:

- Help students access what they know before reading
- Set purposes for their reading
- Assist them to read in an active, purposeful manner
- Help them see what information they correctly learned
- Give them comprehension assistance, if necessary

As for writing, the research authors noted the following three essential ingredients:

- Model for the students what they are to do
- Provide guided practice in writing
- Give feedback to students regarding aspects of their performance that were good or had improved and on features about which they could improve.

The lesson discussed here includes the components of good reading and writing instruction. Furthermore, an organizational device called a *feature matrix* is explained that blends these features.

Who Can Benefit

This tactic would be an appropriate choice for children in the intermediate grades as they are studying in content areas, and for older youths who are studying social studies and science, as well as other subjects. It is a particularly good technique for students who lack confidence or the basic skills required to assemble information and write about it.

Procedures

Reading

1. Select the passage from which to develop a feature matrix. It should be a passage that calls for the comparison of several items of information.

2. Select a few categories from the passage and identify relevant features of those categories. See Figure 46.1 for an example.

3. Display the matrix in skeleton form, with none of the boxes filled in.

4. Ask students to prepare a similar matrix in their notebooks.

5. Lead a discussion with the students at which time they offer suggestions for filling in the matrix. In the example, students put a plus sign in the space if they believed it to be true, and a minus sign if they thought it was not true.

6. Ask the pupils to read the passage from which the feature matrix was developed.

FIGURE 46.1
Prereading Feature Matrix as Filled Out by an Individual Student

SOURCE: From Figure 1 of "Content Area Reading-Writing Lessons," Patricia M. Cunningham and James W. Cunningham, *The Reading Teacher,* February 1987, p. 509. Reprinted with permission of Patricia M. Cunningham and the International Reading Association.

Planets in Earth's solar system						
	Closer to sun than Earth	Larger than Earth	Has moon	Has rings	Orbits the sun	Inner planet
Earth	−	−	+	−	+	+
Jupiter	−	+	+	−		−
Mars	+	−	+	−	+	+
Mercury	+	−		−	+	+
Neptune	−	+		−		−
Pluto	−	+		−		−
Saturn	−	+		+		−
Uranus	−			−		−
Venus	+	−	+	−	+	

7. Encourage students to review their matrices and fill in the slots based on the new information. They should make changes as needed.

8. Engage the class in a discussion of their matrices. Construct a class matrix. Fill in the boxes with either pluses or minuses as the students agree on the marks. If there is disagreement, circle the box.

9. Ask the pupils to reread the passage in an attempt to come to an agreement on the information needed to fill in the circled boxes.

10. Resume the class discussion. If, following this interaction, there is still a circle or two, require students to search out the information at a library or from another source.

Writing

1. Model for the students how a paragraph on the selected topic (in this case, the planet Venus) might be written.

2. Write a lead sentence, at least three more sentences about specific matters, and one summary sentence. Keep the model sentences and the feature matrix on the chalkboard.

3. Ask the students to write a paragraph on a similar or related topic, in this case about a planet other than Venus.

4. Ask students to read their paragraphs to the class. As they read, offer feedback on exemplary or improved aspects of their writing, and give them further suggestions for improving their writing (e.g., combining sentences, using descriptive words such as adverbs and adjectives, relating one sentence to the next).

Monitor

An obvious way in which to monitor the extent to which pupils can fill in boxes on a matrix is to compare their "fill-ins" with those of a standard. Likewise, another rudimentary way to assess students' writing about a passage would be to determine whether they had written the prescribed number and type of sentences that were requested (e.g., one lead sentence, three sentences about specifics, and one summary sentence). Beyond these rather simple measures, data can be kept on the number of words written, the number of related sentences composed, the number of times the pupil drew upon information that was <u>not</u> in the textbook but was relevant to the topic, and, of course, the use of such mechanical attributes as spelling, proper tenses, and agreement.

Modifications/Considerations

Whereas the topic of the feature matrix in the cited study was the planets in Earth's solar system, matrices in other science topics could be easily developed. In health, for example, a matrix could display various foods along with relevant features such as carbohydrate, calorie, or fiber content. Likewise, a matrix could be designed in social studies to illustrate regions, countries, or political leaders, and to show how they are related.

There are organizational devices other than feature matrices. One is a semantic web (see Tactic 30), which is a helpful way to illustrate text made up of subtopics along with a major topic. Another way in which to organize text is with a time line, a device that is common to many history books.

Research

Cunningham, P. M., & Cunningham, J. W. (1987). Content area reading-writing lessons. *The Reading Teacher, 40*(6), 506–512.

47 LEARNING ABOUT OTHER LANGUAGES

Background

This tactic blends all aspects of language: speaking, listening, reading, spelling, and writing. It goes far beyond the ordinary tactic level in that it calls for a vast change in attitude of U.S. children and adults toward languages other than English. The idea behind this tactic is that too many U.S. citizens are totally illiterate in any language <u>except</u> English. Many of us seem to believe that English in the only <u>real</u> language, and that all others—French, Spanish, German—are not only foreign languages, but are inferior, exotic, or useless. Many U.S. individuals, especially those who have lived their entire lives here and whose parents and grandparents were born here, <u>expect</u> people in our country (and, indeed, people in *any* country) to speak our language. People with these attitudes become impatient with "foreigners" in our midst who do not speak English as well as they do, even if they themselves speak with a blatantly provincial accent and a significant disregard for the recognized linguistic and syntactic structures of English. To repeat, the idea behind this "tactic" is to instill in children the notion that there are languages other than English and that it is exciting to learn about them.

Who Can Benefit

Children of all ages and abilities can benefit from this approach. Moreover, their teachers (most of whom know very little about languages other than English) would profit from these ideas. And by all means, the parents of children exposed to these suggestions would gain.

Procedures

- Inform children about the languages that are spoken in different foreign countries. For example, explain that German is spoken not only in Germany but also in Austria, that Spanish is spoken not only in Spain but also in Mexico and many other countries, that Portuguese is spoken not only in Portugal but also in Brazil.

- Explain to youngsters that there are hundreds of different languages. Point out a few facts regarding languages from the 1990 census: Over 30 percent of the individuals in California, Hawaii, New Mexico, New York, and Texas speak a foreign language at home. More than 17 million people in the U.S. age 5 or older speak Spanish in their homes. In my state, Washington, residents speak 180 languages, and 400,000 people (1 in 10) say that they speak a language other than English in their homes.

- Discuss bilingualism in Canada and how this affects their politics and life in general. Inform students that throughout Canada, and this is especially true in the province of Quebec, all signs and advertisements are written in English and French. Moreover, all the information in hotels, museums, cafes, and other public places is written in both languages.

- Related to the preceding item, and particularly to the relationship of politics and languages, inform children that several languages (and religions) are represented in relatively small countries such as Yugoslavia, Bosnia-Herzegovina, Croatia, and Slovenia (all of which formerly made up Yugoslavia) and the Czech Republic and Slovakia (both of which formerly made up Czechoslovakia) and that this has caused serious problems, even warfare.

- Mention that languages are being taught in schools now that have not been taught for many, many years. A couple of examples are the instruction of Catalan in Northern Spain and Provençal in southern regions of France.

- Mention that several U.S. cities and states have passed legislation to make English the official language for carrying out government and business. Discuss the implications of this.

- As children shop in stores, go to places of worship, ride in buses, play at the park, visit the airport, or go anywhere else, ask them to be alert to individuals who are speaking different languages. Ask students to listen, to try and identify the language, and to try and pick out a few words or phrases they have heard before or know the meaning of.

- Make use of students who can speak and read in a language other than English. Ask them to tell the class, in their own native language, about themselves and where they are from. Ask them to teach the other youngsters a few words or phrases. Ask the other students to repeat the words or phrases and have the "student teacher" correct them if necessary.

- Point out, as this notion of increasing youngsters' respect and knowledge of other languages is being promoted, the intellectual, social, and financial advantages of knowing at least a few words and phrases in other languages.

Monitor

Depending on the age, stage, and grade of the youngsters being instructed, the following are a couple of ways in which to monitor the extent to which students are learning about another language:

- Ask children to keep a log of the new words or phrases they have learned. If they are trying to acquire words and phrases in more than one different language, they should make separate entries. Some children might be interested in learning the same words or phrases across two or three languages, whereas others simply might want to add words and phrases to their language repertories that are most interesting to them, regardless of their relationships to other languages. Ask the children from time to time to tell you (or read from their lists) the words or phrases they have written.

- Encourage small groups of children to get together and tell others the words or phrases they have learned. As one child says a word or phrase, the others could identify the language, and more advanced students could say what it meant in English. An even more advanced activity would be for youngsters to say something that added to the word or phrase. As the children engaged in these "discussions," the teacher could keep track of who said what, generally.

Modifications/Considerations

The following are a few ideas for extending the instruction of languages, most of which are more specific than the ones just listed:

- Point out the many similarities (cognates) in words from one language to another. Note that not only are the spellings virtually alike, but also the pronunciations are very similar.

Between English and French:

salad	salade	program	programme
center	centre	group	group
museum	musee	reserve	reserver
guide	guide	visit	visite
member	membre	audiovisual	audiovisuel

Between English and Spanish:

adults	adultos	cooperate	cooperar
tiger	tigre	relations	relaciones
significance	significa	occurs	occurre
utilize	utilizan	important	importa
possibilities	posibilidades	influential	influencia

Between English and German:

speak	sprechen	help	helfen
find	finde	bring	bringen
American	Amerikanische	hunger	Hunger
book	Buch	cold	kalt
can	kann	light	Leicht

- Present a few "school" words that are spelled and pronounced differently in the four languages:

English	French	Spanish	German
read	lire	leer	lesen
write	écrire	escribire	schreiben
spell	épelir	deletrear	buchstabiere
speak	parler	hablar	sprechen
listen	écouter	escuchar	horen
study	étude	estudiar	studieren
think	penser	pensar	glauben
draw	dessiner	dibujar	ziehen
walk	marcher	andar	gehen
run	courir	correr	rennen

- Point out the origin of several of our common phrases: *faux pas, coup de gras, fait accompli.*

- Point out that even in English there are some differences in spelling: *harbor* and *harbour, program* and *programme, labor* and *labour, behavior* and *behaviour, theater* and *theatre.*

- Point out that the use of punctuation and capitalization is different in some languages than in English. For example: In Spanish, a question mark is used at the beginning and at the end of a question, and the mark at the end is inverted. In German all nouns are capitalized. Inform students that a variety of accents are used in several other languages. For example, in German: ä ë ö ü; in French: á à â é è ê; and in Spanish: ã ñ.

- Point out that the alphabets of some languages are different than that of the English language. For example, the Greek and Russian alphabets are quite different, and those of the Asian languages are really different.

- Inform the children that the word order for constructing sentences is different in most languages. For example, to say "Could you speak more slowly?" in German, the speaker would say "Konnten Sie bitte langsamer sprechen?"

- For a week or so, give directions and make comments throughout the day in a different language. For example, the following words or phrases could be given only in Spanish: good morning, please be quiet, please read or write . . ., please line up, pass in your papers, nice work, see you tomorrow.

Research

Barringer, J. (1993, April 28). When English is a foreign tongue: Census finds a sharp rise in 80's. *New York Times,* pp. A1, A10.

Gilmore, S. (1993, April 28). Census shows state is one of 180 tongues. *Seattle Times,* pp. B1, B2.

48 PARENTS: COMMUNICATING WITH SCHOOLS AND GENERAL PROCEDURES FOR TEACHING READING

Background

There are a number of reasons for encouraging parents to tutor their children in reading or in other school subjects. One is that when parents work with teachers, the parents often think better of the schools. Many parents in the past have been suspicious of schools and have criticized the schools' every effort. When parents have some contact with schools, particularly when the interaction relates to their own children, they often become more positive about teachers and the business of education in general.

Another, more important, reason for working with parents is that when parents are assisted in instructing their youngsters in reading, the pupils receive an additional dose of practice. Furthermore, when parents tutor their children, they are continually aware (as often as they have reading sessions) of how their youngsters are progressing. They do not have to wait until report card time to find out how their children are getting along.

When parents tutor their own children, they often become more sympathetic with teachers. If the parents have a few difficulties with their youngsters, they may be a bit more charitable toward teachers who have not yet solved all the problems.

Another positive result of parents working with their children is that the youngsters realize that their parents are interested in them; parents do care. These reading sessions between Dad and Mom and daughter or son are important moments. Still another benefit is that when teachers work with parents and help them instruct their children, the teachers get to know the parents and thus gain further understanding of the children. Consequently, teachers are better able to deal with the students' strengths and weaknesses.

Who Can Benefit

Generally, it is a good idea for teachers to work with parents regarding any education topic at any time; it is probably safe to say that the more communication between school and home, the better. The pupils, however, who would profit most from this coordinated effort of teachers and parents are those who are somewhat delayed in their development, who are not too motivated at school, but who are quite interested in reading with their parents.

Procedures

Following are a number of ideas for setting up training sessions for parents:

1. Explain the purpose.
2. Make the sessions brief and to-the-point.
3. Hold the sessions in a convenient location and provide adequate parking.
4. Allow parents time to ask questions, to talk with one another, and to generally express themselves (but put a limit on this time).
5. Show parents exactly what to do; model the procedures.
6. Direct them to practice the techniques with one another. Give them feedback on how well they do.
7. Give them all the materials, forms, and whatever else is necessary to teach their youngsters.
8. After they begin the program, frequently check in with parents to see how they are progressing.
9. Make yourself or someone else available by telephone so that parents can call for assistance regarding their efforts at any time.

Following are several ideas for parents as they work with their children:

1. Set a regular time for the reading session and stay with it. If a session is missed, make it up.
2. Schedule a time that is convenient for everyone in the family and that interferes the least with other activities.
3. Schedule only three or four sessions per week.
4. Keep the session time short, between 15 and 30 minutes.
5. Tell the child the goal of the instruction.
6. Gather up any necessary equipment *before* the session begins.
7. Have a plan; know what to do when the child does something correctly, and more important, when he or she makes a mistake.
8. Show your interest in reading by reading yourself. Some families have scheduled sustained silent reading (SSR) times; they all read for 30 minutes or so during the evening without answering the door, answering the phone, or especially watching the television.
9. Stay in contact with your child's teacher to learn whether your instruction (and your child's resulting improvement) is being noted at school or to find out if there are certain aspects of his or her reading that you should particularly attend to at home.

Monitor

The easiest and perhaps the most important piece of data parents can keep regarding their children's reading is the number of minutes read per day or week. Beyond that, more specific data that could be acquired might pertain to reading rates, vocabulary acquisition, and the ability to comprehend. More detail on gathering such data can be found in other tactics in this section.

Modifications/Considerations

Tutors other than parents might work with children, including grandparents, neighbors, siblings, senior citizens, or others. Most of the points included here are applicable for them also.

Likewise, most of the ideas introduced here are appropriate for parents or other tutors who might work with children in other subjects, such as math, spelling, or handwriting.

Fredericks and Rasinski (1990) comment on the need for schools and parents to communicate regarding all levels of a reading program. Following are the topics of their discussion: needs assessment, shared responsibility, decision making, constant communication, and continuous participation.

Research

Breiling, A. (1976). Using parents as teaching partners. *The Reading Teacher, 30*(2), 187–192.

Fredericks, A. D., & Rasinski, T. V. (1990). Working with parents: Factors that make a difference. *The Reading Teacher, 44*(1), 76–77.

49 PARENTS: SECOND-BEST ADVICE FOR HELPING THEIR CHILDREN READ

Background

The notion supporting this tactic, or set of suggestions, is that parents can have a tremendously significant impact on their children's ability to read. Fundamental to children's ability to read is a curiosity about reading and the awareness that from reading comes enjoyment, knowledge, and respect. Parents are in the best position to instill these attitudes. Most parents, even single parents, are with their children more hours during the week than are their teachers. In most cases, although certainly not all, there are fewer children vying for the attention of parents than there are competing for the limited moments of their teachers.

Who Can Benefit

All children and youth would profit from the suggestions offered here for their parents, but toddlers, preschoolers, and children of primary age will benefit the most, since these are the ages in which a love and respect for reading are instilled, and this time span is so important for helping children to become "readers" and to become thoroughly aware of print.

Procedures

Perhaps the single most important piece of advice for parents who desire to assist their children to read is to read aloud to them. To amplify on this suggestion, one might encourage parents to read <u>often</u> to their children, to read with enthusiasm, to read materials of various types, and to read the stories or other materials that are requested by their children (even if they are the same ones day after day). Beyond this fundamental recommendation, six others are offered. These are ways in which parents can establish an environment at home that promotes literacy growth.

Find a time and place for reading. Set a routine time and place for reading at home in which <u>all</u> family members participate.

Provide reading materials for all. Ensure that a large stock of appropriate books and magazines are available to all family members. Make use of the local library and other resources.

Allow children to see their parents read. Reading will be valued by children when they realize that reading is important to their parents and their older siblings.

Talk about what is being read. Parents should explain why they chose a particular book, what it is about, and whether or not the book came up to their expectations. Children should be encouraged to do likewise.

Connect reading and experience. Family, religious, and cultural events and holidays are opportunities for parents to enrich the meaning of stories that will be read or have been read. Relate material that was currently read with material that was read at some other time.

Encourage writing. Children should be encouraged to write at home in a number of situations: preparing a shopping list, writing requests for information, writing to relatives and friends, writing poetry and stories, or keeping a personal or dialogue journal.

Monitor

Initially, it might be a good idea to simply keep a family chart showing the number of times that reading sessions were set up and how long they lasted. When that process seems to be an established part of the family's routine, more sophisticated data might be kept, such as the number of stories, articles, or books read, the number and type of questions that were asked about stories, or the number of stories or other instances of writing that were completed.

Modifications/Considerations

The major point addressed here is that it is vital to learn to read, and parents must realize that schools can do only so much when it comes to teaching children this skill. Schools are expected to teach many things, reading being only one of them. If individuals are to learn to read, much of the effort must be their own. Reading is not a skill that is learned in a year or so, then tucked away to be pulled out only when necessary (although that, unfortunately, is the attitude of many individuals who are poor readers). Therefore, if children are to learn to read and to enjoy the process, they must practice doing it day after day after day. That is where parents can help.

Research

Rasinski, T. V., & Fredericks, A. D. (1991). The second best reading advice for parents. *The Reading Teacher, 44*(6), 438–439.

50 PARENTS: SOME SPECIFIC TACTICS FOR TEACHING READING

Background

Three or four parents a week call me at work asking for help with their children. Most of them are concerned about their child's reading. They have heard from the child's teacher that he or she is not doing well in school; they themselves are aware that the child is having problems; someone at school has said that the child is dyslexic; or perhaps an article in the newspaper alerted them to the fact that their child may have attention deficit disorder (ADD). These parents want confirmation. They want to know if there is a cause to which their child's poor reading can be attributed. This is not an unreasonable wish. In a related concern, they want to know where to take their child for an evaluation. Implicit with these desires, the parents want to know if there is anything that can be done to help their child become a more competent reader. This, too, is a reasonable request.

When it comes to recommending someone or somewhere to take their child for a confirming evaluation, I have deep reservations. Although there are dozens of places I could send them that would be more than happy to evaluate the child, it is doubtful that the parents would know much more about him or her following the testing than they do now, and they will be out 500 or so dollars and a lot of time. Certainly, there are times when parents must take their children to specialists, but when it comes to teaching reading, there is a lot parents can do, more than they think they can do, and certainly a lot more than many of the so-called evaluators can or will do.

Who Can Benefit

This tactic is dedicated to those worried parents. It is my great hope that some of them will be able to take the suggestions offered here and help their children to become successful readers.

Procedures

This is the last of 50 tactics in this section on reading. Although only 3 tactics are pointed directly at parents, most of the techniques described in the others could be arranged by parents. Following, however, is a list of the most important activities for parents to follow as they work with their children. They are simple, straightforward, and there is no jargon. They are most useful for children who have some beginning reading skills but who are becoming bored or disgusted with the process and know they are in trouble.

- Locate some books or magazines that the child is able to read.
- Set up a time for the child to read and sit with him or her. If the child stumbles on a word, do not reveal the word immediately. Let the youngster finish the sentence and see if that helps him or her identify the word. If the child still cannot pronounce the word, pronounce it for him or her, then allow the child to continue reading orally.
- Write down the words that the child could not pronounce. Write down a few other words for which he or she may not know the meaning.
- Ask the child, following the oral reading session, to say the words from your list that he or she could not pronounce while reading. Chat about them for a bit.
- Ask the child to define the vocabulary words you picked out. Chat about them for a little while.
- Ask your child to tell you about the story or the passage he or she just read. This could prompt another little chat.
- Ask your child, finally, to predict what the next passage will be about, the one that he or she will read for you during the next session.
- Keep some data (see the Monitor section).

Monitor

The most important piece of data to keep, and I have mentioned this in other tactics, is the number of minutes read per day. It has been my experience with poor readers, even those at the university level, that they do not read much. Many poor readers avoid the process, and understandably so. But practice is absolutely necessary. Help the child construct a simple chart on which the days are written across the bottom and the number of minutes along the left side. Encourage him or her to write in the number of minutes he or she read each day. I would advise that those data be plotted cumulatively. If, for example, the child reads 20 minutes on the first day, put a dot on that day that corresponds to 20. If he or she reads 30 minutes on the following day, put a dot on that day that corresponds to 50, the sum of the two days.

Modifications/Considerations

In addition to these basic, simple, and important steps for teaching reading, most of the other tactics described in this section could be arranged by parents to assist their children. I will name just a few of them.

For oral reading, the repeated reading, reinforcement, and previewing tactics would be especially helpful.

For vocabulary development, the precision teaching technique would be simple to arrange.

For reading comprehension, there are several from which to choose: summarization, the cloze procedure, paragraph restatements, pupils asking questions, even story grammars, text structures, semantic webs, and graphics.

Research

Years of giving advice to parents.

WRITING

This second section, which is a new section with this edition, includes ten tactics on writing. The first tactic, a direct-instruction approach, is appropriate for very beginning writers. In the next tactic, youngsters are encouraged to read their stories to their peers. In the third tactic, youngsters are "reinforced" for writing certain parts of speech. The fourth tactic includes a discussion of a selective grading procedure, and in the fifth tactic, a writing strategy is explained. The sixth tactic outlines approaches for teaching composition. In the seventh tactic, the use of character development to improve writing is detailed. In the eighth tactic, a process for revising text by means of student/teacher conferences is discussed. In the ninth tactic, a method for keeping track of one's writing is presented. The final tactic in this set explains a process for revising essays on a word processor.

2

1 EXPRESSIVE WRITING

Background

This approach is, according to the authors, in stark contrast to other writing programs that encourage students to use memory and imagination as primary vehicles to stimulate and teach writing. In many of these programs, for example, youngsters are asked to write about their summer vacations or to write about the most interesting or frightening thing that has ever happened to them. Although this approach is satisfactory for some children, particularly for those who are better-than-average students, it is not appropriate for many others.

When students are unable to write as fluently or accurately as the teacher might desire, it may be difficult to determine why they were unsuccessful. It could be that these students have not had the experiences that are called for; or perhaps they have difficulty forming sentences and paragraphs; or maybe they are unable to spell and manage other mechanical aspects of writing. Thus the teacher is in a bind. What is he or she to do in order to assist them? Using the method outlined here makes it easier for students to begin writing and easier for teachers to assist them with their efforts.

Who Can Benefit

This approach is designed primarily for very young or remedial writers. It is particularly helpful for those who initially require a step-by-step process to writing.

Procedures

This technique for teaching beginning expressive writing has two unique instructional features. One is that youngsters begin their writing by reporting on events depicted in pictures rather than on events or ideas generated in their imaginations. The other feature is that the task formats for beginning writing are highly teacher-directed; that is, teachers structure, model, and direct each instructional activity.

Following is a suggested sequence of activities:

1. Assign writing tasks that require students merely to select complete, simple sentences. Several sentences from which to choose can be written below a picture that stimulates the writing.

2. Assign sentence completion tasks. The writer completes a sentence either by naming a person or thing or by telling more about a person or thing. Again, provide pictures to suggest what the story is about.

3. Require students to generate or produce complete simple sentences based on events depicted in a picture or series of pictures. Table 1.1 summarizes selected design features used to structure expressive writing instruction for unskilled writers.

4. In the typical 30-minute lesson, include activities for each of the core skill areas with the exception of paragraph writing. (Paragraph writing should be introduced only after students are able to generate acceptable simple sentences.) Table 1.2 shows general guidelines for structuring a writing lesson.

5. For advanced lessons, incorporate multiple strands of writing skills and build on the skills developed early in the writing program. Advanced lessons should involve fewer separate tasks and should engage students in increasingly longer periods of writing. An example that specifies the time, skill, and task requirements of advanced writing lessons is found in Table 1.3.

TABLE 1.1   Design Features of Expressive Writing Instruction

Variables	Beginning Writing Instruction			Advanced Writing Instruction
Degree of teacher guidance	Extensive ──────────────────────────────→ Minimal			
	(Fade as students demonstrate skill mastery)			
Instructional tools	Single picture ──→	Multiple pictures ──→	Topic sentence ──→	Topic
Task format	Selection response ──→	Completion response ──→	Generation response	
Writing product	Words ──→ Sentences ──→ Paragraphs			

SOURCE: Reprinted with the permission of Macmillan College Publishing Company from DESIGNING INSTRUCTIONAL STRATEGIES: THE PREVENTION OF ACADEMIC LEARNING PROBLEMS by Edward J. Kameenui and Deborah C. Simmons. Copyright © 1990 by Macmillan College Publishing Company, Inc.

TABLE 1.2 Activities and Time Allocations for a Beginning Expressive Writing Lesson

Tasks	Core Writing Area	Specific Writing Skill	Time Allocation
Task 1	Writing simple sentences	Identifying a sentence as naming somebody or something and telling more about the person or thing (review task)	5–8 minutes
Task 2	Mechanics of writing	Copying sentences (review task)	5–8 minutes
Task 3	Writing simple sentences	Review of 1–2 examples from Task 1	8–10 minutes
		Selecting sentences that name somebody or something and tell more about the person or thing depicted in the picture	
Task 4	Editing	Identifying and correcting capitalization errors in simple sentences that name somebody and tell more	5–8 minutes
Task 5	Review	Summary of writing, editing, and mechanics tasks	3–5 minutes

SOURCE: Reprinted with the permission of Macmillan College Publishing Company from DESIGNING INSTRUCTIONAL STRATEGIES: THE PREVENTION OF ACADEMIC LEARNING PROBLEMS by Edward J. Kameenui and Deborah C. Simmons. Copyright © 1990 by Macmillan College Publishing Company, Inc.

TABLE 1.3 Activities and Time Allocations for an Advanced Expressive Writing Lesson

Tasks	Core Writing Area	Specific Writing Skill	Time Allocation
Task 1	Writing paragraphs	Review of critical rules for writing paragraphs	3–5 minutes
Task 2	Writing paragraphs	Writing a sequence of 2–3 paragraphs from a topic sentence (e.g., transportation today is very different from 20 years ago)	25–30 minutes
Task 3	Editing paragraphs according to specified criteria	Correcting run-on sentences Checking verb tense Correcting mechanical errors in punctuation and capitalization	5–8 minutes

SOURCE: Reprinted with the permission of Macmillan College Publishing Company from DESIGNING INSTRUCTIONAL STRATEGIES: THE PREVENTION OF ACADEMIC LEARNING PROBLEMS by Edward J. Kameenui and Deborah C. Simmons. Copyright © 1990 by Macmillan College Publishing Company, Inc.

6.   Provide students with self-monitoring checklists to evaluate and edit their writing. A checklist for beginning writers might include the following questions:

- Does each sentence begin with a capital?
- Does each telling sentence end with a period?
- Does each asking sentence end with a question mark?

The items on the checklists would differ depending upon the proficiency of the writer.

Monitor

As suggested earlier, it is much easier for teachers to evaluate the writing efforts of youngsters when pictures and detailed structures are used initially. If the picture is about something with which the child is familiar and he or she is unable to write anything about it, the teacher has an indication that the child has a writing problem. The teacher can then deal with the problem accordingly instead of needlessly providing the child with more information about or experience with the picture.

As with other writing projects, both quantitative and qualitative data should be kept regarding students' ability to write. For the former, teachers or the students themselves could count the number of words, thought units, or certain mechanical features or parts of speech used. As for the qualitative aspect, judges could be asked to rate selected stories written by the children, some of which are from the first days of instruction and others from a later time.

Modifications/Considerations

Teachers eventually should fade out the picture prompts, but the prompts should be a part of the instructional materials as long as necessary. The teacher might use them sparingly after a while, then not at all. Students could inform the teacher when they are ready to "go it alone."

Teachers could have the youngsters develop the pictures. This activity could be done individually or in a group.

Research

Engelmann, S., & Silbert, J. (1985). *Expressive writing 1: Teacher presentation book.* Tigard, OR: C.C. Publications.

Kameenui, E., & Simmons, D. C. (1990). Designing instructional strategies for teaching expressive writing. In *Designing instructional strategies for academic skills* (pp. 418–464). New York: Merrill/Macmillan.

2

READING STORIES AND DISPLAYING STUDENT RECORDS

Background

The notion supporting this tactic is that when youngsters are allowed to read their stories to their classmates and when records of their efforts are posted, students will be motivated to write longer and more interesting stories.

Who Can Benefit

The research that supports this tactic was carried out with 17 members of a second-grade class. Most of the children were seven years old and able to read at or above the second-grade level.

Procedures

For this project a 30-minute writing period was scheduled four days a week. For the first 10 minutes, the class discussed a topic having to do with science or social studies. Following this discussion, during which time the teacher made an effort to draw on the youngsters' prior experiences, students were asked to write about the topic of the day. The writing period lasted for 20 minutes.

When the period was over, the teacher read the papers and made a few corrections and comments. Most of the corrections—and they were kept to a minimum—related to spelling and punctuation. The teacher was not terribly fussy about spelling or even handwriting.

Following each session the teacher counted the number of words and "thought units" each child wrote. A *thought unit* is generally a new idea and is made up of a subject and verb. It need not include the proper punctuation. Indeed, the children were not told specifically to include any punctuation. The tally of thought units was written on the top of each page. The teacher also wrote a qualifying comment on each child's paper, such as "nice," "good work," or "good writing." The teacher charted the following two frequencies for each child: number of words and number of thought units per session.

There were four phases to this project. During the first phase, the writers could read their stories to their classmates if they wanted to. Most of them did. During the next phase, the children could still read their stories, and in addition, the charts showing the number of words and thought units written each day were posted where all the children could see them. In the third phase, the students did not read their stories to their peers, but their charts were still posted. The final phase was like the first: The students could read their stories to their classmates; however, their scores were not posted at that time.

Monitor

As mentioned earlier, the teacher in this project counted the number of words written and also the frequency of thought units per session. Along with these quantitative measures, an indication of the richness of the stories was also acquired through the stories themselves. Following is a story written by a boy during the early days of the project:

Autm leaves are soon so fun it's gust like
someone on the sun.
In 1492 Columbus discovered America.

This next story was written some weeks later:

Most things we can record. But still some thing you
can't record. Some thing we can record by tape
recorder camera chars or pictures. When we ues
a tape recorder we can here the sownds
of animills or people. When we uos
a camera we can see howses bridges or
parcks. If you yous a ckart you can
see how mach you'v grown. But
allmost all things you can record one of thees was.

Modifications/Considerations

Since most of the students' writing improved throughout this project, we might assume that the simple act of providing opportunities to write and giving minimal feedback on students' writing efforts was enough of an intervention. It is possible also, however, that many of the youngsters were stimulated to write longer and better stories because their scores and those of others were displayed during certain conditions. If a teacher noted that some youngsters were not looking for their scores, felt badly about them, or were being teased by others because of their scores, it certainly would not be a good idea to have their writing scores posted.

Another possible motivating aspect of this project was that children were allowed, indeed encouraged, to read their stories aloud to their classmates. Too often, children write only for their teachers; they are not given a real audience.

Research

Lovitt, T. C. (1981). Charting academic performances of mildly handicapped youngsters. In J. K. Kauffman & D. P. Hallahan (Eds.), *Handbook of special education* (393–417). Englewood Cliffs, NJ: Prentice-Hall.

3 SEQUENTIAL REINFORCEMENT CONTINGENCIES

Background

The thought behind this research is that overall, writing will improve if components of writing are identified, and if reinforcement contingencies are successively arranged for those elements. More specifically, the authors of the research paraphrased here were betting that if various aspects of writing were improved, so would writing in general.

Who Can Benefit

The pupils in the 1972 research study were fifth graders who were in an adjustment class. The students in the 1973 research study were fourth, fifth, and sixth graders in regular classes.

Procedures

The procedures outlined here are from the 1972 study. The following features were in effect throughout all phases of the study:

1 The writing period was scheduled twice a week for 60 minutes.

1 The teacher took a few minutes each session to give the pupils suggestions as to what they could write about. They could write on any subject they wanted to.

1 The teacher wrote out on a card any words that the pupils wanted spelled. Each pupil had his or her own card. The teacher kept track of how many times each pupil was assisted.

1 The teacher gathered up the papers at the end of the period and counted the number of words, number of new words, and number of different words used.

There were four phases to the study:

Points for general work behaviors. During this time, students received points for sitting, paying attention, doing good work, and finishing a story. There was no consistent relationship between points and specific aspects of writing.

Points for number of words. Throughout this phase, students were given 1 point for every word they wrote. They continued receiving points for general work.

Points for different words. For this period, students were given 2 points for each different word they used in the story and, as before, 1 point for each word in their story. They no longer received points for general work in this phase. If a student wrote "I like baseball. I like football.", he or she received 6 points for the number of words, and 8 points for the 4 different words, for a total of 14 points.

Points for new words. At this stage, students continued to receive points for the number of words and the number of different words, and, in addition, were given 3 points for each new word they used in the story. A new word was one that the student had never used before in any of his or her stories. To keep track of the words used in the stories, each pupil was given an alphabetized list of all the words he or she had ever used in stories. During this phase, students could refer to this list as they wrote their stories.

Monitor

Several types of data were kept in the 1972 study: number of words written, number of different words used, number of new words used, time spent writing, number of teacher contacts, and number of points earned. In addition to these quantitative measures, two qualitative measures were arranged. For the first measure, a scale made up of the following five components was developed: (1) mechanical aspects, length, spelling, grammar, punctuation; (2) vocabulary, variety, and word usage; (3) number of ideas; (4) development of the ideas; and (5) internal consistency of the story. Each component was scored on a scale of 0 to 5 by independent judges who rated a number of the children's stories.

For the second qualitative measure, a few stories collected from some children during each phase were printed and shown to judges for their evaluation.

Modifications/Considerations

When this study was carried out, the teacher had to manually count each word and somehow keep track of the different and new words written. Today, collecting such information is easy if the pupils write their stories with a microcomputer and word processing program. Those three totals, as well as many other attributes of writing, can be easily obtained from such programs.

In the 1972 study, the most effective intervention—that is, the one that had not only the most effect on the element that was treated but also on overall writing—was giving points for the number of words written. The results for the other two interventions were somewhat equivocal.

In the 1973 study, reinforcement contingencies were successively associated with adjectives, then action verbs, and then a combination of adjectives, action verbs, and beginnings. Data from that investigation, much like that from the 1972 study, indicated that generally, the element or aspect of writing that is reinforced is most affected.

Research

Brigham, T. A., Graubard, P. S., & Stans, A. (1972). Analysis of the effects of sequential reinforcement contingencies on aspects of composition. *Journal of Applied Behavior Analysis, 5*(4), 421–429.

Maloney, K. B., & Hopkins, B. L. (1973). The modification of sentence structure and its relationship to subjective judgments of creativity in writing. *Journal of Applied Behavior Analysis, 6*, 425–433.

4 SELECTIVE GRADING

Background

This tactic is based on the notion that students should write at least a page of text four days a week. A related notion, which is also fundamental to this tactic, is that students should receive adequate feedback on their writing efforts. *Adequate feedback* is feedback that is precise, immediate, positive, and frequent, and that highlights small increments of improvement. Although most educators would agree with both these notions in helping children to develop as capable writers, it is no easy task to give adequate feedback to 28 or 30 youngsters four days a week if they all write one page a day.

Who Can Benefit

The tactic explained here has been arranged for middle-school and intermediate-age youngsters. Considering the modifications that are possible to associate with this technique, it should be suitable for a wide age and ability range of students.

Procedures

Selecting Writing Topics
- Provide students with 3 to 5 topics to choose from each day.
- Allow students to alter the day's topics.
- Allow pupils to write about topics from previous days.
- Allow students to continue writing a story begun on a previous day.
- Limit the discussion and choice of topics to no more than three minutes a day.

Determining Writing Targets and Performance Criteria

- Identify the targets to be emphasized (e.g., action words) through analysis of students' writing.
- Change the target elements periodically. Occasionally, schedule an old target with a new one.
- Determine the criteria (e.g., so many action words per page) from the writings of superior students.

Explain Procedures to Students

- Put up a wall chart to illustrate examples of the aspects of writing that are being featured.
- Explain to the students that you will now grade only four of their papers each day.
- Explain that you will choose the four papers randomly. Do not select one particular child's paper more than two days in a row, and over time, be sure to select every child's paper. Keep a record of whose papers have been selected on which days.
- Each student will receive five points if he or she writes a full page of text.
- If three of the four papers that are checked meet the day's criteria (e.g., 15 or more action words), all pupils will get three bonus points.
- If all four of the papers that are checked meet the day's criteria, all pupils will get five bonus points.
- Develop a plan for exchanging the points. In one class the pupils were given one bean for each point, and they put all the beans earned into a jar. When the jar was filled, the class went on a field trip that they had planned.

Direct Instruction

- Spend some time instructing the featured aspects of writing prior to the timed writing period.
- Show examples from the students' writing to illustrate the use (or nonuse) of the target items.

Timed Writing Period

- Students should write for 10 to 20 minutes each period.
- Allow students to continue a paper or story that was begun on a previous day.

Selecting and Grading Student Papers

- Select and grade four papers each day. (This number could be different depending upon how many students are in the class and other factors.)

- Indicate on those graded papers all instances in which the students acknowledged the target item(s).
- Provide the type of feedback that incorporates the features noted earlier.
- Put some type of score on the top of the paper. It could be a number, a percentage, or something else depending on what the target item was.

Sharing Feedback with the Entire Class
- Return the previous day's papers and announce how many of the four papers met the performance criterion and how many points the students earned. Do not tell the class which papers were graded.
- Give feedback to the entire class based on what was noted in the graded papers.
- Provide instruction on the day's target item.
- Select topics and begin writing.

Monitor

Although some record should be kept of the extent to which the pupils improve with respect to the target items, more global measures should be considered to evaluate the pupils' writing. For example, experts could be called on to read and comment on the pupils' stories. Samples of each pupil's writings could be handed to the expert, who should then attempt to put the samples for each child in the order in which they were written. If a pupil's last stories were judged as among the best, it would seem that in general, he or she was becoming a better writer. The expert could also comment on certain features of each child's writing.

Modifications/Considerations

Several modifications are possible with this general tactic:

- Individualize target skills and/or performance criteria.
- Schedule longer writing periods and require longer stories.
- Find and correct yesterday's errors.
- Rewrite a previous story for publication.
- Allow students to choose nonselected papers for evaluation.
- Post publicly a few excellent stories.

Research

Heward, W. L., Heron, T. E., Gardner, R. III, & Prayzer, R. (1991). Two strategies for improving students' writing skills. In G. Stoner, M.R. Shinn, H. Walker (Eds.), *Interventions for achievement and behavior problems* (pp. 379–398). Silver Spring, MD: National Association of School Psychologists.

5 QuIP: A Writing Strategy

Background

The purpose of this research is to provide a rationale for the reading and writing connection. From a review of research, the author of the cited research drew five conclusions: (1) paragraphs with explicit main ideas are more readily comprehended; (2) main ideas located at the beginning of paragraphs promote understanding; (3) sensitivity to text structure can be taught; (4) the more opportunities children have to structure their own thoughts and writing, the better prepared they will be to interpret the structures of others; and (5) varied writing experiences will lead to a heightened awareness of the author's message and of the framework used to convey it.

Who Can Benefit

The tactic explained here would be appropriate for children as young as second grade. It is a particularly important technique for students in the intermediate grades as they begin reading expository narration.

Procedures

Three steps are involved in this technique: preparation and completion of an interview grid, preparation of an outline, and creation of the paragraphs.

Interview Grid

Students begin by determining a topic (e.g., pets, holiday traditions, forts). They are then instructed to create three questions relevant to the topic, as shown in Figure 5.1. The questions are placed in the left-hand column. Students next seek answers to the questions. Initially, interviews should be about familiar topics (e.g., family or friends). Later, the topics could be less familiar so that sources such as reference books are required to supply answers.

Topic: Forts in the U.S.A.
Student's name: Keith (4th grade)

	Source: *The American Republic*	Source: *New Standard Encyclopedia*
Question 1: A. What were some famous forts in America?	1. There was Fort McHenry where Francis Scott Key wrote the "Star Spangled Banner," and 2. Fort Sumter that started the Civil War.	3. Fort Donelson: Grant's Civil war victory here led to his promotion to general. 4. Fort Bridger: way station on Oregon Trail.
Question 2: B. Why were forts built?	1. Protection from Indians on the frontier.	2. To protect seaports from other countries.
Question 3: C. What kind of forts were there?	1. Star forts have regular designs with many sharp angles.	2. A bastion has works called bastions which go out from the main fort.

FIGURE 5.1 A Completed Interview Grid

SOURCE: From Figure 1 of "QuIP: A Writing Strategy to Improve Comprehension of Expository Structure," Elaine M. McLaughlin, *The Reading Teacher,* March 1987, p. 652. Reprinted with permission of Elaine M. McLaughlin and the International Reading Association.

Outline

The completed grid provides a transition to the creation of an outline, such as the one shown in Figure 5.2. The three questions become the subheadings, and the responses become supporting details.

Paragraphs

After the outline is developed, the material is ready to be shaped into paragraphs. Each heading becomes a main idea followed by supporting information. After all the paragraphs are written, a concluding sentence that restates the major theme should be added.

FIGURE 5.2
Outline Developed from the Interview Grid

SOURCE: From Figure 2 of "QuIP: A Writing Strategy to Improve Comprehension of Expository Structure," Elaine M. McLaughlin, *The Reading Teacher,* March 1987, p. 652. Reprinted with permission of Elaine M. McLaughlin and the International Reading Association.

U.S. military in the 1800s
I. Forts in the USA
    A. Famous forts in America
        1. Fort McHenry
        2. Fort Sumter
        3. Fort Donelson
        4. Fort Bridger
    B. Reasons for forts
        1. Protection from Indians
        2. Seaport defense
    C. Kinds of forts
        1. Star fort
        2. Bastion

Monitor

Foremost with this technique, data should be obtained on the extent to which students write paragraphs that include main ideas and supportive information. Moreover, data should be gathered on the students' ability to integrate the paragraphs so they form a smooth and reasonably logical story. Data should also be kept on the overall or general effect of their stories. For these data, a checksheet could be constructed that prompts evaluators to check the vital ingredients of the total text. Evaluators should also be encouraged to make general comments regarding the students' writing, such as whether or not it makes sense, is convincing, and is interesting.

Modifications/Considerations

Once students have written their paragraphs and have a rather cohesive story, they should, of course, revise their text. As one part of this process, and in an effort to blend their paragraphs into a unified whole, the students should be instructed in how to use such connectives as *whereas, however, moreover,* and *on the other hand.*

According to the author of the cited research, the technique outlined here is particularly suitable with the compare and contrast expository format, which is said to be among the more difficult text structures for students to comprehend.

Not only will this technique assist students in writing, but according to the author, through interviews, outlines, and paragraph writing, students also will come to internalize the structures they encounter when reading. The result will be better comprehension of text.

Research

McLaughlin, E.M. (1987). QuIP: A writing strategy to improve comprehension of expository structure. *The Reading Teacher, 40*(7), 650–654.

6 STRATEGIES FOR TEACHING COMPOSITION SKILLS

Background

Many students have a hard time meeting the writing demands of school because they have problems related to the mechanical aspects of written expression (e.g., spelling, handwriting, punctuation, and capitalization). After recognizing these needs, teachers often spend a considerable amount of time working with students to develop these mechanical attributes. The authors of the tactic paraphrased here take issue with this approach; instead, they recommend a process-oriented writing program, which is one that places initial emphasis on writing stories and less emphasis on the mechanics of composition.

Who Can Benefit

The authors of the cited research have implemented the process-oriented writing approach with students of varying ages in a variety of settings. They recommend it particularly for students with learning disabilities.

Procedures

For this approach the rules of grammar, punctuation, capitalization, and spelling are taught as needed, *within* the context of composing. Three related steps form their program: planning, drafting, and evaluating and revising. It is recommended that 40 minutes a day be set aside for writing.

The Planning Stage

At this time the teacher should focus students' attention on thinking, organizing, and discussing. Students should be encouraged simply to get their ideas down on paper without being over-critical about how they do it. Moreover, students at this stage should be told to consider their intended audience and their purpose for writing to that audience. During this time, the teacher should model for the students how to plan a composition. Following this model, the class as a whole should plan a piece of writing. One example might be to write product advertisements. To start this assignment, the students might be required to bring in a number of advertisements they selected from magazines or newspapers. During this stage students should be introduced to a few planning formats that will help them organize their ideas. Some sample formats are included in Figure 6.1.

The Drafting Stage

At this time students should take a "first pass" at writing a story. They should not be overly concerned with the technical aspects of their composition. However, there is no point in being overly sloppy at this time, because whatever mistakes or examples of poor writing appear will have to be dealt with at some time; they will not go away.

During this phase, students should elaborate on the points noted in their outlines. They could also modify their outlines at this time. As was suggested for the first stage, a group draft could be written. Using that draft, the teacher could first model for the youngsters how he or she would develop the story. Later, the teacher could turn more of the process over to the students, guiding them along the way. If students run across some troublesome spots in the draft, the students may skip them, but should highlight those areas so they can be dealt with later. Students should write on every other line during this phase to make future editing easier. At this time some youngsters could be encouraged to use a word processing program. For those students who have problems writing, they could tape record their stories or dictate them to the teacher or another person who could then write them down.

FIGURE 6.1

Formats for the Planning Phase of Various Types of Student Writing

SOURCE: From "Strategies for Teaching Composition Skills to Students with Learning Disabilities" by A. L. Vallecorsa, R. R. Ledford, and G. G. Parnell, *Teaching Exceptional Children, 23*(2), 1991, p. 53. Copyright 1991 by The Council for Exceptional Children. Reprinted with permission.

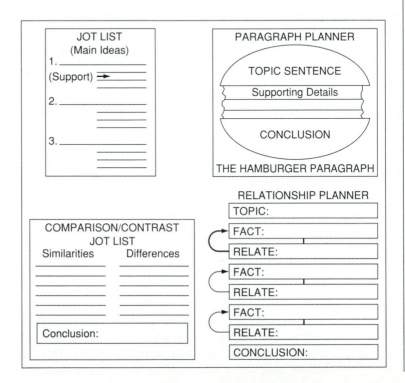

FIGURE 6.2

Evaluation Guide

SOURCE: From "Strategies for Teaching Composition Skills to Students with Learning Disabilities" by A. L. Vallecorsa, R. R. Ledford, and G. G. Parnell, *Teaching Exceptional Children, 23*(2), 1991, p. 55. Copyright 1991 by The Council for Exceptional Children. Reprinted with permission.

I.   Organization of ideas

_____   A.   Topic sentences

_____   B.   Supporting details

_____   C.   Order of ideas

_____   D.   Use of transition words

II.   Style

_____   A.   Vocabulary

_____   B.   Sentence structure

_____   C.   Grammar

III.   Spelling

_____   A.   Spelling demons

_____   B.   Personal trouble words

IV.   Handwriting

_____   A.   Clarity

_____   B.   Spacing

_____   C.   Neatness

V.   Conventions of print

_____   A.   Format

_____   B.   Capitalization

_____   C.   Punctuation

The Evaluation and Revision Stage

Now students should be encouraged to take a close look at their drafts and make decisions about how to improve them. In so doing, they should pretend to be someone other than the author, that is, someone who is unfamiliar with the story. During this phase, some youngsters might be encouraged to use the COPS strategy, where <u>C</u> indicates concentrating on capitalization, <u>O</u> on organization, <u>P</u> on punctuation, and <u>S</u> on spelling. Other students could be encouraged to use a more sophisticated guide to help direct their writing, such as the one in Figure 6.2.

As was true in the preceding two phases, the teacher should demonstrate for the students how to revise a composition. As the demonstration proceeds, the teacher should talk aloud, giving reasons for the changes that are made to the initial draft. When the students are asked to write their own stories, the teacher should set aside time to talk with them about their efforts. He or she should question them about aspects of their writing, and attempt to instill in them the idea of being critical writers.

Monitor

Perhaps the best way to monitor the effects of this type of instruction is to assemble a set of stories from the youngsters prior to their involvement in the technique and then gather together a few stories that were written after the program was in effect. The stories could then be mixed up with the dates occluded and then given to a judge who is unaware of the instructional technique or the teacher's objectives, beyond the objective of assisting students to be "better" writers. The judge's task would be to arrange the stories in order of worst to best. If the treatment was effective, the best stories, according to the judge, would be among the last ones written.

Modifications/Considerations

During the third stage of this process, children could be assisted in polishing their drafts by being instructed in the use of such writing aids as a thesaurus, special encyclopedias (e.g., *The Reader's Encyclopedia*), special dictionaries (e.g., *Dictionary of Contemporary American Usage*), and other references such as *Bartlett's Familiar Quotations*.

Research

Vallecorsa, A. L., Ledford, R. R., & Parnell, G. G. (1991). Strategies for teaching composition skills to students with learning disabilities. *Teaching Exceptional Children, 23*(2), 52–55.

7 USING CHARACTER DEVELOPMENT TO IMPROVE STORY WRITING

Background

The idea behind this tactic is that explicit instruction in character development helps students understand the importance of characters in the stories they listen to or read. In turn, students will be better able to write stories in which characters of various types are involved.

Who Can Benefit

This tactic would be particularly helpful for youngsters who are able to write simple stories—ones in which they write about events, the sequence of those events, and that involve some dialogue. Indeed, this tactic would probably also benefit older students who had never tried their hand at including characters and dialogue in their stories.

Procedures

1. Read to students stories and excerpts from books containing fictional characters.

2. Arrange discussions about the characters in those stories, the purpose of which is to help students understand the elements of character development.

3. Schedule some of the discussions to focus on developing a character's point of view and on making characters the catalysts for action in the stories.

4. Provide explicit instruction in character development. Following are techniques for teaching students to use three character attributes:

    1 *Physical appearance.* Inform students that readers get to know the characters in a story in the same way that a person actually gets to know another person. Tell students to use an author's description of characters to imagine the characters in their

heads. Ask them to give examples of physical attributes that could be used to describe a character for the reader. Write their ideas on the chalkboard.

- *Speech and actions.* Mention to students that they can get to know a person by listening to what they say and observing how they act toward others. As they write dialogue for their characters, ask students to suggest verbs that can be used instead of *said* (e.g., *exclaimed, yelled, moaned, complained, proclaimed, uttered*).

- *Thoughts and emotions.* Introduce a character by asking the students to think about a person they know and like. Tell them to write about why that person is different from others. Then ask students to think about a person they do not like and to write about the reasons for this appraisal.

5. Write thought words on the board such as the following: *wanted, noticed, knew, understood, realized, reasoned, wondered, believed.*

6. Write emotion words on the board such as the following: *happiness, amazement, depression, nervousness, tension, sadness, boredom, jealousy, loneliness, compassion.*

7. Provide story writing practice.

- Give students a list of story prompts or have them come up with their own list.
- Ask students to imagine characters who might be in a story about the selected topic (e.g., inside a burning building).
- Discuss possible problems the characters may encounter as the story unfolds. Inform students that problems can arise from the following: money, family, business, work, school, weather, sickness, abuse, nature.
- Request that students develop a plan for solving the problems they posed for their characters.
- Encourage them to describe how their characters feel as subsequent events are added. Ask them to examine their own feelings about the events. Help students to understand the relationship among characters' thoughts, actions, and reactions.

8. Teach students to evaluate their stories. Request that they read the story and underline words and sentences that answer the following questions:

- What does the character look like?
- What does the character say in the story?
- What does the character do in the story?
- What is the character thinking about in the story?
- How does the character feel about what happens in the story?

Monitor

As is true of many tactics in this book, particularly those that have to do with writing, specific and general features should be monitored. For this tactic, the extent to which students develop the characters in their stories should be assessed. Data should also be acquired on the students' stories in general; that is, how well they are developed in several respects. To determine the latter, judges other than the teacher might be called on to read and evaluate the stories.

Modifications/Considerations

Once students become reasonably adept at developing characters, they should be encouraged to expand on this. To stimulate such an exercise the teacher could tell them a story about some famous or infamous character, one who had greatly influenced others. Students might be informed that there will be a contest to see who can write the most about the character. The contest could also be arranged for teams or groups of students.

Research

Leavell, A., & Ioannides, A. (1993). Using character development to improve story writing. *Teaching Exceptional Children, 25*(4), 41–45.

8 TEXT REVISION USING STUDENT/TEACHER CONFERENCES

Background

Revision of written text is an important aspect in writing. In the past, research suggested that revision skills might be linked to age and cognitive level. The research on which this tactic is based suggests that this philosophy is not necessarily true. Rather, it intimates that all students are able to revise passages effectively if they know *what* to revise. A good way to make students aware of possible areas of revision is through student/teacher conferences during the writing period.

Who Can Benefit

Students in the cited research were two average-ability second-grade girls. That this technique was successful with students of that age suggests that it might be an appropriate approach with other, perhaps older, students who are able to write at least a short, basic composition. The technique explained here could be especially helpful for students who have a difficult time coming up with an original draft.

Procedures

A time period of 60 minutes should be set aside at least twice a week for a "writing workshop."

1. The first 10 minutes of each writing workshop session is devoted to skill development. The teacher selects an important writing skill (e.g., punctuation, capitalization, word usage) or a revision skill (e.g., deletion, addition, modification) and teaches it. This time can also be used to introduce a new topic for writing.

2. The writing portion of the writing workshop lasts for 35 to 40 minutes. During this time, students work independently on their compositions. They may be at different stages of writing and revising.

3. During the writing session, the teacher calls each student to his or her desk, one at a time. The teacher and student hold a conference about the student's current composition. During the conference:

- Both student and teacher read the composition.
- The teacher questions the student and waits for his or her responses. The teacher's questions are of five types: process, basic structure, following, opening, and questions about development. During each conference the teacher focuses on no more than two types of questions. The purpose of the questions is to assist the child in clarifying the meaning of the text, to elaborate on the information, or to determine relationships between information known by the child and information presented in the text.
- The teacher encourages the child to question, to comment, and to demonstrate solutions to unclear aspects of the text.

4. At the completion of the conference, the student returns to his or her desk to make the appropriate revisions.

5. Conferences are held on a weekly schedule, or whenever a child requests one.

6. At the conclusion of the writing period, the students form small groups for 10 to 15 minutes to share their compositions and to react to the comments and suggestions they received.

Monitor

An easy and practical way to monitor the effectiveness of this tactic would be to periodically compare copies of students' work. Over time, the draft copies should be of higher and higher quality. For example, a comparison of a draft from October could be compared to a draft from February to determine any general or specific changes.

Modifications/Considerations

An important consideration to this tactic is that although mechanical revisions should be required of students (e.g., spelling, punctuation, capitalization), all content revisions should be made by students on a voluntary basis. Thus, the teacher must be careful to encourage and suggest rather than to criticize or demand.

The revision approach explained here could be modified in a number of ways. For example, the workshop could be scheduled daily or weekly. Moreover, the teacher personally could hold conferences with all the students, or an aide, a parent helper, or a same-age or cross-age peer could hold the conferences.

Children with learning disabilities might need increased conference time during the initial drafting process. Frequently, many of these students have a difficult time getting started with a "story."

Once students have a final composition, it should be bound in some way and shared with the class; that is, if the author agrees. The bound book of stories might become a part of the classroom library or placed in a special section of the school library. This sharing of completed projects encourages students to do their best work.

If students are allowed to evaluate or comment on the works of their peers, they should be encouraged to make positive comments about the pieces they read.

Research

Vukelich, C., & Leverson, L. D. (1988). Text revisions by two young writers following teacher/student conferences. *Journal of Research in Childhood Education, 3*(1), 46–54.

9 ON WRITING A BOOK

Background

Although this tactic was not carried out with elementary-school-age young-sters, it seems fitting to include it in this collection of writing tactics since I relied on it to record my progress while writing both editions of this book. This tactic was designed to help me write the best possible book and to finish it in a timely fashion. In order to do this, at least with respect to the schedule, the first thing I had to do was determine *when* the book should be completed, and next, decide on *how many* tactics were needed for the book.

Who Can Benefit

Although this tactic was developed for an adult—and one who was writing a rather large book—it also would be appropriate for much younger students working on much smaller-scale projects. It would certainly be a suitable approach for pupils in intermediate grades who are setting out to write reports, stories, or other lengthy pieces of text. The tactic will help individuals complete large writing assignments in spite of the fact that dozens of smaller tasks must be dealt with along with the major project.

One of the main reasons that individuals do not write lengthy and thoughtful pieces—those that require a fair amount of research, organization, and editing—is that they wait for a mythical "extended period of time" that can be totally devoted to the project. They romantically yearn for a summer spent writing in an oceanside cabin or mountain retreat. They eagerly pine for the sabbatical, the summer vacation, or the extended holidays. For most of us, there are no such times, and our writing plans are forever put on hold. This tactic is particularly important for individuals who have busy schedules and who have only a few hours a week to work on their project.

Although the demands are different for fourth, fifth, and sixth graders than they are for professors, there are expectations and assignments just the same. If students are to learn about taking on large tasks and completing them on time, along with handling the dozens of other chores and responsibilities that come up, many unexpectedly, they must be shown how to do it.

Procedures

The procedures for setting up this tactic are quite simple:

1. Determine the day you will embark on the project, the day you will begin committing amounts of time and thought to the task. For the writing of *Tactics I* (the first edition of this book), that was July 11, 1982; for *Tactics II* (the second edition), it was March 1, 1993. I had been thinking about the projects some months before my real commitment, and had been writing notes, making outlines, and gathering together some materials, but those dates were the serious beginnings.

2. Decide how many components there will be in the project. For *Tactics I* there were 112 tactics, and for *Tactics II,* 105.

3. Decide when the project (at least the first carefully written draft) should be finished. For *Tactics I* that was October 10, 1982, and for *Tactics II* it was September 15, 1993.

4. Indicate all this information on a chart. For the *Tactics II* chart, the beginning date was marked as well as the date I intended to have a first draft of all the tactics written. Those dates (March 1 and September 15) and every date in between were marked along the bottom, horizontal part of the chart. Along the left vertical side of the chart I wrote in numbers from 0 to 105, which represented the number of tactics I intended to write. I then drew a straight line beginning with 0 on March 1 that intersected with the ending date, September 15, and the projected number of tactics, 105. This sloping line served as my projection line.

5. Attend to the projection line. It tells the author if he or she is on schedule, falling behind, or ahead of the schedule set to meet the deadline.

6. Along the projection line, write in events that will interfere with the completion of the assignment. During the period I was writing the first draft, I had six out-of-town trips. I wrote in the dates of those journeys. By so doing, I knew that if I was to stay on schedule (above the projection line), I would have to step it up on those days I stayed put in Seattle.

Monitor

With this tactic, monitoring progress is built in. The author is able to see his or her progress, or lack thereof, each day and is aware of how much work remains to be done. It took 80 days to write the first draft of the first edition, and 200 days to write the first draft of the second edition. Other information is readily available from a chart such as those I kept: the greatest number of successive days the author worked on the draft, the greatest number of sections written in a day, the greatest number of successive days the author did no work.

Modifications/Considerations

I also kept charts for writing the second and third drafts of the books. As might be expected, it did not take nearly as long to complete these as it did the first drafts.

Instead of counting "tactics," other units can be charted depending upon the project: words, lines, paragraphs, pages, sections, chapters.

It is important to indicate the other incidents in one's life that will interfere with working on the major effort. Those events that are known at the beginning of the project should definitely be noted on the chart. As others come up, they too should be marked on the projection line. Knowing about these interferences can help the author step up his or her efforts at other times in order to complete the project at the desired time.

Research

Lovitt, T. C. (1984). On writing a book. *Journal of Precision Teaching, 5*(1), 3–9.

10 REVISING ESSAYS PRODUCED ON A WORD PROCESSOR

Background

Several notions form the basis for this tactic:

1. Students will write longer stories or essays with a word processor than they will if they use paper and pencil.
2. They will revise those narrations more often.
3. Their revisions will be more substantive than had they been written with paper and pencil.

The cited study was further based on the assumption that if youngsters with learning disabilities are to get the most from word processing programs as they write and make subsequent revisions, they must be given a strategy for not only detecting and correcting mechanical errors, but also for improving the clarity and cohesiveness of their writing.

Who Can Benefit

The cited research was carried out with three youngsters who had learning disabilities. They were in either fifth or sixth grade and were given writing instruction by trained instructors in resource rooms. Prior to this study the students had considerable experience using a word processor. Each of them was able to move lines of print, center a title, and insert, delete, or replace textual material. Their typing speeds were about 40 letters per minute.

Procedures

General Procedures
- Students wrote essays for topics such as the following: Do you think children your age should be allowed to ride mini-bikes? Should boys and girls play sports together?
- Each student met with an instructor in the resource room for 45 minutes, 3 days a week.

- On days they were to begin writing, students were told to look at the sentence on the card and make up a good essay.
- On days they were to make revisions, students were given an essay they had written and were told to think about any changes they would like to make or anything they would like to fix, and were told to go about revising it.

Instructional Procedures

- *Pretraining.* Students received instruction on the components of a good essay (e.g., that it tells what you believe, tells why you believe it, and has a good ending). Students practiced identifying the three parts in essays.

- *Review current performance level.* Teacher and students examined a few of the students' early attempts to revise essays. Students wrote a goal indicating their commitment to learning a strategy for revising essays.

- *Describe the composition strategy.* Following is the six-step strategy: (1) Read your essay. (2) Find the sentence that tells what you believe— is it clear? (3) Add two reasons why you believe it. (4) SCAN each sentence. (Does it make **s**ense? Is it **c**onnected to my belief? Can I **a**dd more? **N**ote errors.) (5) Make changes on the computer. (6) Re-read the essay and make final changes.

- *Model the strategy.* The instructor models the use of the strategy while revising one of the student's early essays. The instructor models four types of self-instructions: problem definition, planning, self-evaluation, and self-reinforcement.

- *Mastery of strategy steps.* Students memorized the six-step strategy.

- *Controlled practice of strategy steps.* Positive and corrective feedback is given as students practice the six-step strategy while revising one of their stories.

- *Generalization and maintenance components.* Students are asked to inform other teachers and their parents about the new writing and revising strategy. Students discuss with their instructor how to modify the strategy for those times that they write with pencil and paper.

Monitor

Data of several types were kept in the paraphrased study; they follow:

- Changes in writing performance were measured by analyzing students' ability to revise, the quality and length of individual essays, and the proportion of mechanical errors.
- Changes in affect were assessed by examining students' judgments of their ability to write and revise a good essay.

- Generalization to a paper-and-pencil writing task and maintenance of effects over time were appraised.
- Evidence of strategy usage and students' modification of the involved strategy was collected.
- Students' progress in acquiring the strategy during training was monitored.

Modifications/Considerations

Data from this study indicated that not only did the students write more when they were provided the six-step strategy than during a baseline, they also revised more often, and their revisions were more substantive. Moreover, the students made fewer mechanical errors following the use of the strategy, their self-efficacy scores improved, and the quality of their essays following the intervention was improved. Another important point to note is that, according to the authors, the three youngsters had little difficulty in learning the strategy.

Research

Graham, S., & MacArthur, C. (1988). Improving learning disabled students' skills at revising essays produced on a word processor: Self-instructional strategy training. *The Journal of Special Education, 22*(2), 133–152.

SPELLING

There are 10 spelling tactics included in Part 3, which, like the Part 2 writing section, is new to this second edition. The first of these spelling tactics is an explanation of the "time delay" approach, which is an appropriate technique for youngsters having great difficulty learning to spell. The next tactic, also a suitable one for children having problems with spelling, discusses how to involve blending training in spelling instruction. Imitation of children's spelling errors is the topic of the third tactic. For the fourth one, a write-and-say approach is explained. A study strategy is outlined in the fifth tactic, and for the sixth, a fingerspelling method is detailed. For Tactic 7, a standard pronunciation strategy is outlined, and for the eighth tactic, a peer tutoring spelling game is explained. For Tactic 9, the add-a-word spelling program is summarized, and for the final tactic, a reinforcement contingency is detailed.

1 CONSTANT TIME DELAY

Background

Educators of pupils with learning disabilities, or of other children who have great difficulty spelling, must find new training procedures, and possibly ones that do not resemble those traditionally arranged to teach spelling. It has been demonstrated that a number of children have not been able to learn to spell words reliably when their teachers arranged techniques for them that had been commonly used in elementary schools. The constant time-delay procedure is not an instructional method that is routinely scheduled in schools, but its effectiveness has been supported by educators of several types who have collected data regarding a number of student behaviors.

Who Can Benefit

The pupil in the Stevens and Schuster (1987) study was an 11-year-old boy with learning disabilities. He was experiencing severe written-language problems due largely to his inability to spell.

Procedures

General Procedures

1. In the Stevens and Schuster study, the teacher had available index cards on which target words were printed in lower-case manuscript; for the student, small paper strips were available on which the student could write his responses.

2. The teacher worked one-on-one with the student.

3. Fifteen words were selected from ones the student had been unable to spell. The words were randomly organized into three groups of five each.

4. Two one-hour tutoring sessions were conducted weekly with two spelling lessons per session. At least one hour separated the two sessions.

5. Sessions consisted of thirty training trials divided into three blocks of ten trials each. Each set of words was trained in a randomly mixed sequence.

Constant Time-Delay Procedures

1. In the study, when a new set of words was introduced, the words in the first block of 10 trials were presented using a 0-second delay. The teacher said, "Spell _____ " and then immediately held up the printed model of a word. The student then wrote the word. If he did not write it or wrote it incorrectly, the teacher corrected him and wrote it.

2. Subsequent trials for that word set were presented using a 5-second delay. The teacher said, "Spell _____ ," and held up the card after 5 seconds if the student failed to respond immediately.

3. All correct responses—anticipations and waits (see the descriptions in the Monitor section)—were immediately followed by verbal praise from the tutor. When errors occurred—waits and non-waits—the tutor immediately said "wrong," removed the paper strip, and looked away from the pupil for 10 seconds (time out).

Acquisition and Generalization

1. *Acquisition:* The criteria for considering a set of words "learned" was 100 percent correct anticipations for 5 consecutive blocks of 10 trials.

2. *Generalization:* Situations were set up to assess the extent to which the student generalized across settings (i.e., while being assessed by another teacher) and across tasks (i.e., writing words in the context of sentences).

Monitor

Five types of data were kept in the Stevens and Schuster study:

1. **Correct anticipations**—the student begins to print a word before the model is presented.

2. **Correct waits**—the student prints a word correctly within 10 seconds after the model is presented.

3. **Non-wait error**—the student prints the word incorrectly before the model is presented.

4. **Wait error**—the student prints the word incorrectly after the model is presented.

5. **No-response error**—the student does not print a word within 10 seconds of the presentation of the model.

Modifications/Considerations

As indicated earlier, the technique explained here to instruct spelling is quite different from standard practices. Although it requires more time and one-on-one instruction to carry out, the time-delay procedure may be the only one that will assist certain students. In this particular study, 4 hours and 15 minutes of direct instructional time was required to teach the 15 words.

Time-delay techniques have been arranged to teach a number of basic skills. Winterling (1990) demonstrated that a treatment package of time delay, practice in writing or spelling target words, and token reinforcement was effective in teaching sight words to primary-age youngsters with severe learning disabilities.

Research

Stevens, K. B., & Schuster, J. W. (1987). Effects of a constant time delay procedure on the written spelling performance of a learning disabled student. *Learning Disability Quarterly, 10,* 9–16.

Winterling, V. (1990). The effects of constant time delay, practice in writing or spelling, and reinforcement on sight word recognition in a small group. *The Journal of Special Education, 24*(1), 101–116.

2 BLENDING AND SPELLING TRAINING

Background

A fundamental goal behind this research was to determine if phonetic-cue readers could be moved to the cipher stage through either blending or spelling training. A related purpose was to determine if *phonemic analysis skills*—the ability to use auditory skills to segment or blend words without relying on the visual aid of letters—would improve as a result of one or both training approaches.

Who Can Benefit

First-grade children with learning disabilities were the participants in this research. A criterion for selecting the youngsters was that they have difficulty with phonemic segmentation. More specifically, the following seven qualifications were developed to select the participants:

1.   they scored above 85 on the PPVT-R intelligence test
2.   they perfectly named 18 letters
3.   they were correct at least 12 of 18 times saying a letter when hearing its sound
4.   they were correct at least 10 of 30 times saying a sound when seeing the letter
5.   they were able to read at least 8 of 24 CVC nonwords
6.   they were able to spell at least 5 of 6 CVC nonwords
7.   they were able to use auditory skills to segment at least 5 of 10 words

Procedures

Pretraining

Pupils were trained to 100 percent mastery on the two letter-sound identification tasks (i.e., hear-sound say-letter and see-letter say-sound).

Training

In the cited study there were two treatments: blending and spelling. They were similar in that letters were used for training, but differed with respect to their emphasis. *Blending* emphasized print-to-sound relationships and emphasized blending the first two sounds of a consonant-vowel-consonant string. *Spelling* emphasized sound-to-print relationships and forced a letter-by-letter analysis.

1. For each session (25 minutes), three trials were provided to produce either a correct blending or spelling. The teacher provided correction when necessary. After three incorrect trials, the teacher produced the correct blending or spelling and the child repeated it.

2. For blending training, 3-letter tiles were provided; for spelling, 9 of the 18 possible tiles were provided, with three vowels always making up part of the visible set. (Note: All stimuli [words and nonwords] were of the CVC type and were limited to four vowels [a, e, i, o] and all letters were presented in lowercase [consonants = b, d, f, g (hard sound), j, k, l, m, n, p, r, s, t, v, w].)

3. For blending, the child was shown a word in a CVC pattern in which the final consonant was separated slightly from the first two. The child was expected to say the first two phonemes as a unit and add the last phoneme.

4. For spelling, the teacher said a word; the child repeated it, selected letter tiles, and pronounced the sound of each letter selected to spell the word.

Monitor

In the cited study three types of posttraining data were collected: (1) probes for maintenance across time (retention) and generalization across persons; (2) generalization across stimuli (i.e., to other actual words and nonwords); and (3) phonemic segmentation.

Modifications/Considerations

The researchers' data indicated that whereas both techniques were effective, one was not superior to the other. That might indicate that both techniques are necessary.

According to the research authors, beginning reading instruction should focus on letter-sound relationships *within* actual words, rather than with only phonemes, as is the standard practice. Along that line I would recommend that if children are experiencing difficulty discriminating their *b*s from their *d*s, they should be trained to make that discrimination by placing the troublesome letters in words, if not in sentences. The more context the better.

Research

DiVeta, S. K., & Speece, D. L. (1990). The effects of blending and spelling training on the decoding skills of young poor readers. *Journal of Learning Disabilities, 23*(9), 579–582.

3 IMITATION OF ERRORS

Background

This tactic is based on the notion that pairing incorrect and correct spellings will help pupils focus on the specific ways in which their incorrect responses differ from the correct ones.

Many educators believe that students should not be exposed to the incorrect way of doing something. The tactic described here departs from this idea, since according to the research of the cited authors, teacher imitation of students' spelling errors seemed to improve performance for certain types of students.

Who Can Benefit

This tactic would be an appropriate choice for students who have not responded to self-correction, positive practice, or other, more standard instructional techniques. In the research cited here, the students were in primary grades and were pupils with mild retardation and learning disabilities. This tactic could also be scheduled effectively with older pupils who have difficulty focusing on specific errors in particular words. This tactic might be particularly suitable for pupils with whom a sight-word approach to reading has proven effective.

Procedures

A teacher might arrange this tactic as an adjunct to whatever other type of spelling program was being scheduled for a targeted student. This technique may be arranged as a variation of corrective feedback, or it may be expanded to become the core of an individualized spelling program. The following are steps for carrying it out:

1. On Monday, administer a pretest to students on an appropriate number of words. Pronounce each word individually, and require students

to write them on a worksheet. The words may be from a Dolch list, from a basal reader, or from a commercial spelling program.

2. Rely on direct instruction or another instructional format to teach the words from the pretest. Whenever possible, use the correctly spelled words as confidence-builders and as clues to the spelling of other words.

3. Administer a posttest in the following manner:
   - Say the word.
   - Ask students to say the word and write it.
   - Praise students if they write the word correctly and go on to the next word. Words can be put on cards and given to students when spelled correctly.
   - Say, "No, that's wrong," if students write the word incorrectly, and cross out the word with a broad marker. Then say, "Here's what you wrote," (writing the word as an imitation of the students' error) "and here is the correct way to write it" (writing the word correctly). "Where is the error?"
   - Request students to copy the correct model. (Note: Do not use colored pencils or other cuing devices to highlight student errors.)
   - Go on to the next word, and continue until the posttest is complete. (Cards given for correct spellings may be exchanged for appropriate reinforcers, such as books, magazines, or school supplies.)

4. Begin the next session at step 3; repeat sessions daily until 90 percent mastery is reached.

5. Carry error words over to the next week.

6. Emphasize positive responses through meaningful reinforcement and underscore the "noninstances."

Monitor

To assess accurately the effectiveness of this tactic, it is suggested that baseline data be gathered on students' initial ability to learn the spellings of new words and to maintain those words prior to scheduling this procedure. If the same number of words is given for each spelling test, each pupil's score can be charted as a percentage correct. Following the baseline determination and throughout a period when the imitation technique is being used, the teacher should continue to gather these data. By comparing a pupil's scores in one phase with those in the other, the teacher could determine the effects of the treatment.

Modifications/Considerations

This tactic may be especially effective for teaching phonetically irregular words. For some students, it may be better to revise the action of copying the correct model to highlighting specific errors. For other students, it might be effective if the corrected part of the word was written with larger letters. Attend carefully to students' responses, and let your best judgment guide your selection of approaches.

Research

Kauffman, J. M., Hallahan, D. P., Haas, K., Brame, T., & Boren, R. (1978). Imitating children' s errors to improve their spelling performance. *Journal of Learning Disabilities, 11*(2), 17–222 .

Nulman, J. A. H., & Gerber, M. M. (1984). Improving spelling performance by imitating a child's errors. *Journal of Learning Disabilities, 17,* 328–333.

4 THE WRITE-SAY METHOD

Background

Traditional approaches for teaching children to spell, such as the simple memorization of words, do still persist, but they often lack methods of providing immediate feedback to multiple sensory modalities; this feedback is believed to be integral to improved spelling performance. A need exists for cost-effective interventions that are based on immediate feedback and that are applicable to general and special-education classrooms.

Who Can Benefit

Students in the cited study were children of about 12 years of age who had learning disabilities. The students had previously spelled correctly more than 95 percent of words up to five letters in length, but did not do as well on words six or more letters in length. In addition, each subject was able to read the words they were to spell.

Procedures

- Schedule 30-minute spelling sessions.
- On Monday, present each student with a 10-item word list and ask him or her to study the list. The list in the paraphrased study consisted of four common six-letter words, three seven-letter words, and three eight-letter words. Change the word lists each week.
- On Tuesday, administer a test of the words to the pupils.
- Following the test, provide verbal feedback on the incorrect and correct spellings.
- Have students look at the original word list, then instruct them to simultaneously say aloud and write, letter by letter, the correct spelling of any incorrectly spelled word. Have students correctly write each incorrectly spelled word five times.

- Repeat the Tuesday procedure, except this time have students simultaneously rewrite and restate incorrectly spelled words 10 consecutive times.
- Rely again on the Tuesday procedure, except have incorrectly spelled words simultaneously rewritten and restated correctly 15 consecutive times.
- Administer a spelling test on Friday. At this time the teacher simply reads the words to the students and they are expected to write them.

Monitor

If the teacher schedules the same number of spelling words for pupils each week, he or she could keep track of the number (or percentage) of words correctly spelled on the Friday test. If a treatment of one type is scheduled for several weeks, those data could be summarized. Following, if the treatment recommended here is put in place for several weeks, those data could be summarized. Data from the two phases could then be compared for each pupil in the study to determine the comparative effects of the treatments.

Modifications/Considerations

Several alterations are possible from the procedures suggested here: the number of words given each pupil, the number of times students are required to restate and rewrite the misspelled words, the type of words that make up the lists, and the number of days the treatment is in effect. Moreover, criteria to indicate whether or not a word is learned could be imposed. Rather than simply asking the pupils to work on a list of words for one week, they might be required to stay with them until they have been mastered. Furthermore, some measure of retention could be included in the criteria.

Research

Kearney, C. A., & Drabman, R. S. (1993). The write-say method for improving spelling accuracy in children with learning disabilities. *Journal of Learning Disabilities, 26*(1), 52–56.

5 PREDICTING GOOD STUDY HABITS FOR SPELLING

Background

Awareness of one's own knowledge about a particular subject matter can greatly improve how one studies and eventually performs. The study cited here did not specifically teach metacognitive skills; however, their indirect use proved to have an important influence on outcome performances. Students were trained to use a spelling strategy, then were given the opportunity to predict how well they would perform. The inferred feedback students received following their predictions and actions had a positive effect on their study habits. Students studied more efficiently because they were able to determine what a test would require and could decide how to best study in order to do well on the test.

Who Can Benefit

The students in the referenced study were fourth-graders. They were students with learning disabilities and were targeted as poor spellers on the *Test of Written Spelling* (TWS), which measured their ability to spell phonetic and nonphonetic words.

Many students do poorly on spelling tests because they lack a strategy that prepares them for a final test. Other students may have a strategy, but it is a faulty one, and hence they are baffled with their low scores on spelling tests. This tactic would be helpful for them.

Procedures

The researchers tested various study conditions; however, the focus of this tactic is on only the teacher-monitored condition.

Teacher Models the Strategy

1. From a list of 15 words, the teacher says each of the words in turn.
2. The student has the same list. As each word is spoken, the student covers it. Next to the covered word, he or she is expected to write the word and then say it.

3. The student then checks his or her spelling of the word by comparing it with the original one on the list.

4. If the student spells a word incorrectly, he or she erases it.

5. The student then uses a finger to trace the correctly spelled word from the list while saying the word.

6. Once again the student covers the written word and writes it from memory.

7. The student checks the spelling of the word.

8. If the spelling is incorrect the process is repeated. (Figure 5.1 shows an example of a word list–write sheet.)

Teachers should think out loud using the strategy. For example, for Step 3, the teacher would say: "Now I will see if I spelled this right. Later, L-A-T-E-R; later, L-A-T-E-R. I spelled it correctly so now I will trace *later* with my finger."

Students Practice with Teacher Monitoring
Students follow Steps 1 through 8 thinking out loud, as the teacher demonstrates. The teacher should intervene immediately if the student incorrectly performs the strategy. Teacher direction is terminated once the student is able to successfully apply the strategy without assistance on two consecutive words.

The Test
1. Give each student a list of 15 words. (In the cited study, words were chosen that were meaningful to 75 percent of the students, but that were infrequently used in the fourth-grade reading and writing materials.)

2. Inform the students that they have 30 minutes to study for the test.

FIGURE 5.1
Example Word
List–Write Sheet

Name _____			
Words	Write 1	Write 2	
1. later	*later*		
2. steel			
3. queen			
4. peek			
5. change			
6. fond			

3. If students complete the study strategy for all 15 words before 30 minutes have elapsed, require them to select certain words on the list to study again.

4. Ask students to predict the number of words they will spell correctly on the test.

5. Give the test using the following procedure:
   - Say the word
   - Use the word in a sentence
   - Repeat the word

Monitor

The teacher should carefully monitor the student's initial use of the spelling strategy. Immediate feedback and modeling of correct performance should reinforce skillful use of the strategy. A teacher may devise a simple checklist that students use initially to determine whether or not they are completing each step in the sequence. Before the teacher terminates giving direction, he or she should use a checklist to evaluate each student's performance.

Teachers should also compare the students' predictions with their actual test performances.

Students with learning disabilities may overestimate their scores on tests. The teacher should discuss predictions and praise estimations that are close to actual scores. The key is to have students focus on their predictions, then relate the success of the predictions back to the way in which they studied.

Modifications/Considerations

Several modifications are possible with this spelling strategy. For example, the teacher may choose to vary the number of words given, the time allotted for studying, and the allowed time for taking the test. Furthermore, the teacher may choose to give the list at the beginning of the week. Then, throughout the week, the teacher may specify short periods of time for studying words. The teacher may then give the test later in the week. Older students, after some practice, may become skilled enough to use this spelling strategy independently at home. The goal should be to decrease teacher direction and move toward student independence.

The teacher could also put spelling words on a list different from the one on which the students will practice writing. Teachers may choose to put words on flash cards and have students practice writing the words on their own papers. Teachers may also choose to have students practice the strategy with partners. One partner might dictate words while the other writes them down on paper.

Predictions also could become more of a focus. Teachers might have students record their predictions on top of the paper they will use for taking the test. Students could also chart their predictions and actual scores and then determine the differences.

Teachers need to realize that students will have varying needs as far as the amount of prompting necessary to learn the strategy. More competent students may be able to assist the teacher when working with less proficient students.

Modeling should be clear and specific. The teacher should model correctly spelled words as well as incorrectly spelled words. The teacher should also model the predictions, and evaluations of those predictions, with actual outcomes.

Research

Harris, K. R., Graham, S., & Freeman, S. (1988). Effects of strategy training on metamemory among learning disabled students. *Exceptional Children, 54*(4), 332–338.

6 A FINGERSPELLING APPROACH TO SPELLING

Background

Many students, particularly those in special education, avoid any situation in which they might have to write. Often this avoidance is due to the student's inability to spell accurately. It is essential, however, for students to write, particularly in middle and high school. If a student's poor writing is due to a problem with spelling, then every effort should be made to improve the problem. Traditional spelling programs—the auditory approach, the visual approach, the meaning approach, or a combination of these approaches—often are not successful with students who have rather severe spelling deficits. The authors of the cited research suggest that a kinesthetic fingerspelling technique may be a beneficial alternative for some of these pupils.

Who Can Benefit

The students with whom the Isaacson, Rowland, and Kelley (1987) fingerspelling research was carried out were boys and girls of average intelligence in grades four through nine. These students were from 1.5 to 4 years below their expected grade level in spelling, however. The technique explained here might be a reasonable alternative for many students who are having difficulty mastering spelling in one of the traditional programs.

Procedures

The fingerspelling technique is based on the manual alphabet most commonly used by individuals with hearing impairments. There are 26 fingerspelling positions, one for each letter of the alphabet. The following procedures can be implemented once a student has mastered "reading" the manual alphabet as well as producing it.

1. Each student is matched with a partner. The partner may be the teacher, an aide, a parent, or another student.

2. Both the student and the partner select which hand each will use for fingerspelling. Once selected, the hands must not be switched.

3. The partner receives a list of 10 words for the student to practice. The teacher selects words for the pair that are important and useful for the student.

4. The partner shows the student the first word on the list and asks the student to draw one or more vertical lines in the word to divide it into meaningful parts. The student may divide the word in any way he or she chooses. The purpose of dividing words into parts is to help the student keep his or her place when fingerspelling the word. (Dividing the words is not necessary if the student accurately fingerspells without it.)

5. The student looks at the first part of the word and fingerspells it while saying lt. The student then says the first part again, followed by the second part, fingerspelling the second part while saying it. The student says the first part, the second part, and then the third part, now fingerspelling the third part.

6. The partner repeats Step 5 until the student can spell the word from memory.

7. Once the student can successfully fingerspell the entire word from memory, the procedure is repeated for the next word.

Once all words have been successfully fingerspelled from memory, the student is asked to write the words by following the next steps:

1. The partner says the word aloud.

2. The student fingerspells the word to him- or herself while saying the word.

3. The student writes the word. The partner continues until all 10 words are fingerspelled and then written.

4. Once the student is confident that he or she knows the words, the partner administers the final mastery test in which the student fingerspells and writes each word.

The student frequently should review the newly learned spelling words by writing them in sentences and paragraphs.

Monitor

The effectiveness of this technique could be determined by comparing a student's scores on spelling tests taken before the implementation of the fingerspelling technique with scores on tests taken after the technique had been implemented. Because one of the purposes behind the technique is to help improve not only spelling but also expressive writing, data could also be kept on the student's writing over a period of time. The teacher could keep a few writing samples before the technique is scheduled and then collect several samples while the student is involved with the approach.

Modifications/Considerations

The authors of the technique claim that it may take anywhere from 3 to 9 months of daily use before the student sees an improvement in writing ability. Because of this, the need for patience and persistence should be explained to the student at the beginning of the program.

Several modifications could be implemented from this technique. One alternative might be for the student to practice all of the steps alone and then enlist the help of a partner for only the mastery test. Another modification might be for the student to use the technique as a study routine while at home with parents. Yet another change would be allowing the student to use a word-processing computer program when writing the words.

An important consideration of this technique is that it requires a fair degree of fine-motor ability. The technique, therefore, would probably not be a good choice for students with cerebral palsy or other motor-impairing problems.

Research

Isaacson, A. G., Rowland, T. D., & Kelley, P. A. (1987). A fingerspelling approach to spelling. *Academic Therapy, 23*(1), 89–96.

7 USING A STANDARD PRONUNCIATION STRATEGY TO STUDY SPELLING WORDS

Background

Several commercial spelling programs instruct students to pronounce the spelling words they are studying. Moreover, a number of strategies are available that indicate in writing how words are pronounced. Two such written pronunciation strategies are the phonetic method and the standard method. In the phonetic pronunciation strategy, a written word is divided into syllables using sound or dictionary pronunciations. For example, a written phonetic pronunciation for February would be "Feb-you-wary." In the standard pronunciation method, the written word is divided into syllables using the actual letters in the word, such as "Feb-ru-ar-y." The research study on which this tactic is based hypothesized and substantiated that if students study spelling words by using the phonetic pronunciation technique, they often memorize the phonetic spelling instead of the actual spelling. However, when students study standard pronunciations, their spelling memorization improves. The following is a technique that uses the standard pronunciation strategy to study and memorize spelling words.

Who Can Benefit

The students in the cited research were average fourth graders. Although the research authors' data indicated that all the students benefited from the technique, the poor spellers improved more than did the better spellers. Thus, the technique would be most helpful for students with learning disabilities, but could be used with other students as well.

Procedures

Preparation for Activity

1. The teacher selects the week's spelling words. The weekly words from any basal spelling program could be used.

2. Three forms of each word are printed on a 5"×8" card: a standard spelling written in lowercase, a standard spelling written in cursive, and a standard spelling divided into syllables and markings for the long vowels. The word forms should be written so that the standard spellings are written one under the other on the left half of the card, with the divided form written on the right half of the card, as shown:

   morpheme   môr fem
   morpheme (cursive)

3. The cards are placed in a ring binder that has a flap to cover and uncover the standard spellings on the left half of the card.

4. On a separate sheet of paper, the teacher writes each word and a defining sentence to accompany each word.

Study Activity

1. When this strategy is employed, five practice words are used to teach the students to decode conventional spellings. A proper pronunciation entails pronouncing each syllable separately with suitable stress and including the appropriate sound corresponding to each letter. Students should be taught the procedure individually so that the teacher can correct and explain errors if a student performs incorrectly.

2. Students are assigned a study partner. Each pair consists of a tutor and a student, or tutee. The student uses the flip cards. The tutor uses the word list with definitions.

3. The student looks at the standard syllabicated spelling on the first card. The student points to each syllable, pronounces it, and then blends the syllables to say the whole word. Incorrectly pronounced syllables are pronounced by the tutor and repeated by the student.

4. The two standard spellings—manuscript and cursive—are then exposed. The student looks at them and reads the word aloud.

5. The tutor gives the word in a defining sentence.

6. The student copies the correct spelling in lowercase or cursive.

7. The procedure is followed for all other words on the list.

8. Partners change roles and repeat the procedure.

The procedure can be implemented once a week or several times a week, depending on the needs of the individual students.

Monitor

As with many spelling programs, the best way to monitor its effectiveness would be to take baseline data prior to using the tactic and compare those data to data taken during the implementation of the new or special technique. Student interviews might also suggest whether the procedure was popular and effective for the students.

Modifications/Considerations

This procedure can be modified for use with only one or two students in a class, or can be used with the entire class. The teacher can act as the tutor or another student might serve as the tutor. This activity works well during peer-tutoring sessions in which tutors are older students. The procedure could also be implemented as a home study procedure with a parent acting as the tutor. In a classroom setting, a flip-card packet and list of sentences could be constructed for each student and put in a special place in the room; when other work is completed, study pairs can go to this location and use the pronunciation strategy.

An important consideration when setting up this tactic is the amount of time necessary for the initial preparation of the materials, particularly the flip cards. A student helper, parent, or instructional assistant could be drafted to construct each week's cards, or each student might use Monday spelling time to construct his or her own cards. If the word lists being studied come from a basal spelling book, the flip cards could be kept and used year after year. One way to simplify the procedure might be to make up a blank set of flip cards and laminate them. Then weekly words could be written on the cards using a Vis-a-Vis™ pen and then erased at the end of the week.

Research

Drake, D. A., & Ehri, L. C. (1984). Spelling acquisition: Effects of pronouncing words on memory for their spellings. *Cognition and Instruction, 1*(3), 297–320.

8 THE PEER TUTORING SPELLING GAME

Background

In many academic programs, the mastery and acquisition of a skill is highly dependent on the amount of time set aside for the activity, as well as on the amount of opportunities students have to make responses. This is particularly true when it comes to learning to spell words; however, most traditional spelling programs do not focus on maximizing engaged time or opportunities to respond. The authors of the cited research suggest that by incorporating principles of direct instruction into a traditional spelling program, student accuracy and achievement in spelling can be greatly increased.

The peer tutoring spelling game was designed to increase student achievement by maximizing engaged time and opportunities to respond. This occurs through social and token reinforcement, team competition, distributed practice, and an error correction procedure. According to the authors, the program was designed to meet the following criteria:

1. It would not create extra work for the teacher.
2. It would assist all children in the class.
3. It would utilize materials found in the current spelling program.
4. It would supplement rather than supplant current spelling activities.
5. It would be carried out during the usual time period available for spelling.

Who Can Benefit

This technique was successfully implemented with third-grade boys and girls, some of whom were pupils with learning disabilities, whereas others were of average and above-average ability. Although the technique increased the spelling ability of all students, it was particularly helpful for those with learning disabilities. Because the technique can be used with any spelling program, it is appropriate for any grade level that schedules spelling as a separate subject.

Procedures

Tutor Training

Before the tutor spelling game can be implemented, the teacher must train the students in the rules of the game and in the method of earning and scoring points. The game is similar to basketball. The steps for tutoring are as follows:

1.   Each tutor pair is given a list of the week's spelling words.

2.   One student in the pair begins as the tutor.

3.   The tutor says the first word on the list to the partner.

4.   The partner writes the word on paper.

5.   The partner orally spells the word that he or she has written back to the tutor.

6.   If the partner spells the word correctly, the tutor says, "Correct, give yourself a basket (two points)." The partner writes the number two on his or her paper next to the word. If the partner spells the word incorrectly, the tutor points to the word, pronounces the word, and spells the word correctly for the partner. The partner must then correctly write the word three times. The tutor then awards a foul shot (one point). The partner writes the number one on his or her paper next to the word.

7.   The procedure is repeated for each word on the list.

8.   During the game, the teacher circulates around the room, stopping from time to time for 20 to 30 seconds to observe tutor pairs. If a tutor is observed to be giving the words quickly and clearly, giving corrective feedback, and accurately delivering points, the teacher awards one to five bonus or referee points to the tutor.

Once the rules and scoring are explained to students, the teacher may want to model the procedure several times for the class.

Weekly Game Procedures

1.   Each Monday at the beginning of the spelling period, the students in the class are randomly assigned to one of two teams (e.g., the Red Team and the Blue Team).

2.   Once the teams are designated, the teacher pairs the children within each team to make up tutor pairs that will work together during the week. (The members of each pair must be from the same team.)

3.   Students are instructed to find their spelling books and move to a place in the room where they can work with their partners.

4. The teacher sets a timer for 5 minutes, and the first child of the pair tutors the other. When the timer rings, the students reverse roles. The teacher again sets the timer for 5 minutes.

5. During tutoring, the teacher circulates about the room and awards bonus or referee points.

6. At the end of each day's tutoring session, the tutor pairs add up each other's points, including baskets, foul shots, and referee points.

7. The teacher, in front of the class, calls out the name of each team member, and she or he responds by calling out his or her point total. The teacher adds up the points for each team and enters the total on a daily point chart posted on a bulletin board.

8. Steps 3, 4, and 5 are repeated on Tuesday through Thursday.

9. On Friday, the teacher administers the weekly spelling test to all students. When the test is completed, the team pairs switch papers and correct one anothers' responses, giving three points for each word spelled correctly.

10. Again, the teacher has each child call out his or her individual points, which are then summed into the team total for the week.

11. The winning team for the week is announced by the teacher.

Monitor

The effectiveness of this technique is easily monitored by recording and evaluating weekly spelling test scores. In the original research, the authors evaluated spelling performance by setting up a baseline period of about two or three weeks during which the game was not used, an experimental period of three or four weeks during which the game was implemented, and then another week during which the game was not scheduled. Scores from each of these phases could be compared to determine the effectiveness of the game.

Modifications/Considerations

An important consideration to make before implementing this competitive game is to discuss social skills and appropriate team etiquette, such as what is appropriate and inappropriate for winning and losing teams to say and do. The concept of appropriate positive reinforcement should also be discussed. The teacher might even implement a response cost procedure or system of fines for inappropriate behavior or comments.

This game could be modified to fit subjects other than spelling. It could be effectively implemented for memorizing math facts, memorizing social studies facts (e.g., historical dates, the order of the presidents, capitols of states), or recognizing sight words in reading. The amount of tutoring time—5 minutes for each student in the referenced study—could be shortened or lengthened, depending on the nature of the subject being studied and the type of students involved.

Research

Delquadri, J. C., Greenwood, C. R., & Hall, R. V. (1983). The peer tutoring spelling game: A classroom procedure for increasing opportunity to respond and spelling performance. *Education and Treatment of Children, 6*(3), 225–239.

9 USING THE ADD-A-WORD SPELLING PROGRAM

Background

The ultimate goal of any spelling program is to improve students' spelling accuracy in daily written work. Traditional spelling programs generally consist of giving students a list of 10 to 20 words on Monday and having a test on those words on Friday. For many students, this exercise is meaningless, since the spelling lists contain words rarely used by students in their daily written work. The research on which this tactic is based suggests that a student's spelling accuracy and generalization to daily written work can be greatly increased if practice and tests occur daily and if spelling lists are individualized for each student, using words the student frequently misspells in his or her daily work.

Who Can Benefit

The students in the cited research were fifth and sixth graders with learning disabilities. They were instructed in a special education resource room. According to the authors of the study, this technique would also be effective for individuals with mental retardation and behavior disorders, as well as for students without disabilities.

Procedures

To begin the program, each student receives an individualized list of 10 words. The list should be composed of words that the student misspelled in his or her daily expressive writing or other writing assignments. If these sources do not generate enough words for a list, additional words can be selected from a basal spelling book or basal reader. Once an initial list is composed, each day the student will:

1. Copy the first word from the list onto a piece of paper.
2. Fold the paper or cover the word on the paper and write the word from memory a second time.

3. Compare the second spelling of the word with the spelling on the list.

4. If the word was spelled correctly, proceed to the next word and repeat the same procedure. If the word was misspelled, repeat the process with the same word until it is spelled correctly.

5. Take a spelling test over the entire list once the entire list has been spelled correctly.

6. Drop a word from the list when it has been spelled correctly on two consecutive days, then add a new word.

7. Retest each word five days after its removal from the list and once a month thereafter. If a word is misspelled at any time during this review, place it back on the list.

Monitor

An easy way to monitor a student's growth when this technique is in effect is to simply keep track of the number of learned words per unit of time (e.g., week). Moreover, students can monitor their own progress by keeping a personal record of all words they have successfully mastered. By the year's end, their list of learned words should be quite large.

Since the goal of any spelling program is to improve students' spelling not only on their weekly or daily tests, but also as they write more expressive and narrative assignments, the teacher should document the number of words misspelled in daily written work and note the words that are spelled correctly in daily work that appeared on a student's spelling list.

Modifications/Considerations

One consideration for this tactic, particularly for regular classroom teachers with 20 to 30 students, is that of time. This program will definitely require more time to implement than will a basal spelling program. Using a teacher's aide, parent volunteer, or dependable older student could be extremely helpful when administering the individualized lists.

Although the authors recommended 10 words per list, the program could be modified to as few as 2 or 3 words or as many as 20, depending on the ability of the students and the amount of time set aside for learning to spell. The procedure could also be used effectively in a cooperative setting where students quiz each other before taking the daily test.

Research

Pratt-Struthers, J., Struthers, T. B., & Williams, R. L. (1983). The effects of the add-a-word spelling program on spelling accuracy during creative writing. *Education and Treatment of Children, 6*(3), 277–283.

10 FREE-TIME CONTINGENCY

Background

This tactic is based on three related notions: (1) youngsters are motivated by free time, particularly when they have some say about how that time is spent; (2) students are motivated when they can "earn" the opportunity of not participating in regularly scheduled activities, such as practicing spelling words; (3) youngsters who have experienced a few techniques to help them learn to spell words can often select the technique that is most effective for them.

Who Can Benefit

The pupils in the Lovitt, Guppy, and Blattner (1969) study were fourth graders. The technique explained here was arranged for all 32 of the youngsters in the class. As could be expected of most classes this size, the abilities of the youngsters varied widely.

Procedures

There were three phases in the Lovitt et al. study. The first was a baseline phase, during which time the procedures for instructing spelling were quite traditional (as will be detailed later). During the second phase, the students chose their own techniques for studying the new words, and were no longer required to participate in spelling activities when they achieved a 100 percent score on a test. In the final phase, a group contingency was set up during which time all the youngsters were granted extra free time if all of them achieved 100 percent scores in spelling.

Baseline

During this period, the students read a story on Monday from their spelling text that contained that week's spelling words. They also completed a workbook exercise regarding the words (e.g., filled in blanks in sentences that contained the new words). On Wednesday, they were given a trial test over the words. On Thursday, they carried out another exercise from their workbooks and wrote each word several times. On Friday, the final test was given and the pupils' percentage scores were entered in the teacher's grade book.

Student Choice and Contingent Free Time
Throughout this phase, following the presentation of the new words on Monday, the children were asked to complete two workbook exercises and hand them in by Wednesday. No specific classroom time was allotted for the completion of these requirements. During this phase, spelling tests were given on Tuesday, Wednesday, Thursday, and Friday. A student was finished with spelling for the week as soon as he or she achieved a 100 percent score on the test. If, for example, a student scored 100 percent on Tuesday's test, he or she did not have to take the other three tests. Pupils who had mastered the list in this way could do as they pleased at their desks when the subsequent spelling tests were given. If, however, the score on Tuesday was less than 100 percent, the student had to keep taking the tests until he or she achieved a perfect score, or until the Friday test was reached. Students' papers were returned to them immediately following the tests. If they had incorrectly spelled a word, corrections were indicated on the paper. They were not required to study for the next day's test, but were encouraged to prepare in any way they thought would be helpful. Throughout this phase, the teacher entered the day each pupil achieved a 100 percent score (e.g., 1 = Tuesday). If a pupil never achieved a perfect score, his or her Friday score (e.g., 80 percent) was entered in the grade book.

Group Contingency
During this phase, the procedures were like they were in the preceding period, but with one exception. Now, an additional contingency was added: If all of the pupils achieved a 100 percent score at some time during the week, the entire class was allowed to listen to a radio program for 15 minutes.

Monitor

Suggestions for monitoring this approach were offered in the Procedures section; instead of reviewing these suggestions, I will present the results of the Lovitt et al. research in this section. During the first phase of this project the median number of perfect papers from the class of 32 was 12. In the second phase the median number of perfect scores was 25, and in the third phase, it was 30.

Modifications/Considerations

In this tactic students were allowed to select the way in which they studied their assigned spelling words. The reason this approach was generally successful stems from the fact that the youngsters had, for a few years prior to this study, experienced a number of techniques for learning spelling words that had been arranged by their teachers. Presumably the students had recalled those practices, and when they were allowed to choose their own, selected the ones that were most helpful.

An obvious modification that a teacher could make with respect to this tactic would be to individualize, to some extent at least, the assignments. In the study cited here, all students were given the same words and the same number of words. Although the technique was quite successful with these youngsters, it might have been even more successful had some youngsters been given assignments that were more in keeping with their abilities.

In a more recent study, Dangel (1989) showed that the spelling performances of sixth-grade students with learning disabilities were improved when they relied on two student-directed spelling strategies: student-directed planning and monitoring.

Research

Dangel, H. L. (1989). The use of student-directed spelling strategies. *Academic Therapy, 25*(1), 43–51.

Lovitt, T. C., Guppy, T. E., & Blattner, J. E. (1969). The use of a free-time contingency with fourth graders to increase spelling accuracy. *Behaviour Research & Therapy, 7,* 151–156.

MATHEMATICS

In the first edition, the tactics in this section had to do mostly with arithmetic computation. Of the 10 tactics in this part, a few have been rewritten for this edition, and several new ones that have to do with word problems have been added. The first tactic deals with establishing goals or proficiency rates in each of the four arithmetic processes. The next four tactics focus on increasing students' response accuracy to arithmetic problems: verbalizing the problem, slicing back, cuing and fading, and demonstrating and modeling. The sixth tactic explains an approach for challenging the routines of ordinary arithmetic instruction. For the seventh tactic, a reciprocal peer tutoring and group contingency approach is discussed. Mathematics strategies are covered in the next two tactics. One tactic outlines several heuristic strategies and the other explains a mnemonic strategy. The last tactic discusses how real-life situations can guide mathematics instruction.

1 ESTABLISHING ARITHMETIC GOALS

Background

The idea behind this procedure is that teachers should decide on the extent to which pupils should master each of the four problem types (addition, subtraction, multiplication, and division). Teachers need to establish what it takes to be proficient in all of these different areas.

There are at least three reasons for being concerned about proficiency and for encouraging pupils to reach criteria. One is the value to students of becoming automatic when solving a problem. It is highly desirable for a student to be able to solve a problem without having to stop and think about it or to count on his or her fingers; instead, the goal should be for the student to immediately say or write the answer.

A second reason for becoming proficient in a specific skill is that the chances of remembering how to perform it are greatly increased, even if the skill is not exercised very often. Also, if proficiency is reached and then the person does not use the skill for some time (and loses a bit of competency), the time and effort required to recoup that skill are generally not great.

A third reason for attaining proficiency on certain kinds of problems is that the student then is able to generalize more readily about other problem types. When learning the next set of problems, that student has an advantage over pupils who have not mastered other areas.

The criteria for the problem types shown in this tactic came from my experience with six sixth graders in an elementary school. I asked two sixth-grade teachers to loan me their top arithmetic performers for a few hours over a three-day period. I then asked these six students, for one or two minutes each, to work the 78 types of problems selected for the Computational Arithmetic Program (CAP). Next, I averaged their correct and incorrect rates and plotted them. Data for 16 of the problem types are shown in Figure 1.1. The letters across the top are the coded symbols used in the CAP program. MAF means Mixed Add Facts, MSF means Mixed Subtraction Facts, and so forth; the four types of problems then are broken down by difficulty into three sub-categories (e.g., AA, AB, and AC).

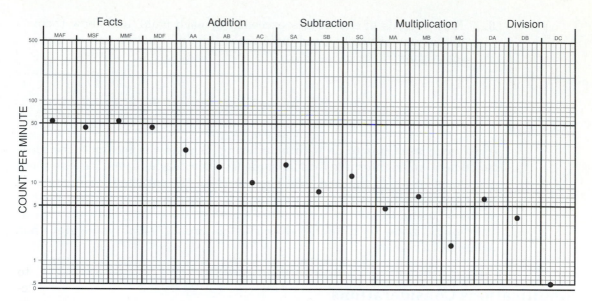

FIGURE 1.1 Nongraded Placement and Individual Evaluation Form

SOURCE: Adapted from *The Computational Arithmetic Program (CAP)* (p. 26) by Deborah D. Smith and Thomas C. Lovitt, 1982, Austin, TX: Pro-Ed Publishers.

Who Can Benefit

Although the targets shown here were obtained from sixth graders (competent ones at that), they also should be considered for other children, even those who are younger or those with learning disabilities, because these scores are not excessively high. There are some teachers, in fact, who recommend that youngsters' rates on basic arithmetic facts be around 100 correct problems per minute. (Note: In my study, the sixth graders' correct rates were only around 50 per minute.)

Procedures

Following are a few ways in which to use the goals, either the ones suggested here or others that you might set.

1. Write them on the pupils' papers so they know what they are trying to attain.

2. Communicate the goals to parents, along with their children's scores and a record of their progress, so that parents know how the students are relating to the standard.

3. Keep records of the targets exceeded by each child, and show them publicly or privately. Used judiciously, this information can be quite motivating.

Monitor

This tactic itself has to do with monitoring. Beyond the fact that the ideas noted here would inform individual students, their teachers, and parents about the extent to which the goals had been reached, the collected information on aims met in certain aspects of arithmetic (or other subjects, for that matter) would be useful to principals and other administrators. With that information they would know by grade level and by classroom which youngsters had achieved their goals.

Modifications/Considerations

Although these scores were gathered from sixth-grade high achievers, other data could be acquired from pupils of other ages and abilities. If, for example, a special education teacher was concerned about helping a child fit into the lowest arithmetic group in a general education classroom, he or she could obtain data concerning the members of that particular group and use them as the target. Or, if a second-grade teacher wanted his or her pupils to be as competent as the current third-grade students within a certain timespan, the teacher could gather data concerning the third graders as well as the second graders at the beginning of the year, and then throughout the year, aim the second graders toward those third-grade rates (or higher).

Of course, one could also acquire standard rates from experts. In math, the most proficient performers might be bank tellers or certified public accountants. Mercer, Mercer, and Evans (1982) have compiled the suggested rates of various researchers in a number of subjects, arithmetic among them. In their review, the range of aims for computing grade two and three facts was from about 15 to 100 numerals per minute. The range for responding to grade three and four facts was from about 40 to 75, and from about 40 to 100 for grade four and five facts. The range for grade five and six facts was from about 40 to 90.

Research

Mercer, C. D., Mercer, A. R., & Evans, S. (1982). The use of frequency in establishing instructional aims. *Journal of Precision Teaching, 3*(3), 57–63.

Smith, D. D., & Lovitt, T. C. (1982). *The computational arithmetic program (CAP).* Austin, TX: Pro-Ed.

2 SAY IT BEFORE YOU DO IT

Background

The idea behind this tactic, as its name implies, is that students' answers are often more accurate when they think about, and actually articulate, what they are going to do before they do it. There is some folk wisdom to support this approach: Many parents and grandparents have chided young ones for clumsy or reckless acts by saying "Henry, if you had only thought a bit about what you were going to do before you did it, you wouldn't have done such a careless thing!"

This idea of saying or thinking before doing fits into two rather sophisticated learning theories as well. Psychologists have for some time promoted the idea of a *mediator*, that is, some thought or event that comes between a stimulus and its response. More recently, psychologists and educators have promoted various *metacognitive* theories. Like their mediational predecessors, these theories stress the importance of saying or thinking before (or along with) doing.

Who Can Benefit

The pupil in the cited research was an 11-year-old boy. He attended a class for children with behavior disorders at the Experimental Education Unit of the University of Washington. This tactic would be a good selection for many youngsters who are just learning a skill and are still in the awkward or acquisition stage of development. These students can perform the skill correctly only if they thoroughly concentrate on it; they have not yet reached the automatic or proficiency stage. As noted in the Montague and Applegate (1993) study, "think-aloud" protocols are helpful for a wide age and ability range of students.

Procedures

1. Define a class of problems that the student should master. In this research, the problems were subtraction items of the type $\square - 2 = 6$, in which the minuends and subtrahends were less than 10.

2. Print 10 or 20 different problems of this type on a practice sheet. Place them randomly so that each item is included half a dozen or so times.

3. Schedule a time for the pupil to write solutions to these problems, and observe him or her carefully while working. If the student incorrectly answers a few problems and the errors seem to be random, or if the errors appear predictably in connection with a certain problem, the student might be a good candidate for this tactic.

4. Require a pupil who makes random errors to verbalize *each* problem before writing the answer. If, however, the pupil consistently erred on only one or two specific problems, direct him or her to verbalize *only* those types of problems before writing the responses. These targeted problems could be circled or otherwise highlighted so the youngster knows which ones are to be verbalized.

5. Coach the pupil on how to articulate the problem before answering it. For example, tell the student to say, "Some number minus two equals six." Then have the child say, "Eight minus two equals six." Tell the child to write down the answer *only* after he or she has verbally cleared the path.

Monitor

Keep data on the pupil's efforts for a few days. If the student correctly answers all the problems, tell the child not to recite the two sentences you modeled before writing the answers. You might, instead, suggest that the student simply *think* about those cues before writing the solutions.

Continue keeping data. If the student falters on some problems, reinstate this tactic. If the child's accuracy holds up, quicken the pace and thus push him or her toward the automatic stage. If, following that advice, the child misses an occasional problem, ask him or her to start thinking a bit more about each of the steps.

Modifications/Considerations

This tactic has a wide range of uses, and could be considered for most subjects. If, for example, pupils have difficulty spelling words containing *ie* or double consonants, they could be taught a rule or two that pertained to those situations and then be encouraged to recite those rules before writing words that contained the troublesome items. Or, if pupils are uncertain about the meanings or spellings of certain pairs of words such as *principle/principal* or *imminent/eminent*, they could be shown a rule or aid and asked to repeat it before using one word or the other.

Some researchers and teachers have taken this idea a bit further by providing youngsters with a number of steps to take before engaging in certain acts. For example, a child with a hot temper might be instructed to follow these steps when provoked:

1.   Think about what brought on the flare-up.

2.   Consider what he or she would ordinarily do (fight).

3.   Speculate on what would then happen (he or she might be sent to the principal's office).

4.   Think of alternatives (apologize, sit quietly, ignore the antagonist, overlook the offense, tell the teacher).

5.   Infer what the consequences of each of those alternatives would be.

6.   Select one of the options.

There are a few tactics in the self-management and classroom management section that rely on this approach.

Montague and Applegate studied the verbalizations of average and gifted students as well as those with learning disabilities and concluded that although the lower functioning students verbalized as much as the others, their verbalizations were qualitatively different, and generally not as helpful.

Research

Lovitt, T. C., & Curtiss, K. A. (1968). Effects of manipulating an antecedent event on mathematics response rate. *Journal of Applied Behavior Analysis, 1,* 329–333.

Montague, M., & Applegate, B. (1993). Middle school students' mathematical problem solving: An analysis of think-aloud protocols. *Learning Disability Quarterly, 16,* 19–32.

3 SLICE BACK

Background

The Slice Back technique is an extremely useful one for teachers to have on hand, and is certainly one of the simplest tactics to implement. The instructor does not have to purchase a new kit or package, study a complex manual on how to administer the technique, or bring in outside consultants, parents, or peer tutors. All the teacher has to do is make the child's assignment somewhat easier by slicing back a notch or two (backing up a few steps) in the program.

The idea behind the Slice Back technique is that it is better for a child to succeed rapidly on numerous components of a problem type than to struggle with the problem type as a whole day after day. A related thought behind this technique is that if a pupil is unable to master problems of a certain type, the teacher does not need to modify drastically the student's assignment in order to ensure progress; instead, the teacher can make a minor adjustment.

Who Can Benefit

The pupil in the example study was a 9-year-old boy in the fourth grade. In most respects he was quite average, but he did have a difficult time while working multiplication problems when it came to the skill of carrying numbers.

This technique is appropriate for a number of other pupils across a spectrum of circumstances, but it is a particularly wise selection for children who have often failed in arithmetic (and other subjects), and therefore need a number of consecutive successes to strengthen their self-esteem. These pupils require an added push and incentive to try, to achieve, and to do well in school.

Procedures

1. Assign problems of a certain class to the youngster. In the example study, the student was given multiplication problems in which three numerals were on top and one was on the bottom. Each problem required different degrees of carrying, for example:

$$\begin{array}{r} 313 \\ \times\ \ 3 \\ \hline \end{array} \qquad \begin{array}{r} 326 \\ \times\ \ 3 \\ \hline \end{array} \qquad \begin{array}{r} 265 \\ \times\ \ 3 \\ \hline \end{array}$$

2. Maintain data on the number of problems the student solves correctly, and record which specific types of problems are done correctly and incorrectly. If the child has difficulty with one or more of the component skills (i.e., carrying), then . . .

3. Slice back by assigning only problems of the type that do not require that skill. For example, $313 \times 3 = \square$ does not require carrying. Expect the student to work on only these problems until he or she masters them, then . . .

4. Assign problems of two types: One type in which the skill is not required, and one type in which the skill is required only minimally. For example, for the carrying skill, assign $313 \times 3 = \square$ and $326 \times 3 = \square$. Require the pupil to practice these items until the mastery goal is attained.

5. Schedule problems of all three types, and continue drilling until the target for each type is reached.

Monitor

Suggestions for monitoring this technique were just offered. Basically, the teacher should obtain data during a baseline period, prior to slicing back. Data on performance should continue to be kept during each phase of slicing, and the pupil should be held to each successive type until the predetermined aims are reached. Finally, when the pupil's performance reaches the aims, problems of the original type can be reintroduced.

Modifications/Considerations

The teacher can slice back as radically or finely as is necessary. In one instance, the research instructor totally misjudged a child's ability and assigned addition problems of the type $379 + 692 = \square$, which involve carrying in every column. After a day or so it was apparent that the child was totally frustrated by these problems. He not only had difficulty regrouping in any of the columns, but he also could not handle some of the basic facts. The teacher therefore altered the assignment significantly by giving him only the basic addition facts.

An example of the other extreme is a girl who was expected to solve problems of the type $126-95=\square$, in which borrowing is required in the hundreds column. Although she did quite well with these problems generally, she stumbled each time there was a zero in the tens column of the top number (e.g., $102-61=\square$). Not only did she err on that item, she made mistakes on the next two or three as well. That teacher simply eliminated all the troublesome problems from her assignment. He gave her that reduced load until she reached proficiency, then concentrated on *only* the zero-type problems. Finally, he scheduled some of the latter items in with the former set, and all was well.

A related way in which to step back from problems that are difficult for children is to teach doubles, neighbors, and two houses away. Doubles are problems such as $3+3$ and $4+4$. Neighbors are $3+4$ and $4+5$. Two houses away are $3+5$ and $4+6$. In a study by Eaton, Partlow, Hermann, and Lankenau (1984), pupils responded to a wide variety of addition problems during a baseline period. During successive phases, the students were instructed on doubles, neighbors, and two houses away. Finally, all the mixed problems were again presented. Data indicated that pupils' performances were greatly improved after they learned these combinations. Incidentally, the aims for these youngsters were 40 digits per minute.

Research

Caufield, H. (1969). Assignment turned in for a behavior management class. Experimental Education Unit, University of Washington, Seattle, WA.

Eaton, M., Partlow, C., Hermann, K., & Lankenau, A. (1984). Doubles, neighbors and two houses away: A quick trip to aim on addition facts. *Journal of Precision Teaching*, *5*(3), 49–53.

4 CUE, THEN FADE

Background

The idea supporting this tactic is that cues, hints, or signals are often necessary for some youngsters to calculate certain facts. Occasionally, some aspect of a problem must be highlighted to attract attention and to help students get off to a good start. Not only do cues direct concentration to specific problems, they also serve to distinguish one type of problem from another.

In music, cues of several types have always been a part of the process. The conductor's main task is to give cues—hand signals, glances, and other gestures. The cues prompt certain instruments when to come in; they signal musicians to play louder, softer, more or less sustained, and faster or slower in tempo; and finally, cues remind the players when to stop.

When I was part of an orchestra, we wrote cues on our music to warn us of particularly difficult spots; for example, we marked passages in which the fingerings were awkward, the intervals were unusual, the intonation was a concern, and so forth. In those tricky places we drew a pair of eyeglasses above the notes as cautions to "look out" and be careful.

Who Can Benefit

The pupil in the example study was a 7-year-old second grader. He was an average student in most respects but was having difficulty with the subtraction subskill of borrowing. His teacher, therefore, provided some cues.

Cues, signals, or hints can indeed be arranged for all types of performers in many areas. See the Modification section for a further discussion.

Procedures

1. Define a type of problem that the pupil should practice. In the research example, it was calculations of the type $23-5=\square$, where the pupil must borrow from the 10s to the 1s column.

2. Assign several of these problems to the youngster each day and keep data on his or her performance. In the research case, the boy first practiced these problems by himself for five minutes. This period was

followed by a one-minute timing, in which the child was given a work-sheet containing 72 problems of the type that needed work (more problems than he could compute in one minute).

3. Make certain that the pupil has difficulty with the skill being evaluated. Consider also whether or not the student has the prerequisite skills for this task. In the case of the example research, it was obvious that the student was unable to borrow, but the teacher was convinced that he had mastered the steps prerequisite to that type of problem. Many times his answer to the problem 23–5 was 22, a very common error.

4. Continue with the practices and timings, but explain to the student the nature of the error that he or she is making. In the borrowing example, the student was told that now he must borrow from the top, not the bottom. He had the basic idea—he was subtracting one number in the 1s column from another (but he had reversed them), and he was bringing down the number in the 10s column to its proper place in the answer. Explain to the pupil that you will write several cues on the troublesome problems of the practice worksheet.

5. The following is an example of cues written on problems that use borrowing.

$$\overline{2}\,\overline{3}$$
$$-\underline{5}$$

In this example, the student was told that the line over the number in the 1s column is a prompt to borrow if the top number is less than the bottom number. The line over the number in the 10s column means that that number is the "provider"; it should be crossed out and a number one less should be written beside it. Later in the calculation, that number will be brought down to the answer space.

6. Show the pupil how to use the cue a few times; say all the steps along the way as you model how to complete the problem. Require the student to go through this process a few times until you are certain he or she has the idea.

7. Tell the student that during the timings, he or she will be expected to use the cues; if the pupil wants to talk while doing the problem, communicate that this is acceptable.

8. For a few days, carefully monitor the pupil's method of solving the problems as well as the finished product. If the child continues to err occasionally, remind him or her to use the cues, or perhaps write in more or different ones. If the child's performance is perfect, drop all the reminders.

9. Fade out the cues. Either remove all hints at the same time or individually. By continuing to keep data on performance and to watch periodically while the child works, you will know if he or she still needs the cues, or portions of them, or if you can eliminate them entirely.

Monitor

Suggestions for monitoring this technique were offered in the Procedures section, but to summarize: Gather data during a baseline phase during which time no cues are used; continue obtaining data during a period when cues are available; and finally, after the performance aim has been reached in the second phase, acquire data during a period when the cues are not offered.

Modifications/Considerations

Dozens of cues in arithmetic can be employed. One cue is to emphasize the operation. For example, when children are required to solve mixed problems on a worksheet (e.g., some subtraction, some addition) they often get confused. In these instances, the – or the + can be highlighted.

Often youngsters have difficulty with place value in addition. With these students, dashes can be written below the answer space, as in the following example.

$$
\begin{array}{r}
5\,4\,6 \\
+\ \underline{6\,2\,1} \\
\text{– – – –}
\end{array}
$$

These dashes indicate that a number should be entered on each line.

Some youngsters also need place value indicators in multiplication, for example:

$$
\begin{array}{r}
4\,3 \\
\times\ \underline{1\,2} \\
\text{– –} \\
\text{– – –}
\end{array}
$$

This set of lines should help pupils who fail to slide over the product of the second computation (i.e., 1×43) to the 10s and 100s columns.

One teacher with whom I worked used cues to help a pupil work on horizontally printed problems of the type $23 + 5 = \square$. He had great difficulty with this particular problem; on occasion he would answer 55, or 73, and even 28. He knew the facts and was aware also that the answers should involve only two digits, but he had a place value problem. So, we drew in these cues:

$$23 + 5 = \square$$

That did the trick; he was able to solve the computations, and after a few days, we removed the cues.

Cawley (1984, p. 237) discusses a number of other cues that can assist children in solving mathematics problems: headings, margin notes, use of contrasting typefaces, or explicit statements saying that a particular fact or idea is important. Kennedy (1984, p. 256) has likewise suggested cues to aid children with learning disabilities in solving addition and subtraction problems.

Research

Cawley, J. F. (1984). *Developmental teaching of mathematics for learning disabled.* Austin, TX: Pro-Ed.

Kennedy, L. M. (1984). *Guiding children's learning of mathematics* (4th ed.). Belmont, CA: Wadsworth.

Smith, J. O., & Lovitt, T. C. (1973). Pinpointing a learning problem leads to remediation. *Teaching Exceptional Children, 5,* 181–182.

5 PROVIDING DEMONSTRATION AND A PERMANENT MODEL

Background

As indicated by the title, there are two components of this tactic. The first part of the approach, demonstration, indicates just that: The teacher shows and tells the pupil how to do something before asking him or her to do it. The permanent model feature is also self-explanatory. It simply means that the teacher writes the problem as he or she solved it on the pupil's page; the pupil then can refer to it from time to time.

Who Can Benefit

The pupils in the Smith and Lovitt (1975) study were intermediate age and were classified as learning disabled. They attended school at the Experimental Education Unit. This approach is best suited for youngsters who have reached proficiency in one or more problem types in a sequence and are just beginning a new, probably more difficult form of problem. The children described in this tactic are probably best categorized as in the acquisition stage. They are fresh, new, fumbling, perhaps even eager learners. Rivera and Smith (1987) reviewed a number of studies that relied on this intervention, and reported that the technique was effective with a wide range of youngsters in learning addition, subtraction, and multiplication.

Procedures

1. Select a problem type that is appropriate for the youngster; that is, choose one for which he or she has thoroughly mastered the preceding steps.

2. Present 25 or 30 examples of this problem type on a worksheet and tell the pupil that these are his or her new problems; the student will work on them until the aim of n per minute is reached.

3. Explain that the student will be expected every day to solve as many of the problems as possible in one minute.

4. Direct the pupil to watch and listen to you carefully as you work one of the problems on the worksheet.

5. Solve the problems that are the farthest to the left on the top row. As you do so, say each of the steps along the way. In the example problem $780 - 247 = \square$, say "Zero minus 7. I can't do that so I must borrow from the number to the left of the zero. When I do this, I cross out the 8 and mark in a 7, and then write a 1 by the 0. Next, I take 7 away from 10 and write the 3 in the answer." Continue this narration until the problem is finished. If the pupil has any questions along the way, you should answer them.

6. Leave that problem as you computed it, including all the crossouts and scribbles, and tell the pupil to refer to it while doing the assignment if he or she runs into a snag and cannot remember certain steps.

7. Eliminate the model from time to time as the pupil begins to show progress and does not need to look at it.

8. Remove, finally, the demonstration aspect of the tactic. If the student falters when you do this (this goes for removing the model as well), then reinstate this element.

Monitor

Initially, the teacher should simply keep track of the number of problems that are solved correctly and those that are answered incorrectly. Along with these data, the teacher should note the various types of errors that are made and use this information to modify the intervention. When the student answers nearly all the problems correctly, the measurement could be shifted to rate or frequency per minute. Relying on these data, the instructor could arrange different techniques to boost the pupil up to the desired rates. See Tactic 1 in this section which describes developing arithmetic goals.

Modifications/Considerations

As was already mentioned, the demonstration and model aspects of this tactic should be taken away when you believe they are no longer needed. The permanent model feature could be phased out gradually. For example, after an answer and the marks for deriving it are left on the pupil's paper for a time, they might be removed gradually rather than eliminating them completely, as shown in the following example:

$$
\begin{array}{r}
{\scriptstyle 2\,1} \\
\not{8}\not{7} \\
-\ 8 \\
\hline
29
\end{array}
$$

See Tactic 4 of this section which describes using cues and fading out their use.

Research

Rivera, D. M., & Smith, D. D. (1987). Influence of modeling on acquisition and generalization of computational skills: A summary of research findings from three sites. *Learning Disability Quarterly, 10,* 69–80.

Smith, D. D., & Lovitt, T. C. (1975). The use of modeling techniques to influence the acquisition of computational arithmetic skills in learning-disabled children. In E. Ramp and G. Semb (Eds.), *Behavior analysis: Areas of research and application* (pp. 283-308). Englewood Cliffs, NJ: Prentice-Hall.

5+9=14

6 ENCOURAGING CHILDREN TO CREATE MATHEMATICS PROBLEMS

Background

Traditionally, three general steps are followed in teaching mathematics:

1. Students are presented information regarding principles, relations, or equations.
2. A few examples are presented for pupils to work out along with the teacher.
3. A large number of problems are presented to students to complete individually.

The tactic explained here challenges the notion that rote practice in arithmetic computation should be the focus of instruction in mathematics for children. Using this tactic, students are encouraged to create problems, often from a model, rather than simply being asked to respond over and over again to a certain class of problems.

Who Can Benefit

The children in the cited research were in grades three through six. Some of them were normal-achieving youngsters, whereas others were pupils with learning disabilities. These techniques would be particularly helpful for students with mild disabilities, because chances are great that many of them have been required to carry out inordinate amounts of rote assignments, ones that have exacerbated the fact that many of them are passive learners.

Procedures

1. Select a type of problem that the youngsters are familiar with and can generally solve without much difficulty (e.g., $6 + 2 = \square$).
2. Place two sample problems of that type on a sheet of paper.

3.   Model the process for solving the problems to make certain that the students know how to do them.

4.   Tell the students to write as many problems of that type as they can in one minute. Emphasize the fact that you want them to come up with different problems of that type, not simply to repeat problems that were given as samples or to repeat others that they came up with.

5.   Ask them to solve the problems they wrote.

6.   As a group, go over the problems. At this time the children should not only state the correct answers for the problems, but also should discuss and identify the characteristics that are shared by the problems.

Monitor

Data of three types should be kept as the pupils create problems:

1.   number of items created
2.   percentage or rate per minute of items correct among those created
3.   number of items repeated

The idea is to increase the number of items created and the percentage (or rate) of items answered correctly, and to decrease the number of items repeated.

Modifications/Considerations

A number of modifications are possible with this tactic:

- Instead of requesting pupils to create problems like the ones in the sample, they could be asked to come up with as many problems as they can that would result in the same answer. For example, if the sample problem was $6+2=\square$, some of the other problems might be $10-2=\square$, $2\times 4=\square$, or $1+3+4=\square$. Moreover, students could be encouraged to create problems from as wide a variety of processes and types as they could.

- Instead of having each youngster solve his or her own created problems, papers could be exchanged and pupils could answer the problems composed by others.

- In an effort to further teach *productive thinking*, problems such as those shown in Figure 6.1 could be given. In the first column, four sample tasks are offered to teach *convergent thinking*. In the second column, four sample tasks are explained for developing *divergent thinking*, and in the third column, four tasks are offered for instructing *evaluative thinking*. Note in this last column that when youngsters are asked to come up with a "bet-

Convergent Thinking

Task 1
See the representation of three:

Find another in the following:

Task 2
See this representation of three:

2 + 1

Find another in the following:

| 1 + 2 | 2 + 3 | 2 + 0 |

Task 3
Read the problem and give the answer.

A girl has 3 grapes.
The girl bought 2 more grapes.
How many grapes does the girl have now?

Task 4
Read the problem and give the answer.

A girl has 3 grapes.
The girl sold 2 grapes.
How many grapes does the girl have now?

Divergent Thinking

Task 5
See this representation of three:

Take these materials and make as many different representations of three as you can.

Task 6
See this representation of three:

2 + 1

Use this set of numbers and make as many representations of three as you can.

2, 0, 1, 6

Task 7
Read the problem.
Complete the task as directed.

A girl has 3 grapes.
The girl __ 2 grapes.
The girl now has 5 grapes.
Write in as many words as you can to make the outcome true.

Task 8
Read the problem.
Complete the task as directed.

A girl has 3 grapes.
The girl has __ 2 grapes.
The girl now has 1 grape.
Write in as many words as you can to make the outcome true.

Evaluative Thinking

Task 9
See this representation of three:

Which of these is a better representation of three?

Task 10
See this representation of three:

2 + 1

Which of these is a better representation of three?

| III | 1 + 2 | 15 − 12 |

Task 11
Read the problem.
Complete the task as directed.
The girl had 3 fruits.
She bought 2 pears
                  peas
                  potatoes
She now has 5 fruits.
Mark the word that shows the better choice and that also makes the outcome true.

Task 12
Read the problem and complete the task as directed.
A girl has 3 fruits.
She sold 2 apples
                  pears
                  peas
                  potatoes
She now has 1 fruit.
Mark the word that shows the better choice and that also makes the outcome true.

FIGURE 6.1 Illustrations of Productive Thinking Activities

SOURCE: From Figure 1 of "Challenging the Routines and Passivity that Characterize Arithmetic Instruction for Children with Mild Handicaps" by R. S. Parmar and J. F. Cawley, 1991, *Remedial and Special Education, 12*(5), p. 25. Copyright 1991 by PRO-ED, Inc. Reprinted by permission.

ter representation" or a "better choice," there is not necessarily a "correct" answer. In these cases youngsters would be asked to explain their choices for whichever responses they selected.

Research

Parmar, R. S., & Cawley, J. F. (1991). Challenging the routines and passivity that characterize arithmetic instruction for children with mild handicaps. *Remedial and Special Education, 12*(5), 23–32, 43.

7 ARRANGING RECIPROCAL PEER TUTORING AND GROUP CONTINGENCIES

Background

The idea behind this tactic is that students' performances in arithmetic would improve if students were placed in cooperative learning groups in which each youngster has an assigned task, and in which a contingency is arranged for the improved performance of the group.

Who Can Benefit

The target students in the example research were low-achieving fifth graders. They represented mixed ethnic groups of boys and girls. There were two criteria for their selection: (1) teacher report card evaluations of unsatisfactory performance in arithmetic and (2) performance within the lower quartile on arithmetic drills during the baseline phase of the study.

Procedures

1. Place youngsters in groups of four. In doing so, the teacher should create groups that are as mixed as possible in terms of gender, race, and temperament. Whereas all the youngsters in the cited research were characterized as low achievers, other cooperative learning studies have sought to mix groups in terms of achievement level as well.

2. Inform students that each member of a group will be assigned a role, and explain the duties of each role:
   - *Coach.* Informs the group of their goal for the day, reminds the members of their strategies for increasing their arithmetic performance, and tells members that if they apply their strategies they will WIN (that is, receive the reward).
   - *Scorekeeper.* Counts the number of arithmetic problems completed correctly by each member and writes this number on each individual's arithmetic sheet.

- *Referee.* Counts independently the number of correctly completed arithmetic problems and records the number by each individual's name on the team scorecard.
- *Manager.* Determines the team's total score and compares it with the team's goal for the day. If met, the manager declares that the team gets a WIN.

3. Train the groups to carry out the various roles. Training should include the following: (a) model and instruct the tasks for all four roles, (b) set up times for the members to practice the tasks, and (c) assess their competency to carry out the roles.

4. Ask the groups to carry out the following tasks: (a) select a team name, (b) devise a "pep talk" for the coach to deliver, and (c) select backup reinforcers from a reinforcement menu.

5. At the beginning of the week, select the roles for each member.

6. Select a goal for the number of arithmetic problems each team needs to win. (The goal choices should represent a narrow range of numbers that is close to the total of individual goals for the group.)

7. Hand out the arithmetic sheets. In the example study the sheets were made up of randomly determined facts. (See the Modifications/Considerations section.)

8. Tell the students to complete as many of the problems as they can in a five-minute period. Tell them to work through the problems from left to right on the top row, then to answer those on the second row, and so forth. Tell them to make some response to every problem along the way, and not to skip any.

9. Following the timing, check the pupils' problems and give the papers to the scorekeepers and referees of each group. They will count the number of correct answers.

10. Inform the groups that after four WINS, the group will receive a group-determined reinforcer (e.g., tokens to play a video game).

Monitor

In the cited study the researchers kept data on the number of correct problems per timing period (which was seven minutes). To establish a sensitive measure of *both* rates of responding, it is more advisable to keep data in terms of correct and incorrect problems per minute. A percentage of accurate responses can then be determined by adding the correct and incorrect rates, then dividing by the correct rate. It is also advisable not only to chart these data, but also to indicate on the individual charts the aims for those rates.

Modifications/Considerations

As the teacher corrects the papers he or she should keep notes regarding the types of problems the youngsters are having difficulty with. As soon as possible—that day or certainly the next day before another timing—the teacher should give the students feedback regarding those mistakes and other matters. Some of the feedback could be offered to the entire class, whereas other suggestions could be given to certain groups or individuals.

As for the type of problems that are given the children, many options are available. If the teacher decides to concentrate on one problem type at a time, a few odd or different problems should be included occasionally, just to keep the children alert.

The teacher probably should keep the youngsters on one problem type until aims are reached. For information on aims, see Tactic 1 in this section. The teacher may want to consider, as is discussed in Tactic 6 of this section, having youngsters spend more time creating problems and less time simply going over the same type of problem. Certainly, there should be some balance between developing proficiency and productive thinking.

Research

Pigott, H. E., Fantuzzo, J. W., & Clement, P. W. (1986). The effects of reciprocal peer tutoring and group contingencies on the academic performance of elementary school children. *Journal of Applied Behavior Analysis, 19*(1), 93–98.

8 ARRANGING ANALYTICAL AND ORGANIZATIONAL PROCEDURES

Background

The standards in mathematics as outlined by the National Council of Teachers of Mathematics underscore the primacy of problem solving and the appropriateness of developing problem-solving skills through inquiry-based techniques. According to the author of the research cited here, *heuristic strategies* are analytical and organizational procedures that precede the calculation phase of problem solving. They are designed to assist learners in conceptualizing problems and organizing their responses to problems. Heuristic procedures are intended to impress upon learners that there are alternative solutions to problems.

Who Can Benefit

The heuristic strategies explained here have a high probability of being effective with students who have learning disabilities. These strategies would assist students in differentiating key information from that which is less important in mathematics problems; forming alternative representations for the information given in verbal problems; designating alternative approaches for solving the problems; and comparing target problems with analogous ones.

Procedures

Following is a brief explanation of seven heuristic strategies:

1. *Analogy.*   Ask students to write problems similar to the recipe-like ones they see in their math books: *Hiram has 7 apples. He gave 5 apples to Dorothy. How many apples does Hiram have left?* Students could sit in a circle and take turns sharing the problems they come up with. As they do so, they can discuss the predictable organizational patterns of the problems they made up.

2. *Annotating.* Require students to underline the verbs found in the problem directions before attempting to solve the problem. Another form of annotation is to ask pupils to bracket the numerical information they need to solve the problem. A third way to annotate problems is to direct students to write an explanation of how they would go about solving a problem.

3. *Detail analysis.* Ask students, as they read problems, to highlight important information with red, and unimportant information with green. Information about which they are uncertain is highlighted in orange.

4. *Deleted details.* Delete some information from problems; some of this deleted information should be necessary for obtaining the solution, whereas other deleted information should be superfluous. The following problem is an example of the latter: *After returning from _____ , a father gave 7 marbles to each of his 7 daughters. How many marbles did the 7 daughters have in total?*

5. *Detail sorting.* Distribute copies of problems to the students. Provide some necessary and unnecessary details within each problem. Students must decide which details are needed in the algorithm to solve it. For example: *A 9-year-old boy and a 7-year-old girl each bought 3 granola bars. How many granola bars did they have altogether?* $3 + ? = \square$.

6. *Symbolized operations.* Give the students worksheets containing problems that include multiple operations. Ask students to mark symbols associated with the process needed to solve the problem (e.g., marking a "plus" sign to denote addition). For example: *Juan bought a lamp on sale for $13.50. The lamp sold originally for $15.50. How much did Juan save?* (−)

7. *Formula designation.* Ask students to write in the margin the formula needed to solve each problem given on a worksheet. For example: *Enzio has 5 pals who work with him. They can clean a yard in 20 hours. If Enzio wishes to reduce the cleaning time to 8 hours, how many helpers does he need?* In the margin, students might write $P \times H = TWE$ (where P is the number of persons required to complete the task; H is the number of hours required to complete the task; and TWE is the total work effort required), $6 \times 20 = 120$, or restate it as $? \times 8 = 120$.

Monitor

Pupils' performance should be monitored in two ways with respect to these strategies. First, data should be kept on the extent to which students can, when given a number of different verbal problems, come up with plausible strategies for solving the problems. Second, data should be gathered on students' ability to actually solve a variety of verbal problems while using any of the strategies they so desire.

Modifications/Considerations

The heuristic strategies can be combined in ways that complement and reinforce one another. Following are two examples:

- *Analyze-estimate-solve.* Children analyze the relevant details needed to solve a problem. They then mark with a highlighter the details they believe are relevant. Finally, they estimate the answer and then solve the problem.
- *Analyze-sort-solve.* Pupils analyze the details required to solve a problem, use highlighters to indicate relevant details, then sort the highlighted data into a computational format that may be partially completed.

Research

Giordano, G. (1992). Heuristic strategies: An aid for solving verbal mathematical problems. *Intervention in School and Clinic, 28*(2), 88–96.

5·9-14

9 USING A MNEMONIC STRATEGY FOR SOLVING WORD PROBLEMS

Background

The RIDGES technique is a simple mnemonic strategy that facilitates the understanding and organization of word problems. As in similar learning strategies, an acronym was developed for this method to help students remember the key steps of the technique.

Who Can Benefit

This tactic could benefit primary and intermediate students who experience difficulty with word problems containing distracters, and that require organization of several steps. It should be of particular assistance to at-risk and remedial students, for they are characteristically lacking in the abilities needed to deal with story problems.

Procedures

Following is the six-step process:

- *Step 1. Read the problem for understanding.* The student should be aware that re-reading may be necessary to grasp the details of the problem.
- *Step 2. I know statement.* Student lists all the information given in the problem.
- *Step 3. Draw a picture.* The student should include all the information from Step 2 in a drawing, but it need not be elaborate. This step is particularly beneficial for students who have difficulty processing abstract meaning.
- *Step 4. Goal statement declared in writing.* The student writes, "I want to know . . ." This statement may give the student a clue for the next step.

- *Step 5. Equation development.* The student writes an equation that allows him or her to solve the problem.
- *Step 6. Solve the equation.* The student "plugs in" the necessary information to reach the goal and solve the problem.

Monitor

As is the case with other learning strategies, the teacher may want to evaluate students' grasp of the process (how well they learned the strategy) and determine the effects of that learning on a product (in this instance, becoming more proficient in solving word problems). To evaluate students' initial understanding, students could be required to recite occasionally the steps of the strategy and explain what those steps mean. As for the effects of learning the strategy, the teacher might set up a two-phase experiment. During phase one, word problems would be assigned prior to instructing the strategy, and during the next phase, the RIDGES technique would be used. Data from the two phases could then be compared.

Modifications/Considerations

During the early stage of the learning strategy, the teacher should occasionally interview students to ensure that the steps are understood. Later, when students have become proficient in using this strategy to solve problems, they should be encouraged to modify it to meet their individual needs.

Initially, the teacher should introduce rather simple word problems, to make certain that students correctly apply the strategy and accurately solve the problems. Later, as students become more comfortable with the technique and with calculating problems, more complex items should be assigned. To make the problems more difficult, require students to carry out two or more calculations, or add redundant figures, words, or phrases to the problems.

As a next step toward instructing students not only to solve word problems but also to understand the development and importance of them, ask students to construct their own word problems. Naturally, these problems should be based on actual circumstances and situations that students encounter.

Research

Snyder, K. (1987). RIDGES: A problem-solving math strategy. *Academic Therapy, 23*(2), 261–263.

10 USING AUTHENTIC LEARNING AS AN APPROACH TO STORY PROBLEMS

Background

According to the authors of the cited research, word problems in basal text-books traditionally do not reflect actual life for at least three reasons. First, they describe situations in a *textual* rather than a *contextual* format. Students interpret the problems from words or graphics that outline a static environment, whereas real-life problems occur in dynamic environments. Second, ordinary word problems are made even more artificial when key words such as *all together* are used. In real life, these words do not accompany the problems. Third, standard story problems have only one correct answer and take only a few seconds or minutes to solve. By contrast, there are often several correct or at least plausible answers to most real-life problems, and many of them take hours to answer. Life problems, according to the authors, are complex and require multiple tasks.

Who Will Benefit

The rationale behind the approach explained here, authentic learning, would be an appropriate one to guide instruction and assessment for children and youth of all ages. The specific method of arranging authentic environments—videodiscs—would be a suitable way in which to deliver instruction not only in math, but also in most other subjects, to a wide range of students.

Procedures

The authors used materials from *The Adventures of Jasper Woodbury* series, which is a set of videodiscs that feature a hypercard-based software for Macintosh computers.

Using this series, students and teachers are free to explore any one of thousands of frames on the videodisc instantly. They can view scenes in any order, view details frame-by-frame, and skip sections of the narration.

One way in which to present such material to children is to organize cooperative groups. Following are the procedures for working with such groups:

1. The teacher asks students to view the *anchor* (i.e., the simulation of a real-life problem) without interruption.

2. During the second viewing, students record in their notebooks information from scenes that depict pertinent information for solving the problem.

3. Students, in small groups, compare notes, discuss possible solutions, and search the episode for more detail.

4. The teacher replays segments of the episode immediately by entering frame numbers into a remote video controller.

Monitor

The most obvious way in which to assess performance on word problems is to check students' "answers" against those of a standard. Beyond that, students could be asked to write down the steps they followed to solve the problems and to explain, if possible, why they used those steps. The latter procedure was used by the authors of the cited research.

Modifications/Considerations

In the program described by the cited authors, sixth-grade students were asked to create their own complex mathematics problems. From these problems, the teachers selected a few that were then videotaped and played later on videodiscs.

As most teachers know, at about the third-grade level when students are asked to create their own "story problems," the results often come as a shock to both the students and their teacher. Many of the students are unable to create such problems. Conceivably, if they had been allowed to work on complex, real-life problems early on, they would not have such difficulty with such an assignment.

A few years ago a teacher friend of mine in Seattle, Sally Horton, asked several of her acquaintances to write word problems that were natural to their work or life. Those problems were indeed complex, and they contained considerable narration in an attempt to fully explain the situation. Quite naturally, there was a fair amount of repeated and redundant information in the problems. For many of the situations, there was more than one "correct" answer. Sally edited some of those problems so that they were more suitable for her sixth graders, and then asked the students to solve them. Moreover, she asked her students to develop similar types of problems based on their own actual experiences.

Research

Bottge, R. A., & Hasselbring, T. S. (1993). Taking word problems off the page. *Educational Leadership, 50*(7), 36–38.

MANAGEMENT

Fifteen tactics make up this section, and some of these tactics came from the first edition. As in the other parts of this book, I have added new tactics to this section and have provided new references for the "old" tactics. The first tactic explains a basic set of procedures that teachers can follow to establish order in their classrooms. The next six tactics are discussions of well-documented approaches for quelling disruptive behaviors: the differential reinforcement approach, or giving something if the rate of student response is low; two overcorrection approaches (positive practice and restitution); two time-out approaches; and the response cost approach, in which fines are used. For the eighth tactic, steps are explained for setting up contingency contracts with children. Tactics 9, 10, and 11 rely on principles of group contingencies; that is, the behaviors of several individuals are taken into account when granting consequences to either individuals or groups. The next two tactics also pertain to groups of children. In the first, a peer-management procedure is detailed, and in the other, there is a discussion of ways to solve interpersonal problems. The fourteenth tactic offers general suggestions for teachers of children with behavior disorders. An intervention ladder is presented in the last tactic. The idea here is to select a method for dealing with behavior problems that is least expensive and most natural.

1 RULES, PRAISE, AND IGNORING

Background

The fundamental idea of this tactic is that when teachers consistently use rules, provide praise for appropriate behaviors, and ignore unacceptable actions, the general behavior of their classes will improve. Another premise behind this tactic is that teachers must change certain behaviors of their own in an effort to alter the actions of their pupils.

It should be noted that teachers often inappropriately use rules, praise, and ignoring. In the case of rules, there are often too many, they are not understood by the children, and they are not consistently enforced. When it comes to delivering praise, many teachers believe they should not give much, maintaining that children should want to do the right thing without needing to be coaxed. Other teachers, when they do praise children, either dole it out at the wrong times or for the wrong reasons. Finally, in reference to ignoring, it is extremely difficult for most teachers to disregard inappropriate behaviors. Customarily, they scold or warn children when misbehavior occurs rather than ignoring it.

Who Can Benefit

In the original study by Madsen, Becker, and Thomas (1968) that demonstrated the effects of these procedures, two classrooms were involved: a second-grade class and a kindergarten class. Both were of average size, and both contained the usual number of unruly citizens in each group who displayed the ordinary kinds of inappropriate behaviors. Some talked out of turn too much, roamed about the classroom at inappropriate times, and tore up many of their papers. Others refused to pay attention, did not begin or finish their work, and handed in messy work. A few fought, swore, stole, and destroyed.

Procedures

In order to get on with the business of teaching, teachers must sometimes change their own behaviors to effectively quell the general inappropriate actions in their classrooms. They must establish a few rules, praise appropriate behaviors, and ignore unacceptable ones. Furthermore, they must do all of these consistently.

1. Establish a few rules and be certain that the children understand them. Use the following guidelines to develop the regulations:
   - Make them short and to the point so they can be memorized easily.
   - Set only five or six.
   - Phrase the rules positively whenever possible (e.g., "Sit quietly while working.").
   - Remind the children throughout the day about the rules.
   - Describe the consequences (i.e., "If you do this, then _____ will happen.").

2. Praise children when they behave appropriately. Some instances of acceptable behavior are answering questions correctly, raising hands to be recognized, working steadily on assignments, waiting one's turn, or submitting neat and accurate papers. The following are some techniques for granting praise:
   - Compliment a child's acceptable behavior immediately following its performance.
   - Deliver a variety of praise statements; be as natural as possible.
   - Praise particularly those students who have had the most difficulty behaving appropriately.
   - Use smiles and other nonverbal means of reinforcement *while* a pupil is performing. Do not interrupt the child's flow of production, however.

3. Ignore inappropriate behaviors such as the following: getting out of the chair without permission, tapping a pencil or other object, pushing a desk, talking to others, turning around, ignoring instructions. Of course, there are dozens of other, more powerful techniques for dealing with undesirable actions. Two are noted:
   - Use a time-out or punishment tactic for pupils who harm others. Do not ignore these behaviors.
   - Praise students who disregard the inappropriate behaviors of their chums.

Monitor

Since the ideas suggested here pertain to all the children in a class rather than to only a few individuals, data with respect to its effectiveness could also be acquired in terms of the group. The data gathered could refer either to disruptions or to more positive behaviors. As with several other tactics in this section, data might be gathered over two or three phases: baseline, intervention, and maintenance. While gathering the data and analyzing it, the teacher may find that after a while, there are only a few disruptions in the class and they are caused by one or two pupils. In such a case, the teacher might find it more profitable to select one of the tactics that relates only to individuals and put it in place.

Modifications/Considerations

In addition to these three general management techniques, teachers could employ other techniques that might contribute to the tranquillity of their situations. Some other basic approaches that teachers have found useful are allowing children to participate in the administration of the classroom as much as possible; making sure youngsters are appropriately placed in the different levels of their academic subjects; showing and telling students what they need to achieve in various activities and then keeping data on their progress; showing students the data kept on their performance; and allowing *them* to maintain their own records whenever possible. Many of these tactics are discussed in other sections of this book.

Along with putting in place the basic techniques of establishing rules, providing praise, and ignoring misbehavior, teachers should discover and develop characteristics of effective schools that are linked with productive classrooms. For example, the following are six activities for teachers to consider:

1. Review and check the previous day's work and reteach if necessary.
2. Present new content and skills.
3. Initiate student practice and check for understanding.
4. Offer feedback and corrections and reteach if necessary.
5. Schedule independent practice for students.
6. Schedule weekly and monthly reviews.

Research

Bickel, W. E., & Bickel, D. D. (1986). Effective schools, classrooms, and instruction: Implications for special education. *Exceptional Children, 52*(6), 489–500.

Madsen, C. H., Jr., Becker, W. C., & Thomas, D. R. (1968). Rules, praise, and ignoring: Elements of elementary classroom control. *Journal of Applied Behavior Analysis, 1,* 139–150.

2 GIVE SOMETHING IF THE RATE OF RESPONDING IS LOW

Background

The theory behind this tactic is that in some instances, to decrease the frequency of a behavior it may be more effective to grant something positive than to give something that is aversive or to take away an event that is positive. Often the classroom manager does not want to eliminate *totally* the frequency of a particular behavior, but merely wants to reduce its rate to a tolerable level.

This tactic, derived from the notion of *differential reinforcement of low rates of responding* (DRL), can be effective when used with either groups of youngsters or individuals. It is a particularly useful technique for a teacher or other manager to have in his or her repertoire, since it provides another way to deal with an inappropriate behavior—by using positive reinforcement to decrease a negative behavior. Few self-appointed school critics would be alarmed by such an approach.

Who Can Benefit

In the sample study, the DRL tactic was arranged for a class of 15 high-school girls enrolled in an office procedures class. As will be indicated later, this tactic can be scheduled not only with individuals and groups, but also for most any type or age of student, and in connection with a wide variety of behaviors.

Procedures

Included here are steps for carrying out the technique that were outlined in the sample study.

1. Define the target behavior. In the case of the students in the study, the behavior of concern was "staying on topic." The teacher became most annoyed when the class's discussions strayed from the scheduled themes. She was particularly vexed that the subject changes were generally about social topics that had absolutely nothing to do with the topic of their class—managing an office.

2. Outline the reward that will be given if the target behavior is reduced. In the study, the teacher told the girls that they would have a free day to talk, Friday, if in the preceding four days they deviated from the day's topic no more than five times per day.

3. Count the number of times the target behavior occurs during the established time period. In the research study, the teacher kept track of the subject changes throughout the 50-minute office procedures class.

4. Announce to the class, after the period in which the target behavior was to be reduced has elapsed, whether or not they achieved their goal. In the study, following the Thursday session, the students were told whether or not they earned the free time to talk on Friday. Do not tell them at other times, however.

5. Decrease gradually the number of times you will permit the target behavior to occur. For example, after the students in the study complied for two weeks with the goal of five or fewer disruptions, the requirement was lowered. First the teacher set it at four, then three, then two, then one and zero. Run each of these stages for at least two weeks.

Monitor

Suggestions for monitoring were indicated earlier. To summarize, the teacher should count the number of times the target behavior occurs and chart that number. As with other tactics in this book, the teacher may see fit to turn over the data counting and recording to a pupil, depending on the teacher's goals for the class or for certain individuals.

Modifications/Considerations

There are numerous modifications that are possible with this tactic. In the research study, the authors also used this tactic with an 11-year-old retarded boy to reduce his outbursts. Following a baseline study that revealed his initial frequency of talking out, the teacher established a program whereby he could earn five extra minutes of play time if he talked out fewer than three times during a 50-minute period.

In another experiment, this time with 10 retarded pupils, these authors set up a situation in which each member of the group received two pieces of candy at the end of the day if their combined number of talk outs was less than 6 during a 50-minute period.

A variant of differential reinforcement has been referred to as selective reinforcement (Jenson, Sloane, & Young, 1988). As an example, it might be that Sam never reads from his book. Instead of reading he often sleeps in class, stares at the clock, or simply flips the pages of a book. Using selective reinforcement, the teacher would select the behavior that is closest to what is ultimately desired, reading, and temporarily reinforce it. In Sam's case, flipping through his book is closer to working than are his other responses, so it is selectively reinforced, and other behaviors are ignored. When the selected behavior has been sufficiently developed, the teacher shifts targets and works on something even more directly related to actual reading.

Research

Dietz, S. M., & Repp, A. C. (1973). Decreasing classroom misbehavior through the use of DRL schedules of reinforcement. *Journal of Applied Behavior Analysis, 6,* 457–463.

Jenson, W. R., Sloane, H. N., & Young, K. R. (1988). *Applied behavior analysis in education: A structured teaching approach.* Englewood Cliffs, NJ: Prentice-Hall.

3 OVERCORRECTION: POSITIVE PRACTICE

Background

The behavior therapist's dream is to identify a tactic that reduces or eliminates behaviors and that has the following three characteristics: it produces strong, immediate, and lasting changes; it is applicable across clients and to different inappropriate behaviors; and it is convenient and acceptable to the person carrying out the therapy. Researchers investigating the effects of overcorrection believe that this technique comes close to filling the bill.

Additional advantages are attributed to overcorrection: it usually is effective in a short time; it can be administered easily by a number of individuals (paraprofessionals as well as professionals); and it can be maintained for long periods by simply warning the subject that it might be used again.

Although the general notions of overcorrection are older than our grandparents (and as simple and logical as many other well-tried ideas), we must credit a few researchers who work in institutions for individuals with mental retardation for developing the rationale and procedures for the reliable use of overcorrection. These researchers have successfully arranged overcorrection techniques of various forms to alter a number of inappropriate behaviors. Because the general methods of overcorrection have been refined, they can now be adapted to most settings, including homes, schools, and diagnostic centers.

According to researchers, there are two types of overcorrection: positive practice and restitution. The form described here is the positive practice variety.

Who Can Benefit

One of the pupils in this sample study was a 5-year-old boy enrolled in a day-care treatment program of a university hospital. He was diagnosed as schizophrenic and hyperactive, and was deficient in motor, verbal, and self-help skills. Furthermore, he engaged in repetitive vocal and motor behaviors that interfered with more appropriate behaviors.

Procedures

1. Define the target behaviors. For the child in the study there were two: inappropriate hand and foot movements.

   The hand movements included frequent contact with his nose, mouth, or eyes; putting his hands inside his pants; repetitively moving his hands back and forth or up and down in the air; tossing objects; clapping his hands; rubbing or scratching his face; and rubbing his index finger and thumb together in a circular motion.

   The inappropriate foot movements included repetitive jumping, hopping, or gliding, and putting his feet above his body when lying with his stomach flat on floor.

2. Remind the child what he or she is doing (e.g., "You're rubbing your face.").

3. Begin training for 2½ minutes. During that time, provide instructions on the alternate behaviors the child is to perform. In the example study, to diminish the inappropriate hand movements, the boy was instructed to move his hands in one of five positions:

   a. above his head

   b. straight out in front

   c. put together

   d. placed at his side

   e. behind his back

   Each behavior (in this case, each position) should be requested two times during the treatment and should be held for 15 seconds. If the child does not follow one of the commands within 2 seconds, physically prompt him or her.

   In the research study, the procedures followed for inappropriate foot movements were much the same as those for the hand activities: After each inappropriate foot movement, the child was seated in a chair, then instructed to lift his feet, straighten his legs parallel to the floor, hold them for 5 seconds, and then return his feet to the floor for 5 seconds. If he did not comply, physical prompts were given. This overcorrection procedure lasted for 2 minutes.

Monitor

During two phases of a project, a baseline and the intervention, keep data on the number of times the pupil engages in the target behavior. In order to determine the lasting effects of the positive practice routine, data could be kept during a third period in which the technique is no longer used. That phase should not begin, however, until the desired frequency of the target behavior had occurred for a few days.

Modifications/Considerations

The positive practice form of overcorrection is suitable for other behaviors, some of which are more likely to occur in schools. One such behavior is that old favorite, talking out of turn. The teacher could (time permitting) carry out a brief training program following each talk out. He or she might, for example, ask the child to name several objects or people around the room (perhaps give their phone numbers or addresses), then answer a few questions, then give a brief speech on some topic.

Another instance in which positive practice could be arranged is for cases of poor sportsmanship. For those boys or girls who have a fit when they strike out, miss a basket, or miss the baseline on a volley, a program could be set up whereby they instead rolled their eyes, muttered to themselves, smiled, went on with the game, praised themselves when they next "did it right," and then complimented their opponent when they executed the behavior properly.

Smith (1989) offers other examples of positive practice:

- To counteract spelling mistakes, have students look up misspelled words in the dictionary.
- To end noisy transition periods, have students spend recess periods practicing quiet transitions.
- To curtail talking out of turn, have students hold a hand in the air for a couple of minutes.

Research

Epstein, L. H., Doke, L. A., Sajwaj, T. E., Sorrell, S., & Rimmer, B. (1974). Generality and side effects of overcorrection. *Journal of Applied Behavior Analysis, 7,* 385–390.

Smith, D. D. (1989). *Teaching students with learning and behavior problems* (2nd ed.). Englewood Cliffs, NJ: Prentice-Hall.

4 OVERCORRECTION: RESTITUTION

Background

Considerable background on overcorrection procedures was included in the preceding tactic. Foxx and Azrin (1973) provide further detail on the rationale of overcorrection by explaining the following features:

1. Because the manager immediately interrupts each instance of unacceptable activity, the duration of reinforcement is brief.

2. As the manager guides the pupil through a brief period of overcorrection, further practice of the inappropriate behavior is prevented.

3. Annoying consequences for the inappropriate behavior result from the overcorrection procedures.

4. Either alternate behaviors are learned by these procedures or the pupil discovers that the old behavior is appropriate in different contexts.

5. The pupil can obtain reinforcement by engaging in the old behavior in a different, more accepted way.

6. If the pupil is pleased and satisfied by his or her new ability to control the old behavior, the pupil may praise himself or herself for doing it.

7. If the student slips back into the old pattern, a brief signal from the teacher is often enough to alter the behavior.

This tactic illustrates the restitution form of overcorrection. When this technique is arranged, the disrupter must correct the consequences of his or her behavior by restoring the disturbed situation to a state vastly improved from that which existed before the disruption. For example, an individual who overturned a table would be required both to restore it to its correct position and to dust and wax it.

Who Can Benefit

One of the pupils in the example study was an 8-year-old girl with severe retardation who was enrolled in a day-care program. She was constantly picking up items and putting them in her mouth or touching them to her mouth. If the object was too heavy to lift, she would go to it and mouth it with her lips and tongue.

Since mouthing of objects or parts of the body can transmit harmful microorganisms, the restitutional overcorrection technique in this case sought to eliminate the possibility of infection.

Procedures

For the case described in the previous section, the following steps were involved in the overcorrection.

1. The child was given a warning when she mouthed something: "No, don't put —— in your mouth."

2. After mouthing something, she was required to brush her gums and teeth with a toothbrush that had been dipped in a mouthwash solution.

3. The child was also required to wipe her lips with a washcloth that had been dampened with mouthwash.

4. Periodically, the child was encouraged to rinse her mouth with the mouthwash and then spit the solution into a cup.

Monitor

A rather ordinary way in which to evaluate the effects of a restitution technique would be to schedule a two-phase project. During the first, or baseline, phase, the restitution tactic would not be scheduled. During the second phase, the technique would be arranged. Data on the target behavior(s) should be taken and charted during both phases. Along with these simple data, information could be gathered on the activities in which the student was engaged that made life better for all those around him or her.

Modifications/Considerations

There are a number of ways a teacher could use the restitution tactic to reduce the inappropriate behaviors of elementary- and secondary-age students. For example, in the case of a youngster who habitually slams doors, following each incident the pupil could be required to go out, wait for a brief period, knock on the door or ring the doorbell to announce his or her presence, wait for the door to be opened, come in, shut the door quietly, greet the person at the door, walk quietly to his or her place in the room, take a seat, and then enter into a conversation.

The restitution tactic is particularly appropriate for all types of vandalism. If a pupil marks on a desk, wall, or floor, he or she could be required to purchase all the necessary materials for the repair work, and then mend not only the damage done but also the wear and tear caused by others.

This tactic could also be scheduled for errors that a student makes in arithmetic, reading, writing, spelling, or music. For example, if a child is learning to play the piano and plays a wrong note, he or she could be asked to return to the beginning of the phrase and redo the entire passage. (Indeed, this is a common way to practice.)

Smith and Rivera (1993) provide a number of other examples in which restitutional overcorrection has been used:

- When a librarian noticed that a book being returned to the library was defaced with pencil marks, he had the responsible student erase all of the pencil marks in that book, and as well as the marks in all the books on the first two shelves.

- The lunch monitor saw several students littering the remains of their lunches on the floor in the cafeteria. During the recess period, she had them pick up <u>all</u> the litter in the cafeteria as well as clean the tables.

Research

Foxx, R. M., & Azrin, N. H. (1973). The elimination of autistic self-stimulatory behavior by overcorrection. *Journal of Applied Behavior Analysis, 6,* 1–14.

Smith, D. D., & Rivera, D. M. (1993). *Effective discipline* (2nd ed.). Austin, TX: Pro-Ed.

5 THE TIME-OUT RIBBON

Background

In recent years the use of the time-out technique as a tactic to reduce or eliminate deviant behaviors has come on bad times. Many school districts have decided to stop using this technique, and others have elected not to begin the practice in the first place. The primary reason for these decisions is that a few unskilled and uninformed persons have misused the approach, and the press has made the most of their mistakes. When the public reads these lurid accounts of time out, they get the idea that whenever a student does something inappropriate, he or she is excluded and imprisoned in a dark, dingy, dungeon-type place, and is kept there for long periods of time unattended. Understandably, this view fosters the idea that time out is considerably damaging to the child involved.

Another more practical reason why time out is on the decline is that many schools lack the necessary facilities for arranging the most common form of the technique, which is absolute exclusion.

The research described here was implemented with the goal of developing a *nonexclusionary* time-out procedure that is effective, humane, and practical. This form of the beleaguered procedure could be arranged in many schools and other applied situations. Smith and Rivera (1993) differentiate between *exclusion* and *seclusion* time out. According to them, the former means that upon substantial disruption, the student is excused from class. The latter means that a pupil who exhibits severe, out-of-control behavior is placed in isolation.

Who Can Benefit

The pupils involved in the Foxx and Shapiro (1968) project were boys with severe mental retardation between the ages of 8 and 18. Their disruptive behaviors ranged from running around the classroom while yelling and hitting themselves to simply being out of their seats. This tactic would be most effective for pupils who are responsive to mild forms of punishment and who are reinforced by their peers.

Procedures

1. Define the inappropriate behaviors of the various children. In the research, these actions covered the gamut: getting out of their seats, yelling, banging objects, throwing things, hitting others, hitting themselves, and crying. There was a different set of target behaviors for each boy.

2. Tie a ribbon around each pupil's neck. Explain that while the child behaves properly, he or she will be allowed to wear the ribbon. During that time, you will praise and compliment the pupil. When the child misbehaves, however, the ribbon will be taken off and placed around your neck. The child will not receive praise or attention regardless of what he or she does when not wearing the ribbon.

3. While a pupil in not wearing a ribbon, refrain from attending to him or her for 3 minutes.

4. Return the child's ribbon at the end of the 3-minute time-out period if he or she has behaved appropriately. Reinforce the pupil as soon as he or she engages in an acceptable behavior.

5. If the child is not behaving properly at the end of the 3-minute period, extend the time out for a minute or so.

6. If the child *really* makes a disturbance during the time-out period (when the ribbon is removed), take him or her to a secluded area.

Monitor

Regardless of the type of time-out procedure being used, it would be appropriate to schedule a three-phase project. During the first phase, prior to the involvement of time out, data on the target behavior should be kept and charted. Continue to gather data during the second phase when the time-out procedure is instituted. This phase continues until the aim for the target behavior has been reached. Data should then be acquired during a third phase, during which time the time-out procedure is not arranged.

Modifications/Considerations

One of the alterations suggested by Foxx and Shapiro was to tie a band around the pupil's wrist that was not as obvious as the neck ribbon; it could be removed and attached much quicker. Signals of other types could be used to indicate that a pupil was in time out and was therefore to be ignored. For example, a colored flag could be raised or lowered on the student's desk.

Another "time-in" signal for certain types of youngsters, particularly those in Little League, is to allow them to wear baseball or other caps; the caps could then be removed contingent on inappropriate actions. Some children are greatly reinforced by their caps and strongly dislike having to take them off.

Such signals—ribbons, wrist bands, caps, or whatever—could indicate that those without these designators are not only "in time out," but also are expected to observe the goings-on of the classroom. For example, they might be required to move to the periphery of a group and watch others in order to learn about proper behavior.

Research

Foxx, R. M., & Shapiro, S. T. (1968). The time out ribbon: A nonexclusionary time out procedure. *Journal of Applied Behavior Analysis, 11,* 125–136.

Smith, D. D., & Rivera, D. M. (1993). *Effective discipline* (2nd ed.). Austin, TX: Pro-Ed.

6 TIME OUT FOR NASTY COMMENTS

Background

This tactic was written up by myself and my colleagues some years ago. One of its premises is that in many instances, a youngster's peers are more reinforcing than are his or her teachers. Another belief is that time out is most successful when a behavior or event that is reinforcing to a child is identified, and then is given or withdrawn contingent on certain behaviors.

Who Can Benefit

The student for whom this tactic was arranged was a 9-year-old boy. He was a member of a self-contained class of 14 youngsters with learning disabilities. The young man had been in special education for 4 years and had received extensive psychiatric treatment. His teachers and psychiatrist had described him, in addition to being learning disabled, as being schizophrenic and impulsive; his verbalizations were laced with sexual and aggressive themes.

Procedures

1. Define the behavior that will be targeted. In this example, this step was difficult since the pupil blurted out a wide variety of unacceptable comments. The teacher decided, however, to deal with utterances that were bathroom or sexually related. Following are some of his favorites: "Boys have penises," "Are you passing gas?", and "I've been to the bathroom; smell my fingers."

2. Inform the pupil that you do not want him or her to engage in this behavior and explain why. In the study, the teacher explained to the boy that he should not say such remarks because many people are offended by them.

3. Identify a student in the class whom the problem child likes.

4. Ask the selected youngster to help you (the teacher) assist the unruly pupil in behaving more appropriately. In the study, the helper was asked to assist the boy in controlling his comments.

5. Direct the new aide to tell the pupil that when he or she misbehaves, the helper will not sit by him or her. For example, in the study the helper was instructed to say, "Ivan, I don't like to sit by you when you say ——— ."

6. Explain to your helper that he or she should slide his or her chair several feet away from the child when that child engages in the inappropriate behavior. The helper in the study was told to move his chair when the unruly pupil blurted out an undesirable remark.

7. Tell the problem child that if the friend moves away, the child can go talk to his or her friend only at the end of a class period; at this time, only appropriate behaviors are to be used. Explain that when the child conforms, the friend will move his or her chair back to the original location.

8. Review this entire program with both the children.

Monitor

As with several other tactics, particularly those that rely on a relatively harsh treatment, a three-phase project should be scheduled: baseline, intervention, and follow-up. The purpose of the baseline is to establish the natural frequency of the behavior. The reason for the second phase is to alter the course of the target behavior to the point that it is now acceptable. The purpose for the follow-up period is to determine whether or not the pupil will behave satisfactorily, with respect to the target behavior, when an intervention is no longer in effect.

Modifications/Considerations

A number of inappropriate social behaviors might be dealt with by enlisting a student helper. Before doing so, however, the teacher should be certain that not only does the pupil of concern like and respect the aide, but also that the helper is compassionate, is truly interested in helping, and will not taunt or tease the problem child.

Student helpers also could be chosen to *increase* certain behaviors of other children, such as beginning work promptly, staying on task, handing work in on time, raising a hand to ask for help, and other commendable activities.

Jenson, Sloane, and Young (1988) discuss the advantages and disadvantages of time-out procedures. Briefly, the advantages are as follows:

1. It is not necessary to know or control the reinforcer that maintains the undesired behavior (although it greatly helps if one knows the controlling event).

2. The technique can be used in a class where points and tokens are not part of the environment.

3. It has been successfully arranged with a wide range of undesired behaviors.

4. It is relatively easy to carry out.

The disadvantages of the time-out technique are

1. It may be so effective in reducing a problem that the procedure could be used to excess.

2. It is easy to bear a grudge and not be "forgiving" when a pupil returns from a period of time out.

3. It is sometimes difficult to find a proper place to carry out the procedure.

4. Some pupils may be very noisy and disruptive while they are in time out.

5. The teacher may have to leave the room or leave the area in which other children are interacting in order to place a child in time out.

6. If the isolation variety of time out is to be used, the teacher must be able to convince the pupil to go into an area of isolation or be able to take him or her there.

7. There may not be a high rate or level of reinforcing activities in the classroom or situation from which the pupil is to be removed.

Research

Jenson, W. R., Sloane, H. N., & Young, K. R. (1988). *Applied behavior analysis in education: A structured teaching approach*. Englewood Cliffs, NJ: Prentice-Hall.

Lovitt, T. C., Lovitt, A. O., Eaton, M. D., & Kirkwood, M. (1973). The deceleration of inappropriate comments by a natural consequence. *Journal of School Psychology, 11*, 148–154.

7 RESPONSE COST OR FINES FOR UNACCEPTABLE ACTS

Background

The basis of this approach is that certain behaviors can be controlled by taking something away from a pupil when he or she behaves inappropriately. This is certainly not a new concept. Often, however, this approach is taken to the extreme and more is taken away than is necessary when a student does something wrong. It is common, for example, for a teacher to cancel a child's entire 15-minute recess if he or she misbehaves.

Considerable research on response cost has indicated that many troublesome behaviors can be reduced by peeling away only a few minutes of free time or a few tokens when the undesired behavior occurs. In fact, in dealing with inappropriate incidents, it is probably more effective to take away recess a minute at a time rather than to deny it entirely in response to one unacceptable behavior.

Another fact to keep in mind when arranging response costs to control behaviors is that something of value must be taken away. Related to this, current research indicates that it is better to take away an event or object that has been given freely to a pupil than to remove something he or she has earned.

Who Can Benefit

In the featured study by Iwata and Bailey (1974), the pupils were 15 boys and girls with mental retardation who participated in a self-contained special class. Most of them exhibited a fair amount of off-task and disruptive behaviors. Furthermore, they often violated the class rules.

Procedures

The following procedures were the ones followed in the Iwata and Bailey study.

1. Define the target behavior. Iwata and Bailey focused on rule violations. Following are four regulations enforced in this class:
    - Remain seated during math class.
    - Raise your hand to get help from the teacher.
    - Do not talk or disturb others.
    - Go to the bathroom only when no one else is there.

2. The pupils were reminded that they should follow these rules.

3. The teacher placed a cup containing 10 tokens on each student's desk at the beginning of the math period.

4. The teacher explained to the students that they would lose 1 token each time they failed to obey a rule.

5. The students were also told that if they had at least 6 tokens left at the end of the 40-minute math period, they would be given a snack. If they did not earn the snack, they were told to go to another area of the room and work on various activities.

6. The teacher informed students that occasionally there would be a "surprise day," but that they would not know in advance when one was scheduled. On those special days, the three or four students who had the most tokens would be given a bonus. The teacher could also decide to give the prize to anyone who still had all their tokens.

Monitor

In order to monitor the effectiveness of this tactic, data could be kept either on the number of points left at the end of a session or on the number of times the pupils disobeyed a rule. Either of these data could be kept for the entire group or they could be kept separately for each student; thus, there might be only one chart for the entire group or there might be one for each child.

Modifications/Considerations

There are a number of variations on this theme: the target behavior could be different; the number of tokens given could change; the prize or reward might be something else. Another modification might be in the form of the token itself. Whereas actual tokens were exchanged in this study, the teacher could also use marks on the chalkboard or on a pad placed on each pupil's desk; a mark could be erased for every violation. Another alteration might be to "charge" more for certain behaviors than for others. For some behaviors, 3 or more tokens could be demanded; for lesser infractions, only 1.

As was indicated earlier, small amounts of time can be subtracted from particular events. For example, a minute of recess time might be taken away for certain actions. Small amounts of time could also be taken from such favored classes as music, art, or physical education contingent on inappropriate behaviors.

Carr and Durand (1985) arranged a study similar to the one paraphrased here. Working with youngsters with behavior disorders, they gave each pupil from 40 to 50 points on Mondays. The exact number was determined by passing a hat. Each pupil drew a slip that indicated how many points he or she had. In addition to those points, they also could earn others by communicating properly. If a student acted out, however, 5 points were deducted. On Fridays the pupils could redeem their points for prizes and privileges.

Research

Carr, E. G., & Durand, V. M. (1985). Reducing behavior problems through functional communication training. *Journal of Applied Behavior Analysis, 18,* 111–126.

Iwata, B. A., & Bailey, J. S. (1974). Reward versus cost token systems: An analysis of the effects on students and teacher. *Journal of Applied Behavior Analysis, 7,* 567–576.

8 CONTINGENCY CONTRACTING AT HOME AND SCHOOL

Background

For certain children, it is often necessary to design a cooperative program between school and home to deal effectively with inappropriate behaviors. This tactic uses contingency contracts, which are based on principles of reinforcement theory, to help teachers and parents squelch certain deviant behaviors of children.

The basis of contingency contracts, originally developed by Lloyd Homme (1966), who adapted the theories of David Premack, is that once the reinforcers for a particular individual are identified, they can be arranged contingent on certain behaviors; as a result, those behaviors will change. Another feature of contingency contracting is that pupils can be involved in setting up arrangements that will affect them, and they will be informed regularly about their progress.

Who Can Benefit

The research supporting this tactic was conducted in a diagnostic and remediation center with pupils from 1st through 11th grades. The procedures their teachers developed were in response to the severe problems exhibited by these youngsters. Many of them were responsible for near crises in either their homes or schools, and often in both places. The problems of these children ranged from running away and being aggressive at home and at school to stealing.

Procedures

1. Decide which tasks the child should perform (e.g., homework, class assignments).

2. Identify the events or materials that he or she likes (e.g., being outdoors, watching television).

3. Develop a two-part contract. One part lists the pupil's duties, including the "payments" given for the completion of each chore (see Figure 8.1). The other part is a list of events that can be earned and how much they "cost" (see Figure 8.2).

4. Explain the features of the contract to the pupil.

5. Tell the parents to give the child points for doing certain things at home (e.g., homework), to mark these completed duties on the chart, and to monitor the child's choices of reinforcers (e.g., television viewing time) and check these off on the sheet.

Week of: _____						
R earned points for:	Mon.	Tues.	Wed.	Thurs.	Fri.	Totals

Homework:
    completed (3 points)
    well done* (5 additional)						

Class assignments:
    completed (1 point each)
    well done* (2 additional)
    with no more than 2 misspelled words or
        careless arithmetic errors (1 additional)						

Listening and complying to directions without reminder (1 point each time)						

Daily grades:
    A (10 points)
    B (6 points)
    C (3 points)
    D (1 point)						

Homework:
        started with no warnings   (5 points)
                one warning   (3 points)
                two warnings   (2 points)
            three warnings   (1 point)
    completed by supper time (2 additional)						

TOTALS						

FIGURE 8.1   Weekly Record Sheet of Points Earned

*BONUS: Baseball glove as soon as R earns 75 points total in these two "well-done" categories.

SOURCE: From "Contingency Contracting with School Problems" by R. P. Cantrell, M. L. Cantrell, C. M. Huddleston, and R. L. Woolridge, 1969, *Journal of Applied Behavior Analysis, 2,* p. 218. Copyright 1969 by Journal of Applied Behavior Analysis. Reprinted by permission of the author.

6. See to it that the child does certain things at school (e. g., class assignments), and send work home with him or her.

7. Put the contract in effect for a number of days, then make some adjustments if necessary. If, for example, the child does not do his or her homework, some changes should be made (e.g., giving more points for homework, fewer for other chores, or adding another reinforcing event to the list).

8. Modify certain aspects of the contract after a few weeks. If the child will voluntarily perform some duties on the contract, drop them from the arrangement. Or, it may be necessary to add different reinforced behaviors to the contract.

Week of: _____							
R exchanged her points for:	Mon.	Tues.	Wed.	Thurs.	Fri.	Sat.	Sun.	Totals
Outdoor time (5 points per ½ hour)								
Television viewing time (5 points per ½ hour)								
Kitchen time (cooking privileges) (5 points per ½ hour)								
Driving (as parents direct) (10 points per ½ hour)								
Going out privilege (10 points per event)								
Staying all night with friend or having one over for night (25 points per event)								
Money (up to limit set by parents) (5 cents per point)								
TOTALS								

FIGURE 8.2 Weekly Record Sheet of Points Spent

SOURCE: From "Contingency Contracting with School Problems" by R. P. Cantrell, M. L. Cantrell, C. M. Huddleston, and R. L. Woolridge, 1969, *Journal of Applied Behavior Analysis, 2,* p. 218. Copyright 1969 by Journal of Applied Behavior Analysis. Reprinted by permission of the author.

Monitor

Obviously, with respect to the last procedure step, data should be kept on the effects of the contract. Most simply, the frequency with which the target behavior occurs prior to and while the contract is in effect should be determined. If, during early measures of the behavior following the involvement of the contract, it is noted that the effects are minimal, adjustments should be made, either by pinpointing another target behavior, selecting different consequences or reinforcements, changing the timing with which these events are delivered, and so forth. Following the change, data should continue to be gathered.

Modifications/Considerations

These contingency contracts can be as simple or as complex as required. For some youngsters it may be necessary to contract for only one or two events, whereas for others the agreements must be more involved.

Anderson (1990) lays out a detailed plan for developing contingency contracts that is similar to the ones just presented. In addition, she reflects on three common questions asked about contingency contracts.

- *Why use contingency contracts?* To teach or train new behaviors, to maintain behaviors that students currently exhibit, or to decrease or extinguish undesirable behaviors.

- *When would I use a contract rather than other techniques?* When simpler or less intrusive management techniques did not work, and a more powerful measure is needed.

- *With which students are contracts most appropriate?* With students in general education classrooms, and in practically all areas of special education, from mildly to severely disabled.

Research

Anderson, J. D. (1990). Contingency contracts: A step-by-step format. *Intervention in School and Clinic, 26*(2), 111–113.

Cantrell, R. P., Cantrell, M. L., Huddleston, C. M., & Woolridge, R. L. (1969). Contingency contracting with school problems. (1969). *Journal of Applied Behavior Analysis, 2*, 215–220.

Homme, L. (1966). Human motivation and environment. In N. G. Haring and R. J. Whelan (Eds.), *The learning environment: Relationship to behavior modification and implications for special education* (pp. 30-39). Lawrence, KS: University of Kansas.

9 THE TIMER GAME

Background

This tactic, which has been used by numerous classroom teachers, was first designed by Wolf, Hanley, King, Lachowicz, and Giles (1970). It is based on the idea that a simple device, a clock, can control certain inappropriate behaviors of children. They demonstrated that this technique also fits into a more general management plan, such as a token economy in which points are granted contingent on certain behaviors and then redeemed for a variety of activities.

This tactic is classified as an independent group contingency, since the contingency is the same for each group member.

Who Can Benefit

In the Wolf et al. study, the Timer Game was set up with a group of 16 low-achieving children from lower class urban homes. The youngsters, most of whom were fourth graders, attended a remedial classroom after their regular school day.

Procedures

1. Define the behavior of concern. In this study, the inappropriate behavior was being out of one's seat. This action was defined as a period in which the child's "seat" was not in contact with any part of the sitting portion of the chair.

2. Discuss this definition with the children, and have them provide examples of the inappropriate behavior and of the appropriate one. In the study, the students were asked to demonstrate being in the seat and out of it (they loved this part!). Continue the discussion and provide examples until the children thoroughly understand the definition.

3. Place a timer clock in front of the room. Throughout the day, set it to go off, on average, about every 20 minutes. (The range of intervals between rings should be from 0 to 40 minutes.)

4. Scan the class when the timer goes off, determine who is working and on-task, and place a mark alongside the names of these children. (The names could be written in the teacher's log book or on the chalkboard.)

5. Award each worker with 5 points, then reset the clock and resume the activity.

6. Allow the children periodically to redeem their points for various events or prizes. (In the example study they could earn snacks, candy, clothes, or field trips.)

Monitor

For the tactic, as was initially explained, data regarding the number of children that are behaving as they should when the timer goes off could be summarized each day and charted. Either the teacher could chart these data or one of the children could take on the assignment. If a child is allowed to be the charter, that chore could be passed around, volunteered for, or earned.

Modifications/Considerations

One alteration that could be made to this technique has to do with the target behavior; any number of inappropriate acts could be dealt with in this manner. In fact, a different inappropriate (or for that matter, appropriate) behavior could be selected for each class member. (If the behaviors are individualized, the Timer Game probably should be used with only a small group of children, unless the teacher has an assistant to help survey the class when the buzzer goes off.)

Another modification might involve the scheduling of points and backup selections. In the example study, the children were awarded 5 points each time they were on-task when the timer rang. That number could vary. Another change might be the time the game is in operation. Whereas it was in effect throughout the day in the example, a teacher might schedule it during only a particularly difficult time. Likewise, the teacher could select different prizes or reinforcers than those chosen by the Wolf group. Jenson, Sloane, and Young (1988) offer several suggestions on arranging reinforcers, one of which is to introduce an element of chance. To do so, a number of possible reinforcers are printed on a card, with more space given to the less valuable item than is given to the most prized. On the occasions when reinforcers are given, each youngster spins a spinner attached to the card. Whatever reinforcer the spinner stops on is the reinforcer for the day.

Wolf et al. adapted the tactic in his study for a single child. For 90 minutes a day the game was in effect, with the timer going off on the average of every 10 minutes. For this child, a 9" × 3" sheet of paper was attached to the wall and the numbers 10, 20, 30, 40, and 50 were printed on it. She was given 50 points at the beginning of each period and was told that 10 of them would be taken away each time she was out of her seat when the timer rang. Later, she could redeem the points that she kept. In some phases of the study, the child could spend the points only on herself; at other times, she could share the points with four other children. Although the Timer Game was generally effective with her, it was even more so during the group sessions.

Research

Jenson, W. R., Sloane, H. N., & Young, K. R. (1988). *Applied behavior analysis in education: A structured teaching approach.* Englewood Cliffs, NJ: Prentice-Hall.

Wolf, M. M., Hanley, E. L., King, L. A., Lachowicz, J., & Giles, D. K. (1970). The timer-game: A variable interval contingency for the management of out-of-seat behavior. *Exceptional Children, 37,* 113–117.

10 THE GOOD BEHAVIOR GAME

Background

This technique is derived from the idea that youngsters are motivated by a number of ordinary classroom events and items. It is also based on the thought that pupils are keenly aware of their peers and will respond accordingly. Further support for this technique is that it is designed for a group; one set of rules and procedures is put into effect for all the members.

Who Can Benefit

This form of group contingency would be appropriate when the general atmosphere of a classroom is chaotic with several children displaying a variety of inappropriate behaviors. It would also be a wise choice for those classes in which the majority of the youngsters are responsible for one another. Furthermore, it would be an excellent tactic for the teacher who wants to quell disruptions in the classroom, but is not a particularly skilled behavioral engineer, and who, in the past perhaps, has not been successful in managing inappropriate behaviors of individual students.

Procedures

The steps explained here, with a few exceptions, are those described in the referenced article. That study took place in a fourth-grade classroom.

1.   Explain to the class that from now on, talking out and leaving their seats without permission will no longer be tolerated. Instead of being overlooked, each incident will be counted.

2.   Precisely define the target behaviors:
     - *Talking out:* talking or whispering without permission; this includes talking while raising a hand, talking to others or to the teacher, calling for the teacher, blurting out answers, or making noises

- *Out of seat:* leaving the chair or a seated position during a lesson or scooting the desk without permission

3. Explain to the pupils that during certain periods, every time you notice that someone is out of his or her seat or is talking out of turn, you will give a reminder of the rule and will write his or her name on a list.

4. Divide the class into two teams, seating one on the left side of the room and the other on the right. Turn the chairs slightly toward the wall so that the members on one team cannot easily see those on the other side.

5. Count the number of misbehaviors that occurred for each team at the end of the designated periods, and announce these counts and who won for the day. The winner is the team with the fewest infractions. If both teams received fewer than five counts, they both win.

6. Grant one of the following to the members of the winning team:
   - Victory tags to wear
   - Stars beside their names on the winner's chart
   - Privilege of lining up first for lunch
   - Thirty minutes of free time at the end of the day

7. Tell the losing team that they will not receive these privileges.

Monitor

Ideas for monitoring this tactic were noted in the procedures section. If these ideas are implemented, each day there would be a tally of the number of infractions for each team. These data, in terms of frequency each day, could be charted. Both teams' scores could be recorded on the same graph or they could be kept separately, depending upon the objectives of the teacher with respect to socialization and cooperation. For another alternative, one of the students on each team could chart the day's total and indicate on the chart whether or not they received a prize.

Modifications/Considerations

There are many ways in which to alter this tactic; one modification has to do with the target behaviors. In the referenced project, the behaviors of concern were talking out and leaving one's seat. Other inappropriate behaviors could be handled by using this technique. In fact, a number of positive social or academic activities could be managed with the same approach. In these instances, the winning side would be the one whose members scored the *most* points.

Another modification of this tactic is in the privileges given to the winning side. In the cited study, a team won such things as tags and free time. In another arrangement—depending on the ages, abilities, and interests of the youngsters—various toys, games, and prizes could be given. The manner in which these awards are chosen could also vary. Whereas the prizes were selected by the teacher in this project, they might, in other circumstances, be picked by the students.

Still another modification might be to change the time the game was in operation. In the example research, the technique was only in effect during the reading and math periods. One could schedule the game during only one period or throughout the day.

Yet another alteration of the Good Behavior Game might be the method for selecting the teams, or, for that matter, the number of groups that participate. In the cited study, there were two teams, and the members were picked by the teacher. Other arrangements could be established in which the youngsters chose the teams or where three or more teams were formed.

A final alteration of this tactic that I'll note has to do with arranging solo contingencies. It is quite likely that there will be a troublemaker or two in a group who generates more negative points for his team than do many of the others. This happened in the original research. In such instances, the teacher could set up an individual contingency and allow him or her to participate as a group member only after demonstrating the ability to be a good citizen. Crouch, Gresham, and Wright (1985) provide more detailed procedures on how to handle the one or two spoilers in a group.

Research

Barrish, H. H., Saunders, M., & Wolf, M. M. (1969). Good behavior game: Effects of individual contingencies for group consequences on disruptive behavior in a classroom. *Journal of Applied Behavior Analysis, 2,* 119–124.

Crouch, P. L., Gresham, F. M., & Wright, W. R. (1985). Interdependent and independent group contingencies with immediate and delayed reinforcement for controlling classroom behavior. *Journal of School Psychology, 23,* 177–187.

11 DISCOURAGING THE "NAUGHTY FINGER" GESTURE

Background

The tactic described here, developed by Sulzbacher and Houser (1968), is another variation of a group contingency. The particular arrangement discussed in this tactic is referred to as an *all group-all group contingency*, since the individual members of the group are dependent on each other for receiving the consequences.

This tactic is designed to deal with not only an inappropriate behavior (raising the fist with the middle finger extended) exhibited by a few pupils in a class, but also the attention given to it by their peers. As many teachers will attest, the commotion caused by class members when others misbehave is often more disrupting to the activity of the room than is the inappropriate behavior to which they are reacting.

Who Can Benefit

The pupils in the "naughty finger" study were 14 children with mild mental retardation in a self-contained classroom. Their ages ranged from 6 years, 7 months to 10 years, 5 months. This tactic, however, could be arranged in most classes regardless of size, depending on the behavior of concern.

Procedures

1. Define the behaviors of concern and explain them to the pupils. In this research, the target behaviors were (1) using the "naughty finger," (2) making verbal references to its use, and (3) tattling or commenting by members of the class when another child lifted the naughty finger.

2. In front of the room, mount a bracket similar to that found on a daily desk calendar. Put 10 cards, numbered 1 through 10, in the bracket.

3. Tell the children that from now on, they will be given a special 10-minute recess at the end of the day. Then say, "If, however, I see the naughty finger or hear about it, I will flip down one of these cards. You will have one minute less of recess whenever this happens."

4. Flip one of the cards immediately following any of the indicated behaviors. Inform the children (briefly) why you did so.

5. Continue with the daily schedule.

6. Tell the children, at the end of the day, how much extra recess they have gained.

7. Compliment the children if they earned some extra time or if they improved their behavior from previous days.

Monitor

Each day, the number of minutes left out of a possible 10 could be recorded on a chart. It would be informative also to keep track of the offenders. It could be that after a while there are only one or two children who are misbehaving. When this is the case, it is wise to arrange some special contingency for just these students while continuing to allow the other children to earn the free time.

Modifications/Considerations

This tactic is quite flexible. For one thing, it can be used with only one child, with a small group, or with an entire class. For another, the target behavior can be different from the one dealt with here; any number of inappropriate behaviors could be chosen. Furthermore, different behaviors can be selected for different class members.

The approach explained by Sulzbacher and Houser might also be used to *increase* the occurrence of a particular action. To do so, the teacher could begin the count at 1, then advance forward each time the acceptable behavior occurs. Such positive behaviors might be giving compliments to others, asking about the welfare of others, or working to develop solutions to vexing social problems.

Another modification might be to choose different people to turn the numbers, either up or down. Instead of the teacher performing the chore, as was the case in this study, an aide, parent, or pupil could be the "flipper." If a pupil is chosen, he or she might be required to earn this privilege by being a good citizen or an accomplished scholar for a specified period.

West et al. (in press) used a classroom clock to curtail the disruptive behaviors of the members of a class. In this study, after students were informed as to what "proper behavior" was, the clock was set at 12 noon and continued to run as long as the youngsters behaved properly. When someone was disruptive, the teacher, using a remote switch, stopped the clock. It was started again when all the class members were behaving as they should. At the end of a period the pupils were allowed to engage in a number of free-time activities for as many minutes as were accumulated on the clock.

Research

Sulzbacher, S. I., & Houser, J. E. (1968). A tactic to eliminate disruptive behaviors in the classroom: Group contingent consequences. *American Journal of Mental Deficiency, 73,* 88–90.

West, R. P., Young, K. R., Callahan, K., Fister, S., Kemp, K., Freston, J., & Lovitt, T. C. (in press). Managing the classroom behavior of secondary-aged students: The musical clocklight. *Teaching Exceptional Children.*

12 HAVING PEERS MODEL BEHAVIOR FOR DISRUPTIVE MATES

Background

Some disruptive children misbehave because they do not know exactly what it is they are supposed to do. Although they generally have a notion about which of their behaviors are not acceptable, they are not always certain which alternative behaviors *are* acceptable. With that thought in mind, the investigator of this research identified some exemplary children to serve as models for their unruly mates.

Another supporting thought of this tactic is that children are often more responsive to their peers than to adults, and sometimes pupils' friends are better able to explain or demonstrate behaviors than are teachers or parents.

A third idea behind this tactic is that if a variety of inappropriate behaviors of a half dozen or so youngsters are to be contained, the teacher will need help. One person cannot possibly manage all the undesired actions alone.

Who Can Benefit

Csapo's (1972) research was conducted in a regular primary classroom. For the purposes of this tactic, attention will be focused on 12 students. Six had displayed a number of inappropriate behaviors (e.g., speaking out of turn, hitting others, banging objects, yelling, grabbing things from their classmates, kicking children, spitting at others). Six other children were selected to serve as peer models. According to their teacher, these peer models were socially mature, reliable, and sensible; they continually exhibited behaviors that were desirable in the classroom.

An added benefit often noted from using peers to assist in managing the unsatisfactory behaviors of their classmates is that the models become helpers; they share the responsibility for changing others' behaviors. Some of the models, prior to being given their new role, giggled and commented loudly when their buddies behaved inappropriately (and often created as much of a ruckus as did the initial troublemakers); however, in their role as models, they became responsible for modifying those undesirable actions, not aggravating them.

Procedures

1. Tell the unruly children that they exhibit a number of behaviors in the classroom that are disruptive not only to themselves, but also to many of their friends. Tell them *precisely* what these behaviors are.

2. Explain to the disruptive students that now they will be sitting alongside someone who will help them. This helper will remind them when they behave inappropriately and tell them to stop. But more important, their partners will act in ways that they should imitate in order to achieve more in school, to not disrupt others, and to avoid incurring your wrath.

3. Notify the disruptive youngsters that they should watch their models and behave as the models do in respect to raising their hands, moving (or not moving) about the room, studying, and so forth.

4. Tell them also to ask their models what to do if, in certain circumstances, they forget how to act or never knew how to handle a situation in the first place.

5. Direct the peer models to behave at their very best and to set good examples for their mates.

6. Also tell the models to answer, as carefully and candidly as they can, any of their companions' questions about behavior.

7. Ask the models to compliment their charges when they do something appropriate, particularly if they previously had not been exhibiting that behavior.

Monitor

In the Stern, Fowler, and Kohler (1988) study, checklists were used to monitor certain behaviors of the youngsters. Data could be taken from these checklists and charted. In keeping with the spirit of that study, the youngsters could alternatively chart the data.

Modifications/Considerations

In the Csapo research, the models helped their peers during the academic part of the day. A modification could be made in the times or places in which helpers are on duty, such as playing outside during recess, sitting with others in the lunch room, riding on the school bus, walking in line from the classroom to the music room, or participating in the music class or in physical education.

Another alteration might be the manner in which the models are chosen and assigned to partners. In Csapo's work, the teacher selected the models and designated the pairs. These chores could possibly be handled by the students themselves.

Models or tutors can be enlisted to accelerate academic growth as well as to modify social skills. In fact, considerable research and general interest has been noted regarding peers as tutors in a wide variety of academic areas. Stern et al. carried out research with fifth graders along this line. The major difference in this study from the one described in this tactic was that the students switched roles. On one day a student monitored a peer, and on the next day he or she was monitored by the peer. In order to monitor their peers, the youngsters were given a checklist of three behaviors that they were to complete three times per session. Using these procedures, the investigators successfully attenuated the off-task and disruptive behaviors of the youngsters.

Research

Csapo, M. (1972). Peer models reverse the "one bad apple spoils the barrel" theory. *Teaching Exceptional Children, 5,* 20–24.

Stern, G., Fowler, S., & Kohler, F. (1988). A comparison of two intervention roles: Peer monitor and point earner. *Journal of Applied Behavior Analysis, 21*(1), 103–109.

13 GETTING ALONG WITH OTHERS: SOLVING INTERPERSONAL PROBLEMS

Background

The Teaching, Learning, and Caring (TLC) curriculum is an interpersonal problem-solving skills training program. It was developed to teach social problem-solving strategies to students with behavior problems. Following are some of the concerns the curriculum addresses: being impulsive, identifying and responding to the affective state of another, generating a range of responses to problem situations, evaluating consequences of behaviors before acting, communicating wants and needs, and responding to the desires of others.

Eight components make up the TLC curriculum: communication mode, empathy, goal identification, cue sensitivity, alternative thinking, skills implementation, consequential thinking, and integration. This tactic outlines procedures for teaching five of these components. (See Table 13.1 for a TLC skill checklist.)

Who Can Benefit

The curriculum described in this tactic was designed for children with severe emotional disabilities (SED) and learning disabilities. It was developed and field-tested for a 2-year period in a program where some students were in a self-contained classroom and others were in general education classes. Because the ability to listen and respond appropriately in typical day-to-day conversations is a prerequisite to adequate social competence, students who have not developed these skills are most likely to benefit from this tactic.

TABLE 13.1 TLC Skill Checklist

COMMUNICATION MODE

1. Repeating the content of another's message
2. Identifying the main ideas of the content of another's message
3. Identifying the stated feelings in another's message
4. Identifying the underlying feelings in another's message
5. Identifying the main idea of the content of one's message
6. Identifying the underlying feeling in one's message
7. Using self-disclosure appropriately
8. Using open and closed questions appropriately
9. Listening to the problems of another for possible reasons for those problems
10. Listening to the problems of another and to hypothetical situations that influence behavior

EMPATHY

1. Identifying words that convey emotions (e.g., jealous, hurt, angry, hostile, shy, afraid, furious)
2. Matching past situations and the feelings associated with the situations
3. Discussing the importance of identifying emotional states as the first step in responding appropriately to them
4. Identifying how you would feel in hypothetical situations
5. Identifying the feelings of others in pictures, films, and hypothetical situations

GOAL IDENTIFICATION

1. Defining own goal(s) when in a problem situation
2. Defining the goal(s) of another when in a problem situation
3. Identifying immediate and long-term goals
4. Sharing identified goals with the student group and accepting feedback
5. Listing the steps to reaching identified goals
6. Charting progress toward reading goals
7. Identifying and describing the needs and goals of others

CUE SENSITIVITY

1. Identifying environmental cues in pictures and responding by asking questions and summarizing content and feelings
2. Identifying environmental cues in real situations that influence behavior
3. Identifying the personal cues people use and what they mean in role-plays and films
4. Identifying the personal cues used by others in real situations
5. Identifying own cues when interacting with others and what they mean
6. Identifying several cues you want to include in your repertoire
7. Identifying cues of others, your typical response to them, and possible alternative responses

ALTERNATIVE THINKING

1. Identifying likely alternatives to solving hypothetical problems
2. Identifying likely alternatives to solving real problems
3. Identifying nonaggressive alternatives to solving hypothetical problems
4. Identifying nonaggressive alternatives to solving real problems

SKILLS IMPLEMENTATION

1. Identifying the best procedure for implementing the selected alternative
2. Identifying a person who implements the alternative well and describing what they do
3. Describing the step-by-step process for implementing the selected alternative
4. Role-playing, practicing, and rehearsing the selected alternative
5. Using feedback from self and others to make changes in the procedures
6. Implementing selected alternative
7. Evaluating the outcome and the procedure

CONSEQUENTIAL THINKING

1. Predicting the likely consequences of a series of events that do not involve them
2. Predicting the likely consequences of hypothetical stories and role-play situations
3. Predicting the likely consequences of interpersonal interactions of others
4. Identifying short-run and long-run solutions to solving hypothetical problems
5. Identifying problems in the long run when implementing short-run solutions to hypothetical situations
6. Identifying the consequences of selected behaviors in interpersonal situations involving others
7. Identifying the consequences of selected behaviors in interpersonal situations involving self
8. Implementing a "stop and think" approach to solving interpersonal difficulties

INTEGRATION

1. Observing models (counselors, teachers, and peers) integrate the problem-solving process in solving hypothetical problems
2. Observing models (counselors, teachers, and peers) integrate the problem-solving process in solving real problems
3. Integrating the problem-solving process in solving group problems
4. Integrating the problem-solving process in solving hypothetical problems
5. Integrating the problem-solving process in solving real problems

SOURCE: From "TLC—Teaching, Learning, and Caring: Teaching Interpersonal Problem-solving Skills to Behaviorally Disordered Adolescents" by S. Vaughn, 1987, *The Pointer, 31*(2), p. 28. Reprinted with permission of the Helen Dwight Reid Educational Foundation. Published by Heldref Publications, 1319 Eighteenth St., N. W., Washington, D. C. 20036-1802. Copyright © 1987.

Procedures

Goal Identification

Purpose: To teach students to identify problems; discern what they and others want when a problem situation arises; establish both long- and short-range goals and differentiate goals from needs

1. Ask students to list academic subjects in which they would like to improve.

2. Help them select one thing they could do immediately to improve their performance in the subjects they have listed.

3. Request students to offer their proposals to the class for constructive feedback.

4. Instruct pupils to keep personal written records of their progress; these records will help them share information in weekly class discussions.

5. Repeat this process, but extend the goal-setting period from weekly to monthly periods, and then to longer periods in the future.

EXAMPLE:

Monthly—Read four books in October

Long-Range—Pass all classes with at least a C average for the semester

6. Encourage students to incorporate personal goals into their plans after they have had some success with academic goal planning.

Cue Sensitivity

Purpose: To help students understand both verbal and nonverbal messages consistently

1. Provide students with the following examples of nonverbal communication:

   Smile = Approval
   Furrowed eyebrows = Confusion
   Touch = Intimacy
   Stepping backwards = Person must leave

2. Cut out pictures from magazines and ask students to identify possible nonverbal messages that people in these pictures could be giving. Direct students to consider dress and body language as well as facial expression.

3. Ask students to summarize a few real-life situations in terms of verbal and nonverbal cues.

   EXAMPLE:

   I knew Bill didn't understand what I was saying to him when he furrowed his eyebrows, so I tried to explain it a different way. The smile on his face when I finished told me that this time he understood.

4. Present several role-play situations for students to observe and have them note verbal cues.

5. Arrange for students to observe each other to identify and evaluate the cues they are sending to others.

Empathy

Purpose: To teach students to recognize their own feelings and the feelings of others

1. Teach students the meanings and applications of words that indicate feelings, such as *frustrated, jealous, perturbed, disappointed, delighted, concerned, furious, outraged,* and *embarrassed.*

2. Ask students to take turns describing emotional situations and how they would feel and react if placed in those situations.

3. Discuss the possible consequences of the various responses given to the situations described in Step 2. For example, in the following situation, students could discuss the consequences of Mike's possible responses. *(Note:* Make sure students understand that Mike's goal should be to select a response that is beneficial to both him and Charlie.)

    Charlie is instantly upset when he sees his girlfriend talking to Mike. Mike knows that Charlie is upset. How could Mike respond to Charlie?

    One answer might be to explain to Charlie that he was only answering his girlfriend's question about a missed assignment. Another might be for Mike to greet Charlie enthusiastically, saying something like, "Oh, there you are, Charlie! I was just telling _____ that I've been looking all over for you.")

Alternative Thinking
Purpose: To provide a strategy for generating solutions to a problem, rather than acting impulsively

1. Make a "problem box" and place it somewhere accessible to students.
2. Ask students to write a note about a problem they are experiencing or have experienced with others (peers, neighbors, parents, or teachers), and place the note, anonymously, in the box.
3. Take one or two notes from the box every day for several days, and have students discuss possible solutions to the problems mentioned in the notes.

Consequential Thinking
Purpose: To help students develop the ability to anticipate the possible consequences of a behavior before engaging in it

1. Write the following questions on the board:
    - "What might happen next if I do _____ (the intended behavior)?"
    - "What will happen in the long run if I do _____ ?"
2. Compile a list of examples taken from the previous lesson on alternative thinking. Discuss these examples in the context of the questions posed in the previous step.
3. Ask students to provide examples from personal experiences of times when they "thought ahead."
4. Conduct a class discussion about the consequences of thinking ahead and not thinking ahead in a variety of situations.

Monitor

This project, like others intended to assist students in getting along with their peers, could be evaluated by arranging a sociometric instrument. Youth could be asked, before and after the training program, to identify a best friend or a person with whom they would like to work, or in other ways rate their peers.

Students might keep a detailed notebook that includes subheadings for each category and notes from the class discussions. As personal situations arise, they could refer to their notebooks for help in deciding how to handle various social situations. Recording their approaches to problem situations and the outcomes would provide ongoing documentation of their growth in this area. For example, they could keep track of the number of times a day they acted with empathy, thought of alternative solutions, or thought about the consequences of an action.

Modifications/Considerations

Teachers may wish to use all or only parts of this tactic, depending on their students' skills. For example, it may be that all of the students in a particular group seem to understand verbal and nonverbal cues and are able to recognize feelings, yet have difficulty setting goals. The teacher could choose to skip Cue Sensitivity and Empathy, and spend more time on Goal Identification.

This tactic also could be expanded by analyzing interpersonal social situations in terms of more than one component. Students might also analyze the behaviors of their "most admired person" in terms of the various components.

Research

Vaughn, S. (1987). TLC—Teaching, learning, and caring: Teaching interpersonal problem-solving skills to behaviorally disordered adolescents. *The Pointer, 31*(2) 25–30.

14 Developing Positive Teacher Mindsets for Surviving in Behavior Disorder (BD) Classrooms

Background

This tactic is based on the idea that teachers, in order to deal effectively with students who have behavior disorders, must develop a *psychological soundness*. That soundness, according to researchers, comes from adopting a rational belief system and developing healthy thinking strategies. Related to this idea is the assumption that perceptions affect behavior, and perceptions and behavior influence self-confidence, interpersonal relationships, and personal well-being. Healthy teacher mindsets, therefore, should facilitate success and survival in managing youngsters with behavior disorders.

Who Can Benefit

As just noted, this tactic should, by assisting teachers to develop positive mindsets, serve to better educate youngsters with behavior disorders. Not only should the approaches noted in this tactic serve youngsters who are legally identified as having behavior disorders, but also they should contribute to effective instruction for children who misbehave or are noncompliant, but who are not legally classified.

Procedures

The following is a summary of 12 mindsets for survival:

1. *Answer? Answer? Yes, I'll find an answer.* Teachers should believe that all problems have solutions and that one problem may have several solutions. To come up with solutions, teachers should: (a) step back and think about the problem, (b) request help from others if necessary, (c) apply various problem-solving strategies, and (d) persist in seeking solutions.

2. *There must be a pony in here somewhere.* There is a story of a boy who was locked in a room filled with horse manure because of misbehavior. He was found later to be digging around in the manure and

whistling. Rather than being gloomy, he was happy, saying "With all this manure, there must be a pony in here somewhere." Although teachers should be realistic about their charges, responsibilities, and energies, they should look on the bright side with respect to their challenging pupils. An optimistic teacher views her students as people who are essentially good and who have positive attributes that need to be nurtured.

3. *Perceptive sensitivity.* The following beliefs are associated with perceptive sensitivity: (a) All children are worth saving. (b) Disruptive behaviors reflect students' past learning history; thus, new behaviors must be taught. (c) Students' behaviors might be healthy, given abnormal circumstances. (d) Students' behaviors are ways to satisfy their needs. (e) Teachers need to view work through their students' eyes.

4. *Progress is progress—recognize it!* Develop the attitude that the next step toward the goal *is* the goal. Teachers who recognize progress in small steps tend to feel reinforced more often and will probably reinforce their students more often.

5. *Conflict is a manageable challenge.* Teaching without experiencing conflict is impossible, and some types of conflict actually stimulate creativity. By accepting these assumptions, teachers of children with behavior disorders should be, or should become, extremely creative individuals.

6. *"No strings attached" caring.* Teachers who expect students to return their gentle caring are often disappointed. Give up the idea. Keep in mind that the child's inappropriate behaviors are not necessarily related to you, the teacher; they are the result of previous learning.

7. *Flexible thinking—I can travel new roads.* Flexible thinking changes the notion of "my way" to "any way that works." By developing this attitude, teachers will add greatly to their repertoire of techniques for managing difficult-to-teach children.

8. *If I'm not making mistakes, then I'm not really trying.* Teachers who recognize and accept their own mistakes are usually willing to take risks and try new techniques. Related to this concept, such teachers are willing to open their classrooms to scrutiny, model self-acceptance, tolerate others who make mistakes, and become more spontaneous in their care of students.

9. *Keep them on the academic track—down time is deadly.* Students should be continually and actively engaged. Teachers should expect students to work and to complete all assignments. Class structure and routines should be well-organized. Free time should be kept to a minimum and made contingent on academic performance.

10. *Pain is not a fearful thing.*   Teachers must overcome the fear of pain that may be caused by students. Fear of being hurt is one of the quickest mental paths to burnout. According to some researchers, fear causes either avoidance or aggressive behaviors.

11. *Life is bizarre and funny.*   Humor is necessary for classroom survival. Since humor tends to decrease anxiety and depression, students with behavior disorders can benefit from the teacher's sense of humor.

12. *Think straight.*   Flush junk thoughts. Teachers must think straight and avoid such junk thoughts as the following: (a) "I must do well and win approval for my performance or else I will be rated as a terrible person." (b) "Other people should treat me with consideration and kindness, just the way I want to be treated; if they don't, they should be punished." (c) "Life in general should be hassle-free, and I should get practically everything I want just when I want it and without great effort."

Monitor

Data of two types should be kept with regard to the involvement of these mindsets. For one, teachers should monitor the extent to which they adhered to the 12 principles while they were teaching. These data could be either qualitative or quantitative; that is, they could write a summary of how well they followed the suggestions or could actually tally the number of times they relied on the various "rules." The other type of data should pertain to pupils. For that, since the involvement of the suggested mindsets is intended to influence every student in a group, the data should pertain to all the youngsters in a class; each incident of inappropriate behavior could be tallied.

Modifications/Considerations

According to the authors of the cited report, when teachers develop mindsets such as those summarized here they will facilitate hope, joy, acceptance, self-efficacy, and progress in their classrooms.

Research

Webber, J., Anderson, T., & Otey, L. (1991). Teacher mindsets for surviving in BD classrooms. *Intervention in School and Clinic, 26*(5), 288–292.

15 THE INTERVENTION LADDER

Background

The idea behind this tactic, which is actually a collection of several management tactics, is that a number of approaches are available that teachers might arrange to curb inappropriate behaviors of students. In choosing approaches, teachers should, when possible, select the least expensive and most natural interventions possible to deal with inappropriate behaviors.

Who Can Benefit

Most directly, teachers, particularly those who must manage difficult-to-teach children in their classes, stand to benefit significantly from learning about these techniques. Of course, the children themselves, the ones with whom the tactics are arranged, stand to gain from the skillful arrangement of these methods. That is especially true if the children, with the help of the techniques, begin to behave more productively, both socially and academically.

Procedures

Smith and Rivera (1993) listed behavior management techniques in two intervention ladders. The following is a summary of the eight techniques listed in Part I. They are noted from least restrictive to most restrictive.

- *Specific praise.* Provide students with positive statements and feedback about their proper conduct.
- *Ignoring.* Systematically and consistently, do not pay attention when the pupil engages in the target behaviors.
- *Rules.* The teacher and students determine the classroom rules that are to be followed.

- *Contingent instructions.*   When a pupil engages in a target behavior, quietly and on a one-to-one basis tell the student specifically not to engage in that activity.
- *Contingent observation.*   Remove a disruptive student from a group activity, but still allow him or her to observe the proceedings.
- *Criterion-specific rewards.*   The student earns a special privilege only when he or she reaches the desired level of the target behavior.
- *Fines.*   The student loses privileges when he or she engages in the target behavior.
- *Group contingencies.*   There are three variations on this technique: dependent (a person earns privileges for peers), independent (each individual earns a privilege when he or she achieves the goal established for all members), and interdependent (the group earns a reward when all members meet the established goal).

Following is a brief summary of the techniques listed on Part 2 of the intervention ladder:

- *Peer management.*   The research authors summarize three types: tutoring (one student assists another in an academic area), behavioral managers (a student whose classroom behaviors are generally appropriate dispenses praise to a peer whose behaviors generally are not as appropriate), and environmental restructuring (all class members are instructed and rewarded for encouraging a classmate's appropriate behaviors).
- *Self-management.*   Three types were noted: self-regulation (individuals monitor their own behaviors, and seek to avoid situations that precipitate inappropriate behaviors), self-evaluation (pupils correct their own performances, record their frequencies, and chart the resulting data), and self-reinforcement (students reward themselves for appropriate behaviors).
- *Overcorrection.*   Four types were noted: positive practice (extensive practice of the desired behavior), restitution (pupil engages in target behavior and related behaviors), exclusion (student is excluded from class when he or she engages in an inappropriate behavior), and seclusion (for severe behaviors, the pupil is placed in an isolation room).
- *Punishment.*   The application of an aversive event is contingent on the occurrence of an undesired behavior.
- *Exclusion.*   Three types are described: in-school supervision (removal of a pupil from one or more classes and requiring him or her to spend the time in a designated school area), suspension (removal of an individual from school for a day or so), and expulsion (removal from school either permanently or for an indefinite time).

Monitor

In order to monitor the effects of any of these techniques, the teacher should rely on suggestions offered for evaluating other tactics in this section. The most fundamental way to monitor this tactic's effectiveness would be to gather data on an individual, individuals, or an entire group (depending on the circumstances and the tactic) throughout three phases. The first phase would be the baseline, a period during which the intervention is not in effect. The second phase is when the intervention is scheduled, and the third is the time during which the intervention is removed, or the maintenance phase.

Modifications/Considerations

Several of the techniques briefly summarized here are explained in considerable detail in other tactics in this section: Rules (Tactic 1), Fines (Tactic 7), Group Contingencies (Tactics 9, 10, and 11), Peer Management (Tactic 12), Self-Management (Tactic 13), Overcorrection (Tactics 3 and 4), and Exclusion (Time out) (Tactics 5 and 6).

Two forms of exclusion noted here, suspension and expulsion, should be used rarely and probably less often than they are in many schools. Schools and teachers must do everything possible to keep students in schools, if not in schools as they are now organized, in schools of different types. There is ample evidence to show that when youngsters are "kicked out" of school, their futures are indeed dim.

Research

Smith, D. D., & Rivera, D. M. (1993). *Effective Discipline* (2nd ed.). Austin, TX: Pro-Ed.

INDEPENDENCE

There are 10 tactics in this section on independence, otherwise known as self-management. Although most of these tactics were included in the first edition, they have all been rewritten and new references have been added. The first tactic is an explanation of the "countoon," a graphic device that facilitates self-recording. The second tactic also provides a means with which to assist children in keeping track of their own activities. Tactics 3 and 4 offer ways to involve very young children in managing their own behaviors. The fifth tactic shows how to self-record work and how to offer cues to access praise. Dealing with the transition from one situation to another is the topic of the sixth tactic. The context of the seventh tactic is composition; youngsters are given ways in which to improve their writing. Tactic 8 explains how to use choice as a motivating element. The ninth tactic presents a discussion of self-determined reinforcement. The last tactic of this set offers ideas for arranging organizational checklists that promote self-instruction.

6

1 COUNTOONS

Background

Before explaining this tactic, credit must be given to Harold Kunzelmann, Marilyn Cohen, and others at the Experimental Education Unit of the University of Washington for coming up with this clever idea and its label. The word *countoon*, in case it seems a bit cryptic, is a combination of the words *count* and *cartoon*.

Two ideas lie behind this graphic device and its ability to help teach pupils, even young ones or those with disabilities, to identify and count the frequencies of certain behaviors. One thought is that most individuals are highly motivated when they keep track of their own behaviors. When they see a record of their progress over time, they often alter their course; they begin doing more or less of the charted behavior depending on their goals.

Another supporting idea for teaching pupils to self-record is that teachers are greatly assisted in carrying out their own duties when pupils are able to record their own behaviors, which ordinarily include actions that are in most need of change. If the teacher has dozens of pupils and several of their behaviors must change, the teacher needs help. He or she cannot monitor and modify all of them alone.

Some children have difficulty tallying occurrences of their own behaviors. They either forget to do so from time to time, or they are not totally clear as to what they are supposed to record. The cartoon aspect of this tactic is valuable for those youngsters because it gives them a sequence of pictures and other aids that remind them of the specific behaviors they are expected to count.

Who Can Benefit

This tactic is particularly good for young children: 4- or 5-year-olds can be taught to monitor many of their own behaviors with countoons. These drawings have also been used successfully with children with developmental delays, particularly those who have a difficult time communicating verbally but who do understand pictures. It is important that the students with whom this technique is used have some understanding of the passage of time and some grasp of cause and effect.

Procedures

1. Identify the behavior that needs to be dealt with, that is, a behavior that should decrease or increase in frequency.

2. Explain to the child that this behavior should be modified, and explain in what way the behavior is to change. For example, communicate to the child whether he or she should do either less or more of the behavior.

3. Draw a countoon to illustrate this behavior. These drawings have three components: What I Do, My Count, and What Happens.

COUNTOON

What I Do | My Count | What Happens

1	2	3	4	5
6	7	8	9	10
11	12	13	14	15
16	17	18	19	20
21	22	23	24	25

- **What I Do** is a three-frame episode of the target behavior. In this countoon example, the teacher intends to put a stop to a girl's finger snapping. The first picture shows the child sitting and not making the noise. In the next frame, she is snapping her fingers, and in the third frame, she is once again sitting quietly.
- **My Count** is a frame that contains numbers. In this example, the numerals 1 to 25 are printed.
- **What Happens** is a picture that illustrates what occurs when the child engages in the target behavior. In this example, there is a picture of a girl working on math problems. The consequences in this case were that every time she snapped her fingers, she had to compute 10 subtraction problems correctly.

4. Tape the countoon to the pupil's desk. Tell him or her to mark a line through the 1 the first time he or she engages in the target behavior; if the target behavior occurs again, the student crosses off the next number, and so forth.

5. Carefully monitor the student's counting for the first few days. Correct the child if he or she does not check off a number, marks the wrong one, or does something else incorrectly. Give some praise for recording behaviors accurately. At the same time, scold the child a little for misbehaving and remind him or her to administer the consequence (in this case, working on the math problems).

Monitor

Initially, the teacher or supervisor should keep data on the extent to which the student carries out aspects of the pictorial cues. Shortly thereafter, data should be obtained on the task to which the cues are related, either a behavior that is to be attenuated or one that is to be developed. As soon as possible, the student should be encouraged to chart or in some other way keep track of how often he or she engages in the target behavior. Thereafter, other self-management steps could be developed.

Modifications/Considerations

Countoons have been drawn to help decelerate a wide variety of behaviors, including banging one's head, squirming in a chair, talking out of turn, picking one's nose, jumping out of one's seat, tattling on classmates, throwing books or pencils, tearing papers, scooting chairs, whistling, banging on desks, and breaking pencils. Countoons have also been drawn to encourage selected behaviors: writing the alphabet or practicing certain letters, learning arithmetic problems, giving compliments to other children, saying "please" or "thank you," standing quietly in line, and learning to spell words.

Alberto and Sharpton (1987) described how *pictorial prompts* could be arranged to teach certain vocational skills, such as dusting furniture, folding laundry, and stuffing envelopes. To design such pictorials, they suggest an eight-step process:

1. Prepare a task analysis.
2. Decide on the type of pictures to be used.
3. Prepare pictures for each step of the task analysis.
4. Prepare pictures of materials that are needed to carry out the task.
5. Check the accuracy and clarity of the picture prompts.
6. Design a "finished" card to indicate that the task is completed so the student will not repeat it.
7. Include a picture of the prize to be gained when the task is successfully completed.
8. Require the student to perform the task in a variety of situations with a number of supervisors.

Research

Alberto, P., & Sharpton, W. (1987). Prompting strategies that promote student self-management. *Teaching Exceptional Children, 19*(4), 54–57.

Kunzelmann, H. P., Cohen, M. A., Hulten, W. J., Martin, G. L., & Mingo, A. R. (1970). *Precision teaching: An initial training sequence.* Seattle: Special Child Publications.

2 GETTING IT ALL TOGETHER: ORGANIZATION CARDS

Background

There are a number of students who simply cannot "get it all together"; they are disorganized. Before children can do their reading, mathematics, and so forth, they must first organize and assemble all the necessary equipment. This tactic is for them.

It is important for adults to be organized, too—this goal is not reserved for children in schools. The carpenter, for example, must carefully consider which tools or materials are necessary to accomplish the job before going off to work. The same can be said of musicians, bricklayers, electricians, television repair people, and other workers who journey about. They must always be certain they have the necessary equipment on hand.

Organization is also a requirement of individuals who are simply out to have fun. A tennis player will not find much enjoyment in a game of tennis without a racket, a hiker will go very hungry without lunch, and a theater-goer will not enjoy Ibsen without a ticket.

Obviously, it is vital to learn, rather early on, how to determine what tools or toys are required for a task or game, and then assemble those items before setting out. Get organized!

Who Can Benefit

This tactic is especially appropriate for youngsters who are extremely dependent on their teachers. These types of students are constantly waving their hands or performing annoying antics in attempts to gain their teacher's attention.

Procedures

Six variations on a theme are briefly described here. These techniques were all designed to help students gather together their tools before beginning to work. All the methods are alike in several respects: each student has a self-monitoring card that is attached to his or her desk or is placed in a notebook; each student is given a reward for fulfilling the requirements on the card; and finally, the students recorded their own behaviors.

Variation I

In this variation, the student kept the self-monitoring card in a work folder. She was allowed to work on an instructional module of her choice for 25 minutes at the end of the day if the three requirements listed on the card were met for 6 days (see Diagram 1 in Figure 2.1).

Diagram 1

Self-monitoring/reading
Name _____

Day A   Day B

On time _____   On time _____
Materials _____   Materials _____
On task _____   On task _____

Diagram 2

Teacher _____
Name _____

                              Days
                    1 2 3 4 5 6 7
1 book   _____
2 notebook   _____
3 pencil   _____
4 on time   _____

Diagram 3

          1   2   3   4
Mon.   _____
Tues.   _____
Wed.   _____
Thurs.   _____
Fri.   _____

Did you bring:
1 Pencil   3 Paper
2 Pen   4 Library book

Diagram 4

Name _____ Grade ____ Day ____

                    Brought
Yes   No   paper/packet
Yes   No   pencil/pen
Yes   No   text books
Yes   No   check list

Diagram 5

Name _____ Prepared ³/₄

1 Desk clean when coming and going
2 Have a pencil with eraser
3 Paper or notebook
4 Card signed completely

Diagram 6

Name _____

                    M   T   W   T   F

Homework
  assignment   _____
Paper and pencil _____
Science   _____
Ready in 2 minutes _____

FIGURE 2.1 Organization Card Variations

Variation II

In this version, the child carried a self-monitoring card with her. If she was able to fill in all four entries for 7 consecutive days, she was allowed to go to a neighborhood fast-food store during lunch break (see Diagram 2 in Figure 2.1).

Variation III

In this variation, the child, who carried her self-monitoring card with her, was rewarded for fulfilling all the duties on her card for 5 consecutive days. If she did this, she was allowed to choose an instructional module of her choice to work on (see Diagram 3 in Figure 2.1).

Variation IV

The student here was in a science class; he carried his card with him. If he was able to circle three of the four YESs on his card, he could play chess or the game *Space Maze* for 10 minutes. He could accumulate up to 50 minutes before having to use this accumulated time (see Diagram 4 in Figure 2.1).

Variation V

In this variation, if three of the four tasks on the card were completed on any day, this boy earned 5 minutes to read a 1960s newspaper. (You never know what will reinforce some people!) The teacher kept the child's card and gave it to him at the beginning of the period (see Diagram 5 in Figure 2.1).

Variation VI

In this version, when the student entered the room, the self-monitoring card was on his table. He then checked off the items that were accomplished, and after a few minutes the teacher picked it up. The boy earned 5 minutes of free time for meeting the four criteria and could cash in the accumulated time on Fridays to read magazines or books or to experiment with an electronic kit (see Diagram 6 in Figure 2.1).

Monitor

The manner in which any of these items is evaluated could differ. For the variations described in this tactic, it was simply a "go or no go" situation. A more elaborate scheme might be developed so that the evaluator gives credit to students for various degrees of accomplishment.

Modifications/Considerations

Several variations on the self-monitoring tactic are noted here; many others are possible. Cards or sheets such as the ones illustrated in Figure 2.1 can be made for preschoolers, graduate students, and all ages in between. Shields and

Heron (1989) describe several strategies that can be used to improve organizational and time-management skills: logs and charts, work stations, color coding, timers, and guided notes.

The form in which reminders, such as the ones described in this tactic, are written could vary. For example, individuals could use 3" × 5" cards, notebooks, appointment books, or chalkboards. These notes, in whatever form, might be placed in a number of different locations: on the refrigerator door, on the dashboard of the car, on the front door of the house, or in a billfold or purse.

Certainly the number of items on these lists could vary. There might be a few that pertained to only a class period or two during the day (as was the case here), or the list might include duties that should be accomplished throughout the day, week, or month.

Research

Shields, J. M., & Heron, T. E. (1989). Teaching organizational skills to students with learning disabilities. *Teaching Exceptional Children, 21*(2), 8–13.

Some of these ideas were from teachers in the CHARTS project (1977–1980) from schools in Olympia, Clover Park, Federal Way, and Seattle, Washington School Districts. CHARTS (**CH**anging **A**chievement **R**ates of **T**eachers and **S**tudents) was a 3-year, federally funded project for learning disabled children. I was the principal investigator, and it was headquartered at the Experimental Education Unit of the University of Washington.

3 SELF-INSTRUCTION FOR PRESCHOOLERS

Background

Some self-control procedures can be self-mediated. Simply stated, many individuals can perform certain chores better and more predictably if they talk to themselves as they do these things; that is, by saying the steps as they perform the task, they can better accomplish the goal.

I catch myself "self-mediating" every now and then. While at the office, I'll say, "Tom, tonight you ought to work on this report, so you need to put this article and that pamphlet in your briefcase. You should also take your power book and this reference list home. That should do it for the report, but now what about the other stuff—your running shoes, the mail that needs to go home?", and on and on.

Several years ago Curtiss and I (Lovitt & Curtiss, 1968) conducted a mathematics study that emphasized self-mediation. We described the procedure as "saying the problem and answer before writing the answer." The student's accuracy in that study was greatly improved as a result of rehearsing the problem orally before writing the solution (see Part 4, Tactic 2).

Who Can Benefit

The pupils in the project described here were three preschool boys enrolled in a Head Start program. According to their teachers, they were highly disruptive.

The training procedures and self-management steps the researchers used in this project also would be quite appropriate for other young children, and for older youngsters with disabilities. These self-mediated steps are particularly suitable for students who have difficulty transferring what they have learned in one setting to another.

Procedures

This program teaches four components of self-instruction:

1. Asking questions about the task
2. Answering those questions
3. Providing self-instruction
4. Granting self-reinforcement

In the instructional program that follows, the teacher and pupil go over these four components six times (in storybook fashion) in an effort to shift the management responsibility from teacher to pupil.

Self-Instruction Steps

1. Model the task for the child while talking aloud to yourself. For example, say "Mrs. B. wants me to draw a picture of a dog. How do I do that? I must get a crayon and some paper. Now I need to look at the picture and draw one like it. First I will draw the head, then . . . That looks pretty good. Nice work." During this phase, if the child attends to you, praise him or her and give the child a raisin or small piece of fruit. Continue this reinforcement action during the next five steps.

2. Require the pupil to perform the same task as the one you modeled while you orally instruct him or her each step along the way.

3. Ask the pupil to perform the same task and talk aloud about each step. Meanwhile, whisper the steps as the student does them.

4. Have the student repeat this assignment, this time whispering each of the steps; at the same time, you mouth the words, without making a sound, that describe each step.

5. Ask the youngster to repeat the task again while making lip movements about the steps while you do nothing.

6. Require the child to perform the task one more time, this time just thinking about the steps.

Instructional Schedule

To teach these components, work with each child individually for about 60 minutes: concentrate on the task for 25 minutes, take a 10-minute break, and return to work for another 25 minutes. Teach a variety of tasks in these sessions, with the difficulty level increasing from one task to the next. Such tasks can range from copying lines and figures to grouping objects or ideas.

Monitor

As indicated in the Modifications/Considerations section, data should be kept, when possible, on the various elements of the instructional program so that teachers can make necessary changes in the program. Beyond those data, information should be acquired on the target behaviors to which the self-instructional strategies are applied: decreasing inappropriate social behaviors or increasing academic performances.

Modifications/Considerations

All six steps noted here to teach self-instruction may not be required. Keep data on how well the pupil generalizes these instructional steps to different situations or behaviors, and use that information to decide which steps are actually helping the pupil. The number of required components may depend on a number of factors, including the developmental level of the pupil. Very young children might need all the steps listed here, whereas more advanced students might get along with fewer.

The number of steps used could also vary according to the task that is being taught. The number of steps needed to instruct motor-type tasks might differ from the number necessary to teach verbal skills, and so forth.

If some pupils receive intensive training on self-instruction for a few skills, they might also come up with their own scripts, possibly different from the plan offered here.

Manning (1988) demonstrated that when self-instructional strategies were taught to primary-age youngsters, many of their annoying, off-task behaviors in classrooms were curbed.

Research

Bornstein, P. H., & Quevillon, R. P. (1979). The effects of a self-instructional package on overactive preschool boys. *Journal of Applied Behavior Analysis, 9,* 179–188.

Lovitt, T. C., & Curtiss, K. A. (1968). Effects of manipulating an antecedent event on mathematics response rate. *Journal of Applied Behavior Analysis, 1,* 329–333.

Manning, B. H. (1988). Application of cognitive behavior modification: First and third graders' self-management of classroom behaviors. *American Educational Research Journal, 25*(2), 193–212.

4 THE TURTLE TECHNIQUE FOR MANAGING AGGRESSION

Background

The Turtle Technique, which aims to reduce aggressive behavior in the classroom, is supported by several assumptions. One of the most important is that children, even those who are very young and who exhibit severe behavior problems, can be taught to manage certain aggressive behaviors. Another assumption is that meditation and relaxation training are useful toward this management. In the practical realm, this technique relies on youngsters to help change the behaviors of other children. Teacher feedback, encouragement, support, and reinforcement are also incorporated as vital ingredients for effecting change.

Who Can Benefit

The youngsters in the sample research were 11 primary-age pupils who participated in self-contained classes for students with behavior disorders. According to their teachers, they all frequently exhibited aggressive behaviors.

Procedures

Introduce the Turtle Technique in two stages.

Phase one.

The *turtle response* is a label describing the technique of pulling the arms and legs in close to the body, putting the head down on a desk, and imagining that one is a turtle withdrawing into its shell. Children can be taught to use this technique in four circumstances:

- when the child believes an aggressive exchange with another is about to occur

- when the child is angry with him- or herself and is about to have a tantrum
- when the teacher calls out "turtle"
- when a classmate calls out "turtle"

Introduce the turtle response to students by reading this story to the children:

> Little Turtle was very upset about going to school. When he was there he got into trouble because he fought with his mates. Other turtles teased, bumped, or hit him. He then became angry and started fights. The teacher then punished him. One day he met the big old tortoise who told him that his shell was the secret answer to many problems. The tortoise told Little Turtle to withdraw into his shell whenever he felt angry, and rest until he felt better. Little Turtle tried it the next day and it worked. He no longer became so angry that he started fights, his teacher now smiled at him, and he began to like school.

After reading the story, demonstrate the turtle response and ask the pupils to practice it as they say the word *turtle*. Then explain the four circumstances in which the response should be used. Act out all four situations via role-playing, and praise the children as they acquire the technique.

Phase two.

Teach the youngsters muscle relaxation. Ask them to alternately tense and relax the various muscle groups. Then teach students to relax when in the turtle position.

After introducing the Turtle Technique, instruct the pupils in problem solving. Have students use the following two steps:

1. Generate a number of alternate strategies for coping with problems.
2. Predict the consequences for each choice.

Monitor

Early on, as children are being taught and then allowed to self-manage aspects of their lives, they should be instructed not only to identify a problem, but also to count and record the number of times they encounter that problem. In the case of the Turtle Technique, this data-keeping translates to the number of times they or others activate the turtle response. Furthermore, children should be taught to note the circumstances that trigger the response. Determining the trigger would enable them to not only deal with problem situations, but also to possibly avoid them.

Modifications/Considerations

For older or more mature youngsters, the turtle response could be modified. Rather than actually assuming the turtle posture, children could use a more subtle one, or they could simply imagine an escape into a safe, appealing situation.

Another adaptation of this technique is to associate it with other actions or thoughts. Some individuals might be instructed to use the Turtle Technique to deal with circumstances that are frustrating and debilitating, but that are not necessarily violent.

Another modification of the method lies in how the response is cued. Here, the teacher or other children signaled the use of the technique. It could also be prompted in a less obvious way, and perhaps handled by only the child involved or by others he or she had designated.

An important consideration in administering this technique is managing the youngsters who are not required to assume the turtle response. It is very important to reinforce them for not attending to the "turtles" and for leaving them in peace; it is certainly not productive for them to tease these children. Indeed, it is these youngsters—the ones who are not aggressive and do not require this radical technique—who might benefit most from the adaptations mentioned.

Osborne, Kosiewicz, Crumley, and Lee (1987) reported that a self-monitoring technique, one in which youngsters marked periodically whether or not they were on-task, was effective in attenuating several disruptive behaviors of young children.

Research

Osborne, S. S., Kosiewicz, M. M., Crumley, E. B., & Lee, C. (1987). Distractible students use self-monitoring. *Teaching Exceptional Children, 19*(2), 66–9.

Robin, A., Schneider, M., & Dolnick, M. (1976). The turtle technique: An extended case study of self-control in the classroom. *Psychology in the Schools, 13*, 449–453.

5 SELF-RECORDING WORK AND CUES FOR PRAISE

Background

There are two features of this technique that make it unique. One characteristic is that self-recording is integrated with a token economy. Throughout the example study, the students were rewarded with tokens for recording their behaviors.

The second characteristic of this technique, and perhaps the most noteworthy, is that the pupils were taught to cue the teacher to give them reinforcement, and then students recorded these cuing incidents. They were instructed, in other words, to "blow their own horns." The purpose for this should be obvious: If individuals are reinforced by praise and if they receive more of it, the behaviors for which they are praised will increase.

Throughout this project, the pupils self-recorded two behaviors—working and cuing—in a number of settings with different managers. The aspect of several managers is important when one considers alternative methods of dealing with students across a variety of settings. One option is to instruct the various managers on how to work with a pupil; another is to train the student to deal with the managers in a number of different situations. The latter approach, the one explained here, has considerable merit.

Who Can Benefit

The pupils in the cited study were girls between the ages of 14 and 17 who were in a facility for youth with behavior disorders. They were placed there primarily because they were either truant or disruptive. In this facility, the girls received training in four settings: a classroom, workshop, office, and kitchen. Each setting had a different manager. The procedures described here also would be useful for a wider age range of students and in other settings.

Procedures

The steps for teaching both the work and the cues are listed here.

Work

1. Introduce self-recording by first presenting a rationale for doing consistent work. The girls in the study were informed that if they were to succeed outside the facility in which they were placed, they must be effective and steady workers.

2. Discuss the exact meaning of *work* with the students. Definitions of work and how it was measured differed for the girls and for the various situations, but for the most part, work "units" were counted. A unit could be earned by completing any job listed in the kitchen, performing specific chores in the workshop, or finishing certain increments of work in the classroom.

3. Give the students charts on which to record the amount of work or number of work units completed during each period.

4. Arrange a system whereby the students are paid a specified number of tokens for each task. These ratios could be individualized for the various students and behaviors.

5. Institute a plan for fining the pupils if they do not self-record accurately. The established fines should be a modest amount.

6. Set up an arrangement so the students can periodically exchange the tokens they earned for a variety of events, items, or privileges.

Cues

1. Discuss the importance of receiving praise from teachers.

2. Explain what cues are and give some examples: "How did you think I did today?" "Did you know I finished all my work?"

3. Point out appropriate occasions for prompting teachers: when a task is completed, at the end of a work period, or when a teacher is standing nearby and is not busy.

4. Using role play, demonstrate how to give cues at appropriate times; also demonstrate cues that are inappropriate.

5. Provide the students with booklets in which they can record the cues they give during each period.

6. Grant the pupils tokens for giving a certain number of cues and establish a place and time for exchanging tokens for rewards.

Monitor

In a situation similar to that of the cited study, data should be self-recorded for both aspects of this technique: work and cues. For the work, the student could keep a chart pertaining to a general category of activities, such as grades. More specific records could also be kept; for example, keeping track of reading or chores at home is an option. With respect to cues, data could also be general and specific. For the former, a record could be kept of the times the student elicited responses from individuals. For the latter, data could be detailed so that they referred to responses from specific individuals. Information about the timing and substance of each cue also could be kept, as could the result of each cue.

Modifications/Considerations

The idea of cuing others could be adapted to several situations at school, in the home, or in the workplace. Children could be taught, for example, to prompt their teachers or parents when they successfully completed some task. Related to this, pupils could be taught a number of specific phrases for cuing these types of individuals.

Gettinger (1985) showed that the spelling performances of 8- to-13-year-old students improved when they directed aspects of their own programs; that is, things were better when they cued themselves. In Gettinger's study, students circled in red the part of a word they had misspelled (after they had checked their papers against a list of correctly spelled words) and said, "This is the part of the word I need to remember." Students then pointed to the circled letters on their papers and studied the differences between their misspelled words and the correct words.

Something that must be kept in mind while teaching youngsters to cue others to praise or otherwise reinforce them is that this can certainly be overdone. The consequences of overdoing this technique could definitely be counterproductive.

Research

Gettinger, M. (1985). Effects of teacher-directed versus student-directed instruction and cues versus no cues for improving spelling performance. *Journal of Applied Behavior Analysis, 18,* 167–171.

Seymour, F. W., & Stokes, T. F. (1976). Self-recording in training girls to increase work and evoke staff praise in an institution for offenders. *Journal of Applied Behavior Analysis, 9,* 41–54.

6 SELF-MONITORING TRANSITIONS

Background

The idea for this tactic was stimulated by a school with which I worked several years ago. In this system, the teachers were attempting to teach in spite of several pull-out programs. Of the 29 students in one fourth-grade class, for example, 26 were pulled out for one reason or another at some time during the day.

Understandably, teachers in similar circumstances are fed up (to put it mildly) with "pull outs" from their classrooms. Some of their children must leave the classroom for speech therapy, others for Chapter I instruction, still others for instrumental music and a variety of other purposes. Not only are teachers irked by the numbers of children who scurry in and out of the room, they are not at all happy about having to remind these pupils of their many extra appointments.

When teachers do forget to prompt their itinerant pupils, someone—a music teacher, librarian, resource teacher, or therapist—often puts blame on them or the pupil. Teachers do not need the additional chore of managing their students' schedules, and they can certainly do without the slings and arrows for forgetting! Hence, this tactic is for them.

Who Can Benefit

This approach has been used with youngsters who go to and from resource rooms, but it also would be useful for pupils who must regularly leave the classroom for any reason.

Procedures

1. Discuss with the child the reasons for setting up schedules and why people should strive to stick to them. In this context, consider with the youngster the importance of leaving promptly for his or her scheduled event, and for returning promptly to the classroom. Point out that

when the child is on time at both locations, he or she can take full advantage of the activities that have been planned. Explain also that when he or she arrives late for his or her special program or activity, the teacher must delay the lesson because there are other youngsters in the group and the instruction must wait until all the students are there at the same time. Emphasize the fact that when the child is late, he or she takes away instructional time from his or her classmates.

2. Give the child a card on which the days of the week are printed across the top. Underneath each day make four boxes. One box is for recording whether or not the child arrives on time for the special program, and another box is for recording whether or not the child returns promptly to the regular room. The other two boxes relate to performance in each location. Also, write on the card the time that the student should leave both locations. For example, a student may have to leave at 10:00 from his or her regular classroom to go to the resource room, and leave at 10:45 from the resource room to return to the regular classroom.

3. Mark an X in the appropriate box every time the student arrives on time in either room. Mark an O in the appropriate performance box each time he or she does appropriate work.

4. Arrange for one or more prizes that can be earned for accumulating a certain number of Xs and Os. These prizes need not be unnatural or expensive. For example, if a student has earned at least eight marks during a week, permit the pupil to remind his or her classmates when it is time for music. The child might also be allowed to lead the youngsters to the music room.

Monitor

Teach the children who participate in out-of-classroom programs to use a simple graph to keep track of their accomplishments, in addition to carrying their own cards with them. Encourage them later to evaluate their efforts. Ask them to tell you whether they are improving in respect to performance or punctuality. If the execution of either duty is not progressing, ask the students to speculate as to why this is so and to suggest possible solutions for the problem.

Modifications/Considerations

This tactic could be considered for children who must leave their classrooms and go to another location for any special purpose. Several examples of such instances were given in the Background section.

The card the student carries from one place to another might vary. For younger children or those who cannot tell time, clock faces with the hands filled in to match their departure times could be printed on the cards.

Furthermore, the number of boxes for the various observations beneath each day could be different. Some teachers might add a third box to be filled in if the pupil brings the necessary equipment to complete his or her assignments (e.g., paper, pencil). Still another slot could be added to show whether the child behaved properly in the particular situation.

Some children might, after their teachers evaluated their actions for a while, be taught to judge some or all of their own behaviors. Later, as they become accurate in their assessments, they could schedule their own rewards.

Fowler (1986) demonstrated that a self-management regime was effective in assisting kindergarten children to effectively deal with four transition activities: clean up, book time, restroom, and snack time.

Research

Fowler, S. A. (1986). Peer-monitoring and self-monitoring: Alternatives to teacher management. *Teaching Exceptional Children, 52*(6), 573–580.

7 SELF-INSTRUCTIONAL STRATEGY TRAINING

Background

The cited study in this tactic shows how self-instructional strategy training can be used to teach composition skills to students with mild disabilities. This type of training emphasizes flexibility and individualization as the teacher initiates instructional procedures such as modeling, graduated difficulty, feedback, social reinforcement and self-reinforcement, and maintenance and generalization of new skills. Students learn to use appropriate strategies for planning, editing, and revising text effectively. The responsibility of making assignments and of self-monitoring are gradually transferred to the student.

Who Can Benefit

Significant improvements in the composition skills of sixth-grade students with learning disabilities were demonstrated in the cited study. The cognitive skills and strategy training would certainly benefit younger students as well.

Procedures

The strategies taught and steps followed in the research situation are illustrated here.

Developing a Composition Strategy Training Session

1. Begin with a thorough task and learner analysis.
2. Determine the goals of training.
3. Select the training task and components.
4. Establish a sequence of learning activities to reach the goals.

Steps to the Introduction, Acquisition, and Evaluation of Skills and Strategies

1. Provide pretraining.
2. Review the current performance level of the student.

3. Describe the executive composition strategy.

4. Model the composition strategy and self-instruction.

5. Require mastery of the strategy.

6. Provide controlled practice of the strategy steps and of self-instruction.

7. Encourage independent performance.

Example—Story Grammar Training

Step 1. Provide pretraining.

Students receive pretraining on defining, identifying, and generating story grammar elements.

- Introduce a chart depicting a mnemonic to be used for the seven story grammar questions. For example, the mnemonic W-W-W, What = 2, How = 2 (which represents Who-When-Where questions, two What questions, and two How questions) might be used. The seven question types follow: (1) Who is the main character and who else is in the story? (2) When does the story take place? (3) Where does the story take place? (4) What does the main character want to do? (5) What happens when he or she tries to do it? (6) How does the story end? (7) How does the main character feel?

- Ask students to memorize the mnemonic and recite the meaning of each element.

- Initiate practice lessons where the students identify story grammar elements in existing stories.

- Ask students to look at a picture and generate story elements (while recording ideas).

Step 2. Review current performance level.

- Before pretraining, examine baseline performance on a number of story grammar elements.

- Discuss with students the goal and the significance of training.

Step 3. Describe the executive strategy.

- Provide a five-step writing strategy: (1) Look at the picture. (2) Let your mind be free. (3) Write down the story part reminder (mnemonic). (4) Write down the story ideas for each part. (5) Write your story; use good components that make sense.

Step 4. Model the composition strategy and self-instructions.

- Write a story while thinking out loud; include examples of creativity, problem definition, planning, self-evaluation, and self-reinforcement self-instructions.

- Discuss the model's performance.

- Ask students to record their own self-instructions.

Step 5. **Mastery of the composition strategy.**
- Provide a chart depicting the five-step strategy.
- Ask students to practice the steps until they are memorized.

Step 6. *Provide controlled practice.*
- The students and teacher set a goal to include the seven elements of composition in their stories.
- The students and teacher work together to compose a story while using the five-step strategy and self-instructions.
- The students and teacher independently count the story elements of the completed story.
- Compare counts and then graph the results.
- Compare the baseline and the goal-setting performance.
- Discuss the student's satisfaction with story writing.

Step 7. *Encourage independent performance.*
- Ask students to compare stories independently while using the five-step strategy and self-instructions.
- Fade teacher feedback after the student has produced two or three stories.
- Evaluate performance as the student sets a personal goal for each story; graph the results to illustrate any changes.

Monitor

The goals of this strategy are reached when the skills learned are transferred to different settings and situations. With cooperative planning between special and general education teachers, a behavioral contract can be written to assess the student's skills and evaluate the procedure of self-instructional strategy training.

Modifications/Considerations

The student is taught processes that may be especially effective in producing the transference of skills to other subject areas. Interaction between the teacher and the student while setting goals should be done in a positive, collaborative manner. When describing the executive strategy, the advantages must be made clear to the student to help develop understanding. A peer may model the strategies to be learned. During the discussion of the model's performance, the teacher and students could collaborate on any changes that may make the procedure more effective. Paraphrasing the strategy and self-instructions should be allowed. When controlling the practice, a teacher initiates independent goal setting, self-monitoring, and self-assessment. Prompts and guidance should be provided as necessary; a teacher should fade the cues until independent performance is achieved.

Research

Harris, K. R., & Graham, S. (1988). Self-instructional strategy training. *Teaching Exceptional Children, 20*(2), 35–36.

8 CONTINGENT CHOICE OF SELF-MANAGEMENT TASKS

Background

The research behind this tactic presents a slightly different wrinkle on the business of self-management. It demonstrates how self-management—being able to perform certain elements of instruction for yourself—can be quite reinforcing. When certain components of self-management are arranged contingently, that is, when pupils are required to do something first before being able to engage in an aspect of self-management, many pupils will perform a required duty. Think of that! The teacher and the pupil gain on two fronts; it is truly a win-win situation.

In certain circumstances, when a teacher arranges something to entice a child to perform, even when the desired results are ultimately achieved, the teacher may feel that he or she had to "give away the store" to accomplish the goal. The project explained here is not at all like that. In this example, the teacher profits twice and so, eventually, does the pupil. The student's academic performances improve and he or she learns about scheduling daily lessons. This type of self-regulated learning, according to Paris and Oka (1986), combines cognitive strategies and motivational dispositions in the classroom to preserve feelings of self-worth.

Who Can Benefit

The pupil in the cited research was an 8-year-old boy in a class for youngsters with learning disabilities. The tactic described here—scheduling various subjects—would be appropriate for youngsters who are already, or who are beginning to be, independent. It is also a good approach for pupils who have sampled self-scheduling and are reinforced by it.

Procedures

1. Set up a consistent schedule for the student. For a period of time, follow the schedule with great regularity; for example, have reading at 9:00, followed by math at 9:45, and so forth.

2. Post the schedule and ensure that the child knows the routine. Occasionally, ask the student to tell you what subject follows reading, math, or some other activity. Once in a while, have the student recite the schedule from beginning to end.

3. Allow the student, when you are certain that he or she knows generally what a schedule is and specifically what his or hers happens to be, to set the time for one or two subjects. You might explain, for example, that tomorrow the student can work on math and reading at any time during the day that he or she wishes to. Offer this privilege every once in a while and emphasize its importance. Convince the student that it is quite an honor to schedule one's own activities.

4. Arrange self-scheduling on a contingent basis. Now, rather than simply allowing students to schedule activities *regardless* of how well they do in their subjects, set up the privilege so that students must achieve at certain levels before they can schedule their own times for learning.

5. Arrange this contingency initially so that if a student reaches the target in one of six subjects, he or she may choose when to schedule that subject for the next day. If the child meets the aim for two subjects one day, he or she may schedule the times for both of them the next day, and so forth.

Monitor

Data should be kept on the extent to which the pupil earns the privilege of self-scheduling. Furthermore, data should be obtained that relate to the development of competencies in subjects such as reading or mathematics.

Modifications/Considerations

One change possible with this technique is the number of subjects in which a student must be proficient before being allowed to set up the schedule. In this tactic, it was a one-to-one correspondence. A teacher could also establish a "go or no go" situation in which the child can schedule the times of *all* subjects only if he or she reaches the target in *all* of them the day before.

In the project explained here, the student's choices related to scheduling subjects such as reading and math. The options allowed the student could be more specific and detailed. For example, a child could be required to attain a certain performance level in an activity, and then be allowed to choose which song the group would sing, whether to work on multiplication or division, whether to read poetry or prose, or whether his or her group plays soccer or baseball. The choices could be even further refined: whether to write with a pencil or pen, whether to sing a song in the key of B flat or C, whether to read this story or poem or that one, whether to use cursive writing or manuscript-style writing, or whether to use zone or man-to-man defense in a basketball game.

In other tactics, arranging certain self-management components in a contingent manner was discussed. Just as the student here had to earn the privilege of scheduling, a pupil could be allowed to earn other self-management tasks. For example, a pupil might be allowed to correct his or her own work in arithmetic *if* performance in reading is satisfactory. Or, a student could choose his or her reinforcement in a phonics program *if* improvement in spelling is demonstrated.

Research

Lovitt, T. C. (1973). Self-management projects with children with behavioral disabilities. *Journal of Learning Disabilities, 6,* 138–150.

Paris, S. G., & Oka, E. R. (1986). Self-regulated learning among exceptional children. *Exceptional Children, 53*(2), 103–108.

9 SELF-DETERMINED REINFORCEMENT: PUPILS SET THE RATE OF REWARD

Background

One of the highest levels of self-regulation is the ability to select for oneself the terms of reinforcement. In determining one's own reinforcement, there are two related elements. One element is selecting *what* the consequence will be: free time, a tangible object, or something else. The other element is deciding *how much* of this item will be given and when it will be delivered; in other words, deciding what the contingency aspect of the arrangement will be. This tactic has to do with the latter aspect, that of self-selecting the contingency or ratio.

Who Can Benefit

This tactic, particularly as it is arranged here, is most useful for students who have been involved with and understand token economies. Before youngsters are allowed to choose their own ratios or time for work, they must have some experience with these arrangements. They should understand, for instance, exactly what 1 minute is and what 10 correct answers are when they are granted 1 minute of free time for 10 correctly answered math problems. Accordingly, they must be able to figure out, at least generally, how much time they will earn for 20 or 30 correctly solved problems.

Procedures

1. Arrange a token economy with a pupil. Specify for him or her how much of something must be done in order to receive some payment (Table 9.1).

2. Put the token economy into effect. Make arrangements for the following:

   - a place to take the free time
   - a time for the free time to occur

TABLE 9.1 Contingency Specifications

	Contingency Manager	
Subject Area	**Teacher-Specified**	**Child-Specified**
Math	10 problems: 1 min. of free time	10 problems: 2 min. of free time
Reading		
(no errors)	1 page: 1	1 page: 2
(errors)	1 page: 1	1 page: 1
Spelling	18 words: 1	5 words: 1
Writing	20 letters: 1	10 letters: 2
Language Arts	10 answers: 1	10 answers: 2
Library book	1 story: 3	1 story: 6
	3 questions: 1	3 questions: 2

- a scheme for keeping track of the earned time and the amount spent
- a set of rules for proper behavior in the free-time area
- the accompanying consequences for disobeying the regulations

3. Run the token economy for several days. During this time, talk with the pupil about the contract and the various ratios. The objective of these conversations is to make certain that the child understands the plan. Ask questions such as: "How many different ratios are there on your contract?" "How many points do you earn for 10 correct math problems?" "How many points would you receive for 20, or 30?" "Which subject gives you the best (or the worst) payoff?"

4. Allow the pupil to select his or her own ratios. Start with the first item on his or her contract and work through the others. In Table 9.1, the contract begins with math; ask the student what the ratio is, correct any misunderstanding, and then tell the student to specify his or her own ratio. Explain that by specifying the ratio, the student can change either the number of units that must be completed or the number of minutes that will be received for finishing those items. After the ratio is set for the first subject, move on through the others.

Monitor

Initially, data of some type should be kept regarding the extent to which the student understands and can carry out the self-delivery of consequences or contingencies. These data might be in the form of interviews or conversations. When the pupil understands reliably how to manage the program, data should be obtained on the extent to which the associated skill or behavior is affected; that is, track how much the student has improved in reading or writing, or how much better he or she has controlled behaviors that were to be attenuated.

Modifications/Considerations

In the research study, the pupil was allowed to arrange ratios in all six subjects. Other teachers might allow pupils to specify a ratio in only one activity at a time. Further, no limits were imposed on the ratios this pupil set. As indicated by Table 9.1, although the student set higher payoffs in most of the subjects than had the teacher, none of the increases were unreasonable (at least according to the teacher). Other teachers, when offering this option to their pupils, might establish some limits above which they would not accept a child's choice. These restrictions would not have to be disclosed to the pupil until after a selection exceeded the boundaries. Another modification of this plan might be for the teacher and pupil to negotiate each of the ratios. In the example study there were no conferences; either the teacher or the child set the ratios.

Heward (1987) reviews a number of ways in which the self-delivery of consequences can strengthen and weaken behaviors. For strengthening behaviors, he notes that students can self-determine the number of tokens, points, or minutes of free time they can earn. To weaken behaviors, Heward mentions that individuals can take away points, place themselves in time out, and perform undesired tasks.

Research

Heward, W. L. (1987). Self-management. In J. Cooper, T. Heron, & W. Heward (Eds.), *Applied Behavior Analysis* (pp. 515–549). New York: Merrill/Macmillan.

Lovitt, T. C., & Curtiss, K. A. Academic response rate as a function of teacher- and self-imposed contingencies. (1969). *Journal of Applied Behavior Analysis, 2,* 49–53.

10 ORGANIZATIONAL CHECKLIST FOR SELF-INSTRUCTION AND SELF-EVALUATION

Background

Some teachers schedule two curricula at the same time: a subject, such as reading, and a component of pupil management. Not only do teachers who run tandem programs get double mileage out of their efforts (teaching the subject as well as self-management), they can tailor instruction. These programs enable teachers to prescribe materials at different levels for their many and diverse students.

Who Can Benefit

Organizational techniques such as the one explained here can be arranged for practically anyone; they are particularly beneficial, however, for students who are disorganized. Such techniques are also extremely helpful for teachers who wish to individualize their students' lessons.

Procedures

The plan explained here was written by Carolyn Lint, who developed this tactic when she was a resource teacher in a Clover Park elementary school. It was used in a self-management workshop I conducted several years ago. The teachers' assignment for these sessions was two-fold: first, they were to individualize their programs for their students as much as possible; second, they were to define all the steps required of the pupils to do the specified work, from the time the students gathered up their materials to the time they evaluated their own performances.

The following is an explanation of the nine points of a spelling plan in which the organizational checklist was used. Each student had a copy of this program. A sheet was attached to every desk, and on it the steps of the program were listed. Five boxes were printed alongside each step, one for each day of the school week. As the student completed the first step, he or she checked it off and went on to the next, and so on.

1. *Obtain a worksheet.* Each pupil picked out his or her spelling worksheet from the teacher's folder; the teacher kept individualized sheets that listed the words for each student. The majority of students were given 10 words; some were assigned 15 words and a few only 5.

2. *Study the words.* Each student studied the words independently for 10 to 15 minutes. During this time, the pupils used a variety of tactics. The "copy-cover-write-compare" approach was one of the favored techniques: The student copied the first word on the spelling list, covered it with a hand, wrote it from memory, then compared his or her effort with the correct spelling.

3. *Take out the test paper.* Next, the pupils took out a test paper. Each student had a stack of these in his or her desk. These test papers were simply 4" × 11" sheets on which the numbers 1 through 15 were listed down the left side. A line was drawn to the right of each number, and two lines were printed on the top of the sheet. The children wrote their names and the date on the two lines.

4. *Locate your partner.* After the students practiced their assignments, they located their partners. (Prior to this program the pupils were asked to select mates. They were told to find someone whose spelling ability was about equal to their own and who they could work with comfortably.)

5. *Administer the tests.* The students then tested one another. First, one student read the spelling words to his or her partner, who wrote them down; then they reversed roles. Students who were reading the words were instructed to pronounce each word at least twice and to say them as clearly as possible. As soon as a pupil finished writing a word, his or her partner announced the next word, and so forth.

6. *Correct the papers.* When the pupils had written their words, they took out the worksheets they had used earlier for study and checked their answers against it. As they did so, they put a *C* to the left of each correctly spelled word and circled the parts of any words that were incorrectly spelled.

7. *Record the score.* Next, students counted up the number of correctly spelled words and wrote that figure on the top of their papers.

8. *Graph the scores.* The students then marked the number of correctly spelled words on their graphs. Along the vertical axis of these charts the numbers 0 to 15 were printed. Across the horizontal axis, several lines were printed; each line indicated a day of the week.

9. *Practice on words.* Finally, the students practiced on the words they had misspelled. One method for practicing was described earlier. In another technique, the pupil first identified the incorrect aspect of the word, then wrote the entire word correctly a few times, then used it, along with other words, in a sentence.

Monitor

As with several other tactics in this book, it would be a good idea for teach
to keep data regarding not only the process of carrying out the interventi
but also the ultimate effects of involving that intervention. In other word
data should be kept on the extent to which the pupils can make use of t
checklists, and more importantly, data should be acquired on how well the
perform on the task related to the checklist or form (e.g., spelling, handwri
ing, reading, or mathematics).

Modifications/Considerations

Steps such as the ones listed and described here have been created for elemen-
tary- and secondary-age students in many different subjects, including handwriting, arithmetic, reading comprehension, social studies and science labs.
Blandford and Lloyd (1987) developed cards for youngsters to use as they
wrote. The following questions were on these cards:

> Am I sitting correctly? Is my paper positioned correctly? Am I holding my
> pencil correctly? Are all my letters sitting on the line? Are all my tall letters
> touching or nearly touching the top line? Are my short letters filling only
> 1/2 of the space? Am I leaving enough, but not too much space between
> words?

Their data indicated that the children's handwriting improved markedly
when the cards were introduced and the improvements persisted over time
while the cards were available to students.

Research

Blandford, B. J., & Lloyd, J. W. (1987). Effects of a self-instructional procedure on handwriting. *Journal of Learning Disabilities, 20*(6), 342–346.